Work Organisations

25

Work Organisations

Resistance and control

Graeme Salaman

Longman
London and New York

Longman Group Limited,
Longman House,
Burnt Mill, Harlow, Essex, U.K.

Published in the United States of America
by Longman Inc., New York

© Graeme Salaman 1979

First published 1979
Second impression 1981

British Library Cataloguing in Publication Data

Salaman, Graeme
  Work Organisations
  1. Organisation 2. Industrial sociology
  I. Title
  301.18'32   HM131   78-40873

  ISBN 0-582-48992-X

Printed in Singapore by Selector Offset Printing Pte Ltd.

Contents

Preface

This book grew out of my work on two Open University courses, and while it differs in many important ways from my contributions to the two courses in question – *People and Organisations* (DT 352), and *People and Work* (DE 351) – nevertheless my involvement in those courses was of enormous importance in raising my interest in the subject matter of the book, and in establishing the general direction that interest would take. This makes the conventional procedure of academic acknowledgement rather difficult, since many people were involved in the two course teams, all of whom contributed ideas, insights, criticisms and suggestions which, directly or indirectly, explicitly or implicitly, have influenced or coloured this work. My first acknowledgement, then, must be to all members of the course teams of *People and Organisations* and *People and Work*. Only those with any experience of Open University course teams at their best will be able to appreciate what stimulating and exciting experiences they can be.

Although to single out individual members of the course teams whose influence was of particular importance is difficult, it remains true that this book, and its subject matter, orientation, and theoretical position was influenced by contact and discussion with certain individual members of the course teams who might well be surprised at the final direction and form my thoughts have taken. The majority of these people have not seen this book prior to publication. Clearly, they can have no responsibility for it. Nevertheless, in important ways, the book grew from contact – through the course teams – with Charles Perrow, David Hickson, Martin Albrow, David Silverman, Ken Thompson, Dave Elliott, Geoff Esland, Alan Fox, Theo Nichols, John Child, Terry Johnson, and Richard Hyman. It was, as can be imagined, a stimulating and valuable experience to work with such company.

Once the book was in draft, it benefited enormously from the criticisms, suggestions and support of four people: Richard Brown, David Dunkerley, Alan Fox, and Alan Waton. Again, the final responsibility must be mine, of course, but the encouragement and kind criticism these four offered played a significant part in shaping the structure and content of the book.

Finally, my thanks to Frances Kelly of Curtis Brown for all her patience and perseverance, to Alice Nolda at Longman for her support and encouragement, to Barbara Kehoe and Carol Johns for typing early drafts and Moira Hilder for not only typing the final version, but for many useful suggestions on matters of style and grammar.

Acknowledgements

We are grateful to the collection Haags Gemeentemuseum –
The Hague for permission to reproduce the photograph on the
cover of this book from 'The Revolt', Luigi Russolo.

To Rena, Alexandra and Sophia

The sociology of organisations

Chapter 1

The importance of organisations

This book is about work organisations in capitalist societies – mainly the UK and the USA, for these two countries supply most of the examples discussed in the book, and the generalisations presented here are particularly applicable to these two countries. The book is about the internal, structural features of these organisations, especially the design of work and control, since these structural features are of most significance to organisational employees, and are most revealing about the nature and priorities of modern organisations.

The focus of this book is on work organisations. Much organisational theory and research is concerned with organisations in general, including charities, voluntary organisations, churches, political parties, etc. This is a perfectly proper delineation of the field, but it is not one which is used here. This book is about work organisations, the common features and processes of such organisations, the determinants of those features and processes and their relationship to the society within which the organisations occur. Such an interest would not be best served by including other non-work types of organisation: the book is not about organisations *per se*, but about the large-scale organisation, design and control of work.

It is usual for books on organisations to begin with some statement of the urgent need for a sociological understanding of these phenomena which, increasingly, dominate the lives of citizens of modern industrial societies. What, after all, could be more necessary than an understanding of the factories, governments, political parties, multi-national organisations and universities that determine so much of our everyday lives? Peter Blau is one of a number of writers on organisations who have argued for the importance of the study of 'the efficient structure of modern organisations, which enables the giant ones and their combinations to dominate our lives, our fortunes, and our honour. To restore the liberty of men, we must free them from the domination of **powerful organisations**' (Blau and Schoenherr, 1971, p.357).

But what does it mean to say that organisations are important? What is it that the sociologist interested in organisations should study? Organisations matter in all sorts of different ways to many different groups and interests. As members of the public we tend to be affected by organisations in numerous different ways, and to hold various – and sometimes conflicting – expectations of them. Sometimes organisations are blamed for being too efficient, too cold, impersonal and procedure-bound. Other times, we complain of 'feather-bedding', nepotism, inefficiency and bias. Sometimes we complain, as Perrow (1972) has noted, that 'there ought to be a rule' covering this or that excess or incompetence. Other times we find supportive audiences for stories of 'red-tape' and bureaucracy.

Organisations are important both for what they do, and for what they fail to do. And this importance takes a variety of forms for different groups at different times. But this general, lay, or public assessment of the importance or problems of organisations is not itself sufficient to inform a sociological approach to organisations. Of course, the sociologist must take account of such frustrations and experiences. But a sociological approach to organisations must not, if it is to be useful or perceptive, accept available common-sense conceptions of the problems of organisations. Such a confusion of sociological issues and interests with what are presented as obvious, common-sense, practical organisational problems carries a number of dangers.

First, it can result in the sociologist developing or employing an ill-considered conception of organisations, and an approach to them, which reflects, and derives from, these issues and priorities. So, for example, a sociologist concerned with organisational efficiency (a common-sense issue) might define organisations as phenomena which are striving to achieve certain goals, where structure and technology etc. are derived from this prime goal. He would then attempt to uncover the factors which obstruct or confuse the harmonious cooperation of all members of the organisation in playing their interrelated parts in their achievement of the goal. His approach to organisations follows from his acceptance of common-sense issues and priorities. The problem with this, of course, is that common-sense is not necessarily a good basis for academic study. An understanding of the most pressing practical problems is not likely to be gained by conceptualising organisations in terms of the problem, but by rigorous attempts to improve our understanding of basic organisational issues and matters of definition and conceptualisation – which may frequently seem far removed from questions of, say, efficiency.

Ironically, then, one of the deficiencies of assuming that socio-logical interest in organisations is synonymous with what is taken to be general, societal interest in them, is that an understanding of these general issues may well be hindered by an approach which re-lies upon inadequate, unrealistic conceptualisation in terms of the issues themselves, rather than on the available body of sociological theorising and discussion.

A second danger which accompanies the confusion of sociological problems of organisations with social problems lies in the identification of the social problems themselves. Although we are frequently reminded of the enormous personal and societal significance of large-scale modern organisations, of their threats to liberty, fortunes, honour; it appears that, despite the rhetoric of concern for the implications of organisations for employees' health and well-being, or for the survival of democratic processes etc., the most pressing practical problem (from the point of view of the organisational researcher) is one of organisational efficiency. Too often, sociologists have committed themselves – and their analyses – to the study of practical organisational problems as these are seen and defined by one group: senior members of organisations. What is presented as an issue of general interest and concern can be seen as a sectional priority.

This leads to the third danger – that by incorporating sectional priorities and problems in their analyses, the sociologists accept and legitimise the significance of this sectional issue (for example, efficiency) and, if their conceptualisations follow their choice of issues, serve also to legitimise existing organisational structures. So, for example, most studies of organisational structure (which frequently take as their point of departure the conviction of the inevitability and necessity of existing organisational forms, and focus on the determinants of inter-organisational variations) justify and de-politicise organisational inequalities and deprivations. These are seen as cruel consequences of the need for efficiency. They are only of importance when it can be demonstrated that they stand in the way of efficiency. Then the liberal's plea for 'humane' work practices will be given attention.

All this is not to argue for a sociology for sociology's sake. The best sociology, as will be discussed later in this chapter, has always had a major interest in the impact of social structures and processes on the individual. Indeed one sociologist has very sensibly defined the subject matter of sociology as the relationship between history and biography. But such a venture will not be assisted by a facile commitment to ill-considered notions of (frequently partial and sectional definitions of) 'common-sense' practical problems and the ramshackle conceptual structures which accompany them. Such a commitment results in questionable findings and recommendations and the perpetuation and justification of current organisational forms.

To say this is not to deny any interest in the social consequences of organisations, the nature and origins of organisational structure, or any other issue of obvious social importance. As we shall see, a genuine sociology of organisations has very definite societal and organisational relevance and significance. What, however, are these proper areas of sociological interest? What are the sociological problems of organisations? Broadly speaking there are two – the nature, origins and consequences of organisational structure, and the relationship between organisational structure and society. As the next chapter will show, these are the issues around which the early sociological theorists – notably Marx and Weber – built their theories of organisations.

A sociological approach to organisations centres on the concept of organisational structure. This concept is used to describe the regular, patterned nature of organisational activities and processes. Obviously, organisations are composed of people, but the regularities displayed by members of an organisation are the result not of their personal preferences or psychologies, but of their exposure to various organisational controls, which more or less successfully limit, influence or determine their behaviour. From the active interplay of organisational members and organisational controls, organisational structure is produced – the regular ways in which activities, responsibilities and authority are distributed, jobs specified and described, and activities bound by rules, procedures and expectations.

Not only are organisations structured, they are structured in different ways. Some organisations have numerous levels of authority and responsibility, some have few; some organisations contain elaborate and specific rules and procedures, others have few, and so on. The sociologist, as we shall see, is interested in the nature of organisational structure, and its variations and consequences. This topic constitutes the main theme of this book.

Organisation and society

The second sociological problem of organisations concerns the relationship between organisations and society, what Benson has described as 'the connection of organisations to the larger set of structural arrangements in the society' (Benson, 1977a, p.14). Under this heading the sociologist seeks to understand the relationship between organisational activity and societal stability or instability; the societal implications and determinants of organisational structure, the role of extra-organisational forces and groups in buttressing, or threatening, organisational structure and process; the implications of organisational activities and ideologies, for society at large, and the relationship between societal structures, groups and interests and organisations.

Although such an interest might seem obviously important and necessary, there have been few ostensibly sociological accounts of organisations which have taken such issues seriously. One exception is the American sociologist, Talcott Parsons, whose analysis of the relationship between organisations and society is worth discussing not only because of its rarity, but because it clearly and explicitly articulates some highly prevalent (but usually implicit) misconceptions about the nature and functions of organisations in modern society.

Parsons has adopted a common-sense approach to types of organisations and classified them by the sort of *output* they supply to the larger society. He argues that 'An organisation is a system which, as the attainment of its goal, "produces" an identifiable something which can be utilized in some way by another system' (Parsons, 1970, p.75). He goes on to add that organisations can be classified in terms of the sort of goals which are achieved by the production of various goods or products. He remarks that what from the organisational point of view is a goal, 'is, from the point of view of the larger system of which it is a differentiated part or sub-system, a specialized or differentiated *function*' (p.76, my emphasis). Now this sort of conception and classification of organisations – in terms of the sorts of goods or services they produce for the society within which they exist – may seem plausible, at least at first sight. After all, it retains many of the attributes of common-sense, lay, theorising about organisations that talks of educational organisations, military organisations, industrial organisations and so on. And Parsons' categories reflect such distinctions. He suggests a four-fold classification of organisations into: organisations oriented to economic production, organisations oriented to political goals, pattern-maintenance organisations (i.e. those with 'cultural', 'educational' and 'expressive' functions) and integrative organisations which include those that handle the adjustment of conflicts, like the law, or that achieve social control like political parties.

But this classification, and the 'common-sense' that it reflects, is based upon and reveals a serious and common misconception in lay and sociological thinking about organisations: that their importance is restricted to the 'obvious' functional contribution they make to the social system of which they are a part. To see, say, economic organisations simply in terms of their production of various goods and materials is to ignore their political importance. To classify an organisation as concerned with pattern maintenance is to miss the critically important point that such organisations play a significant role in perpetuating a particular form of social and economic arrangement. It is nonsense to suggest that only 'political' organisations (in Parsons' sense) play a political role. All large organisations in modern industrial societies play political roles, either directly through the exploitation of labour, or, more insidiously, through educating people to develop 'appropriate' and 'responsible' attitudes, or in disseminating ideological conceptions of health, sickness, madness, criminality, entertainment and so on.

Parsons claims that he wishes to 'define an organisation by locating it systematically in the structure of the society in relation to other categories of social structure' (Parsons, 1970, p.81). But his insistence on restricting his interest to classifying organisational 'outputs' and relating these to society's 'needs' leads him to ignore, as many other organisational researchers have done, the relationship between organisations and the pattern of interests and domination within their host society. The crucial point to appreciate is that organisations not only produce certain goods and services, they also constitute the modern means of exploitation, domination, distraction, and knowledge construction.

A view of, say, the Ford Motor Company, as an organisation which has been granted a societal mandate to supply society with a very necessary commodity – cars – would seem somewhat inadequate sociologically. And yet this is the equivalent of the sort of analysis suggested by Parsons and executed by other organisational researchers.

Perrow's comments on the relationship between society and organisations serves as a useful antidote to the blandness of this sort of thinking. Rather than seeing organisations as essential and valuable institutions oriented to achieve 'what society needs', Perrow reminds us that organisations play a massive part in shaping the world we live in. Perrow notes that organisations are tools that some few people use to impose their 'definition of the proper affairs of men upon other men. The man who controls an organisation has power that goes far beyond that of those that do not have such control. The power of the rich lies not in their ability to buy goods and services, but in their capacity to control the ends towards which the vast resources of large organisations are directed' (Perrow, 1972, p.14).

Organisations are tools. The question that must then be asked is whose purposes are being served by these tools? Whose interests are dominant? Strangely, such questions are rarely asked in that sub-speciality described as organisation theory or the sociology of organisations. It is true that one influential work argues that organisations should be classified on the basis of *cui bono* – who benefits? And this work, which delineates four basic categories of persons who might benefit from any organisation: members, owners, clients and the public at large (Blau and Scott, 1963, p.42), goes some way towards facilitating an understanding of the relationship between organisations and these groups. But it still fails to illuminate the relationship between organisations and the overall societal structure of interest and domination. Blau and Scott, like many organisational analysts, are worried that organisations might corrupt and distort democratic processes. It is for this reason, at least, that they feel a sociology of organisations to be important. They remark:

'The centralisation of power in the hands of management that

organisational giants make possible, . . . poses a challenge to democracies. An efficient administrative machinery vests tremendous power in the hands of the few – be they corporation managers, government officials, military officers, party bosses or union leaders – and thereby undermines the sovereignty of the many to whom the few in a democracy are expected to be responsible. Acquiring knowledge about bureaucratic organisations is an important first step in meeting the threat they pose for democratic institutions (Blau and Scott, 1963, p.15).

But such a view of the importance of organisations will not be presented here. For this writer, the importance of organisations lies not simply in the threat they pose for democracy (as defined in terms of modern mixed-economy societies with parliamentary systems). It is the relationship between organisational activities, processes and 'outputs' and the perpetuation and construction of a particular form of social and economic domination that constitutes the importance of organisations. It is odd that such a view of organisations should require emphasis. In many other subdivisions of sociology and the other social sciences there is increasing interest in the ways in which particular occupations, professions, and organisations serve class interests. With industrial and commercial organisations of course such an evaluation is more obvious (though, even here, some organisation theorists would argue that industrial organisations are merely supplying societally necessary 'outputs'). But Baran and Sweezey suggest a more direct and relevant approach to industrial organisations when they write:

One can no longer today speak of either industrialists or bankers as the leading echelon of the dominant capitalist classes. The big monopolistic corporations, which were formed and, in their early years, controlled by bankers, proved to be enormously profitable and in due course, through paying off their debts and plowing back their earnings, achieved financial independence and indeed, in many cases, acquired substantial control over banks and other financial institutions. These giant corporations are the basic units of monopoly capitalism in its present stage; their (big) owners and functionaries constitute the leading echelon of the ruling classes (Barab and Sweezey, 1972, p.435–6).

Such a view of organisations, and their relationship to capitalism, is not, of course, new, indeed it is almost the received wisdom in some branches of sociology. But, oddly, it is rare within organisational sociology, where concepts like capitalism are rarely employed and where, if moral concern is expressed, it is about the survival of liberal values and institutions, not for any sort of radical social change of organisational structures.

Recently, however, a number of analyses of such ostensibly

apolitical organisations as social welfare organisations, schools and hospitals, have argued for their essentially political role in disposing of troublesome social problems, preparing children for their future positions within an inegalitarian social order, developing notions of health, mental illness etc. Broadly speaking these organisations are seen as buttressing and legitimating existing societal patterns of domination and exploitation, reflecting class-based values, assumptions and interests, dealing with, or disposing of, the casualties of class society, developing ideologies, etc. (See, for example, Bowles and Gintis, 1976).

Clearly, such accounts of non-industrial organisations constitute an extension of the argument more usually applied to industrial organisations: that it is misleading to regard their activities as they are defined by senior members of the organisation (as supplying various necessary goods or services to society as a whole), and that they must be seen in terms of their *political* role in maintaining certain structures of privilege and deprivation, self-fulfilment and frustration, domination and subordination, within class society.

To say this is not to exhaust the possible links between organisations and society. The political significance of organisations is not limited simply to the nature of the goods, services, ideas or 'outputs' they produce. There are also close links between the internal structures of organisations and the society within which they operate. These links will be explored in subsequent chapters. Particular attention will be paid to the relationship between organisational inequalities and inequalities in society at large. The point to stress can be put this way – to what extent are organisational structures with their usual features of hierarchy and extreme inequality in the distribution of rewards, risks, delights and deprivations, determined by interests, values and philosophies of senior organisational members? This question will be considered in Section II.

It must of course be noted that most writers on organisations pay some attention to the social context of the organisations they study. But the relationship between organisation and society is usually conceptualised in terms of system (the organisation) and environment (the larger society), with the 'environment' supplying 'inputs' (personnel, materials, technologies, legal conditions, political pressures, etc.) to the organisation, and the organisation supplying a variety of 'outputs' to feed its societal context. The relationship is seen in highly specific and neutral terms. The nature of the society that is defined as the environment, and the part played by organisations in general in maintaining this form of society, is not considered relevant. The 'environment' is seen *in terms of the organisation*, as a source of needs, pressures, markets. It is conceptualised in terms similar to those used by senior organisational members in their planning and deliberations.

Most writers would agree, then, that 'the environment is very important to organisations' (Hall, 1972a, p.297). And, like Hall, they would probably define this 'importance' in terms of 'the range of (environmental) conditions that appear to have important influences on organisations' (Hall, 1972a, p.297). But, in their concern to establish 'the relative strength and direction of the influence of each factor (technological conditions, legal conditions, political conditions, economic conditions, demographic conditions, ecological conditions and cultural conditions)' (Hall, 1972a, p.306), they demonstrate that their focus on the organisation as the unit of analysis, and the theoretical perspectives they employ, coupled with their concern for practical outcomes, distracts them from any genuine sociological interest in the relationship between the nature of society and the contribution of organisations to its maintenance and development. This trivialises their analysis.

Chapter 2

Organisations and classical sociological theory: Marx and Weber

It is now appropriate and necessary to discuss in some more detail the major features of a classical theory of organisations. As will be discussed in Chapter 3, many of the elements of this theory of organisations have been overlooked, although they are currently being rediscovered. First, however, we must consider the major elements of a genuinely sociological theory of organisations as this is represented in the relevant writings of Marx and Weber. This exposition is not included out of mere habit, or empty pious respect for revered but largely irrelevant pioneers. On the contrary, the point of this chapter is to argue for the relevance of the insights and approaches of these two theorists.

Weber

Weber's work on the nature and basis of bureaucracy constitutes an important attempt to categorise the principles which find expression in bureaucracy, and their relationship with external, societal, beliefs and principles. Weber's work on bureaucracy is enormously important for the influence it has exerted and the argument it has stimulated, yet certain significant features of his work on bureaucracy have tended to be overlooked in the eagerness to discover ambiguities or contradictions in the model, or to assess its empirical validity.

Weber's writings on a particular type of organisation – bureaucracy – establish and articulate many of the elements of a genuine sociology of organisations. Firstly, he was concerned not with detailed empirical variations between organisations, but with the overall tendencies and principles which he could discern, as being expressed in the ideal-typical bureaucracy. He was prepared to risk empirical inaccuracy in order to attempt a categorisation of dominant features of the phenonenon. This approach has the advantage that it not only facilitates a more ambitious level of theorising about the nature, consequences and functions of bureaucracy in general (a level of discussion which is obstructed by the constant search for, and explanations of, minute intra-organisational variation) but also that it opens up and permits an exploration of the relationship between these general, ideal-typical, organisational forms, and the society within which they occur.

This is the second sociological element of Weber's approach: it relates the major features of the form of organisation under discussion to developments in society. His analysis of bureaucracy is an integral part of, and cannot be understood except in terms of, his analysis of large-scale social developments, especially the process of rationalisation 'the growing precision and explicitness in the principles governing social organisation' (Albrow, 1970, p.43).

In relating a specific pattern of control and legitimation within organisations to features of the society within which these bureaucratic organisations occur Weber develops a level of sociological theorising which is significantly different from the more detailed analyses of intra-organisational variation which have so preoccupied more recent writers. A surprising number of recent accounts of organisational structure, or classifications of organisational types, pay little, if any, attention to the societal context within which they occur. There is rarely, if ever, any suggestion that large-scale organisations might reflect values, priorities or principles derived from the host society. The activity and structure of organisations is usually explained in neutral and context-free terms – i.e. in terms of the requirements and imperatives of the task, and the 'need' to perform it efficiently.

Weber's approach differed radically from such analyses. For Weber, bureaucracy was a form of organisation characterised by particular structures and legitimations of control, a form where rationality was represented at its purest. He remarks that 'the purely bureaucratic form of administrative organisation is formally the most rational known means of carrying out imperative control over human beings' (Weber, 1964, p.337). Some have argued that Weber regarded this rationality as synonymous with efficiency, a charge which, if well-founded, would seriously weaken the claim that Weber was an early originator of the genuinely sociological approach to organisations which sees organisational structure not as the outcome of the search for efficiency but in terms of priorities, problems and interests based in the society outside the organisation.

But, as Albrow has remarked (Albrow, 1970, pp.61–6), the notion that Weber regarded rationality and efficiency as synonymous is highly questionable. He points to the complexity and subtlety of Weber's writings on rationality, and demonstrates that Weber defined rationality not in terms of the appropriateness of means to ends but in the application of certain formal principles of administration (p.63–4). To this extent Weber was not concerned to describe efficient organisational structures as such, but to demonstrate the organisational expression of certain values and ways of thinking current within society. He describes the mutually interdependent ideas upon which bureaucratic forms of control and authority depend, as well as specifying the organisational forms taken by a system of thought which was prevalent in the society at large: 'Bureaucracy offers the attitudes demanded by the external apparatus of modern culture in the most favourable combination' (Weber, 1964, p.216).

It is, of course, true that while Weber regards bureaucratic forms of control and organisation as reflections of aspects of modern culture he is clear that such developments are not specific to capitalism, but are part of the process of modernisation. Despite the historical links between capitalism and bureaucracy, Weber saw socialism as even more dependent on bureaucratic forms (pp.338–9). Nevertheless, in explaining broad organisational patterns in terms of social values and priorities rather than in the neutral rhetoric of the organisations themselves, Weber made an important contribution to a genuine sociology of organisations.

Marx and Lenin

However, if Weber established the broad parameters for a sociology of organisations, it is Marx who supplied the ingredients for a critical sociology of organisations. Marx's contribution stems from two somewhat disparate sources: his work on state bureaucracy, and his analysis of the relationship between capitalism and the design of work.

The first of these discussions has been accorded considerable attention because of its theoretical and political significance. The analysis of the nature and function of bureaucracy constitutes a central controversy within Marxist thought, and one which divided the early Marxist writers and politicians (Albrow, 1970; Eldridge and Crombie, 1974; Mouzelis, 1967). Marx's major interest in bureaucracy was limited to state administrative bureaucracies. For him these structures were, under capitalism, instruments of class rule and oppression: the administrative apparatus is a part of the State, and the State is class-based, an expression of class interests. What, then, of bureaucracy under socialism? Marx asserts the necessity for the proletariat to 'smash' the established 'state edifice', not simply perfect it; but does not present a single un-ambiguous statement of the role and nature of bureaucracy under socialism (Albrow, 1970).

As Eldridge and Crombie put it: Marx does not supply a clear answer to the question 'how, in organisational terms, is the proletariat to proceed?' (Eldridge and Crombie, 1974, p.138). These authors suggest that Marx saw a number of options, depending on local circumstances (pp. 138–9) and they note that the important debate within Marxism concerning the nature and organisation of the Party, and its relation to working-class consciousness constitutes an expression of Marx's discussion of the nature of political organisations and bureaucracies (see: Luxembourg, 1972). The two major axes of the debate are represented by Luxembourg's emphasis on the spontaneous *emergence* of the Party from the experiences and struggles of the working-class on the one hand and Lenin's insistence on the need for a limited organisation of professional revolutionaries, the revolutionary vanguard, on the other.

Lenin's views on the nature and origins of hierarchy and control within organisations in general are developed in *The State and Revolution*. In this work, his remarks are not restricted to party, or state bureaucracies, but refer to general issues of organisation – the inevitability of hierarchy, the possibility of democracy within organisations, etc. Lenin argues for the necessity to destroy previous, capitalist, state bureaucratic machinery, but asserts the need for the workers to administer the state themselves.

From the moment all members of society, or even only the vast majority, have learned to administer the state themselves, have taken this work into their own hands. . . . from this moment the need for governments of any kind begins to disappear. . . . The more democratic the 'state' which consists of the armed workers, and which is 'no longer a state in the proper sense of the word', the more rapidly does every form of state begin to wither away (Lenin, 1965a, p.122).

Lenin was clear that discipline, hierarchy and control were necessary in a socialist society. He is scornful in his attack on the 'anti-authoritarians', and quotes with approval Engels' remarks on the need for hierarchy and coordination. 'Take a factory, a railway, a ship on the high sea, said Engels – is it not clear that not one of these complex technical establishments, based on the employment of machinery and the planned cooperation of many people, could function without a certain amount of subordination, and, consequently, without a certain amount of *authority or power?*' (Lenin, 1965a, p.73, my emphasis).

Under socialism, this necessary domination and control is practised differently, however – officials would be elected and liable to dismissal, and their level of reward would not exceed that of ordinary workers (p.92).

It is clear that this debate about the nature and origins of state bureaucracies within Marx's work, and amongst Marxists, is of relevance to a more general sociology of large-scale organisations. Firstly, the debate considers the relationship between organisational structure (in this case bureaucratic structure) and societal types. A major area of interest is to what extent bureaucratic structures as they occur within Capitalism would, or should, be necessary under Socialism. It is with reference to this issue that Marx, Engels and, later, Lenin use the example of the Paris Commune to stress how existing bureaucratic structures must be destroyed and replaced by new forms of administrative structure.

From the very outset the Commune was compelled to recognise that the working class, once come to power, could not go on managing with the old state machine: . . . this working-class must, on the one hand, do away with the old repressive machinery previously used against itself, and, on the other, safeguard itself against its own deputies and officials, by declaring them all without exception subject to recall at any moment (Engels, in Lenin, 1965a, p.91).

In short, traditional bureaucratic forms are seen as inherently opposed to socialist priorities, and as intrinsically oriented towards capitalist interests and values.

Secondly, the Marxists in their discussion of the optimum and necessary relationship between the party and the working class, can be seen to be involved in a discussion which has direct and obvious implications for more general explorations of organisational structures which build on, and emerge from, *members'* needs and interests but which do not rigidify into permanent structures of privilege and hierarchy, i.e. the debate about participation and democracy within organisations.

Thirdly, the Marxist approach to bureaucracy makes the highly pertinent point that bureaucratic activity, which is presented as above politics, as neutral, expert administration, is essentially and irredeemably political. The State itself, which is usually seen as 'an organ for the reconciliation of classes' (Lenin, 1965a, p.8) is in fact an organ of class rule. Because it is political, it must be smashed and replaced. This point needs particular emphasis since, by its very nature, bureaucracy is not only political in its activity and structure: it is also mystifying – presenting itself, and being seen as beyond interests and sectional priorities, as mere administration. In pointing to the ideological nature of such notions and justifications of organisational structure and activity, and to the political implications of certain organisation forms, Marx was establishing some of the essential elements of a radical sociology of organisations.

Finally, the debate touches on the question of the determinants of organisational structure, in that Marx and other Marxists attempted to separate the degree of control, hierarchy and coordination that stemmed from the nature of the task or technology, from that which followed from the capitalist nature of the organisation, or its activities. This remains a highly significant area of debate. As we shall see it is one that Marx gave more comprehensive attention to in his treatment of the relationship between work and capitalism.

Marx: efficiency, control, the division of labour

Marx's analysis of the nature and role of the division of labour which is highly relevant to this analysis demonstrates considerable development from his early writings in the *Economic and Philosophical Manuscripts* to his more thorough and mature writings in *Capital*. It is his later writings that are most pertinent to this analysis. Marx maintains that the nature of capitalism has direct and unavoidable consequences for the division of labour and the structure of employing organisations. This follows from two interrelated features of capitalism. Firstly under capitalism labour *power* is purchased by the employer in order to achieve profit. Labour power is a commodity, a factor of production, to be used profitably. The employment relationship is determined by the employer's search for profit, and the forces of the market. It is this that supplies the 'rationality' of capitalism, and the 'rationality' of organisational structure and process.

By 'labour power' Marx refers to the 'aggregate of those mental and physical capabilities existing in a human being, which he exercises whenever he produces a use-value of any description' (Marx, 1954, p.164). The significant aspect of this emphasis on labour *power* rather than mere labour itself is that it points to the crucial significance of management, direction and control. If it is a potential, or capacity, that is purchased by the employer, then it is necessary to organise, direct and design the way in which the potential is realised. The labourer or employee no longer, under capitalism, sells his labour incorporated in a commodity, but his labour power as a commodity. As Marx notes, in order to sell commodities (other than labour power itself) the employer must have ownership or control of the other necessary factors of production – raw materials, capital etc.

Secondly, the purchaser of labour power buys it to *use* it, to achieve profit. This has one crucial implication – the conflict of interest between the employee who sells his labour power and the employer who purchases and uses it in order to realise, and maximise, surplus value from it. The interest of employee and employer are inherently and essentially in conflict. The purchase of labour power by the employer in order to achieve profit determines the nature of work under capitalism. Firstly, 'the labourer works under the control of the capitalist to whom his labour belongs: the capitalist taking good care that the work is done in a proper manner . . .' (Marx, 1954, p.180). Secondly, 'the produce is the property of the capitalist and not that of the labourer, its immediate producer . . . From his (the capitalist's) point of view, the labour-process is nothing more than the consumption of the commodity purchased, i.e. of labour power' (p.180).

As a result the design of work, and of organisations, reveals one highly significant feature which has considerable influence over a variety of organisational processes: the search for greater efficiency is inherently sectional, or political, irredeemably interrelated and in-volved with the search for more reliable and efficient forms of *control* and exploitation. Control, efficiency (from the employer's point of view) and exploitation become inseparable. Because, in capitalism, the organisation of work involves the purchase and use of labour potential for the achievement of profit for the owner – or his agents (thereby establishing systematic conflict of interest between employer and employee) – the work of the employees must be strictly directed and coordinated, and since their commitment must be uncertain they must be exposed to constant discipline and surveillance, by members of the organisation specially delegated to the task. As Marx puts it:

The directing motive, the end and aim of capitalist production, is to extract the greatest possible amount of surplus-value, and consequently to exploit labour-power to the fullest possible extent. As the number of cooperating labourers increases, so too does their resistance to the domination of capital, and with it the necessity for capital to overcome this resistance by counter-pressure. The control exercised by the capitalist is not only a special function, due to the nature of the social labour-process, and peculiar to that process, but it is, at the same time, a function of the exploitation of a social labour-process, and is consequently rooted in the unavoidable antagonism between the exploiter and the living and labouring raw material he exploits (Marx, 1954, p.313).

This interdependence and coincidence of efficiency and control has implications for a number of aspects of organisational structure and process: the three most important are the degree and extent of the division of labour, the use of machinery and technology, and the role of management. Each of these deserves attention.

For Marx the division of labour under capitalism demonstrated certain characteristic features directly related to the elements of capitalism described above. Under capitalism there is a tendency for the work of the employees, for the mass of the work force, to be de-skilled, for labour to be cheapened, to be reduced to the frequent repetition of a small number of processes or activities. Capitalism, writes Marx, revolutionises work by converting the 'labourer into a crippled monstrosity, by forcing his detail dexterity at the expense of a world of productive capabilities and instincts' (Marx, 1954, p.340). Discretion and skill are concentrated in a few employees, and systematically and purposively denied the rest: 'Intelligence in production expands in one direction, because it vanishes in many others. What is lost by the detail labourers, is concentrated in the capital that employs them' (p.341). And this 'lordship of capital over labour' increases the productive power of labour at the expense of the employees concerned, and serves to dominate and subjugate as it exploits. Marx is quite clear that under capitalism the extreme division of labour which involves the large-scale de-skilling of jobs, and the consequent separation of

hand and brain work – the former concerned with detailed execution of procedures designed by the latter – serves the twin goals of
productivity and discipline and control. Even the concept of
efficiency itself must be seen to contain ineradicably political – i.e.
class – elements and interests, despite the efforts of the employers
and their ideologues to present the division of labour and the objectives it serves as beyond politics, or class, as aspects of an inevitable
and desirable search for a generally beneficial level of efficiency
and productivity. It is critical to stress, Marx writes, that 'Division
of labour within the workshop implies the undisputed authority of
the capitalist over men, that are but parts of a mechanism that
belongs to him' (Marx, 1954, p.336).

For Marx, the division of labour within organisations cannot be
understood except in terms of the 'division of labour' in society as
a whole:

*Division of labour in society is brought about by the purchase and
sale of the products of different branches of industry, while the
connection between the detail operations in a workshop, is due to
the sale of the labour-power of several workmen to one capitalist,
who applies it as combined labour-power. The division of labour in
the workshop implies concentration of the means of production in
the hands of one capitalist; the division of labour in society implies
their dispersion among many independent producers of
commodities (Marx, 1954, p.336).*

The class-based, political aspects of the structure of organisations
and the division of labour also extend to Marx's analysis of the role
and consequences of machinery in employing organisations.
Machinery raises the degree of exploitation of labour; it also serves
to cheapen, and de-skill, labour. Just as the extreme division of
labour reduces the autonomy and skill of the mass of the employees
while enabling control and direction to be concentrated in the hands
of a small minority of the owners, or their agents, so the installation and use of machinery reduces skills, concentrates work decisions and permits a division of employees into 'workmen who are
actually employed on the machines (among whom are included a
few who look after the engine) and into mere attendants (almost
exclusively children) of these workmen' (Marx, 1954, p.396). An
important consequence of the use of machinery (and of the extreme
sub-division of labour) is the easy transferability of labour: 'Since
the motion of the whole system does not proceed from the workman, but from the machinery, a change of persons can take place
at any time without an interruption of the work' (p.397).

The use of machinery also has implications for the employer's
capacity to control and dominate the work force – as well as to
regulate and direct it. Marx notes the role of machinery in strike

breaking, and in facilitating the concentration of organisational decision-taking.

Marx's argument that the design of work and the use of machinery in large-scale organisations can only be seen in terms of the employer's efforts to direct the labour power he purchases to cheapen labour and to achieve ever greater profits also applies to his analysis of the role of management. If, on the one hand, there is discernible a 'tendency to equalise and reduce to one and the same level everything that has to be done by the minders of the machines' (Marx, 1954, p.396) there is also a resultant expansion of the coordinating, supervising and controlling functions of management. The two processes are mutually interlocked: the 'mere appendage' can only play his part in a capitalist environment with the direction and supervision of management.

Marx does not claim that all management and coordination stems from the exigencies and elements of capitalism. He recognises that

All combined labour on a large scale requires, more or less, a directing authority, in order to secure the harmonious working of the individual activities, and to perform the general functions that have their origin in the action of the combined organism, as distinguished from the action of the separate organs. A single violin player is his own conductor; an orchestra requires a separate one (Marx, 1954, p.313).

However, he stresses that under capitalism management necessarily does more than merely coordinate and integrate the activities of those collectively involved in a cooperative activity. Under capitalism management takes on new functions, functions which follow from the class nature of the employment relationship, and which are reflected in the class-based antagonisms between the detail labourer and the manager. Under capitalism management works to ensure a satisfactory level of profitability, and to increase it, to impose and maintain discipline on those whose labour is being used, to direct and determine their work activities, and to regulate the speed and nature of their work operations, the standard of their work, etc. Capitalism, he writes, requires managers as an army requires officers, to command in the name of the capitalist. The formal power of the manager comes not from the technical functions he serves, but from his position as employer – or as agent of the employer. The form of organisation characteristic of capitalism – with the division of members into 'hand' and 'brain' workers, the former reduced to detailed operations, the latter allocated control, design, supervisory and coordinating functions – is not an inevitable or neutral phenomenon. It is 'a method employed by capital for the more profitable exploitation of labour, by increasing that labour's productiveness' (Marx, 1954, p.317).

Weber and Marx compared

Despite the obvious differences between Marx's and Weber's approach to and analysis of large-scale organisations, these two theorists can be seen to share certain interests in organisations, to ask similar questions of them, and to focus attention on similar processes. These areas of common interest represent the basic parameters of a truly sociological approach to organisations, an approach which has recently shown signs of re-emergence.

First, both theorists were concerned with describing and explaining general principles and features of organisational structure. They were more interested in the broad tendencies demonstrated by and within employing organisations than with small-scale intra-organisational variations. This focus of interest makes them vulnerable to the criticism, from the less ambitious, empirically-minded student of organisations, that their models of organisations, or the processes isolated, show greater empirical variation than they seemed to appreciate. This line of attack is particularly common in recent American reactions to Weber's ideal type of bureaucracy (see Albrow, 1970). Such criticisms miss the point. In drawing attention to certain basic features of large-scale organisations (for Weber the elaborate, detailed and formal specification of authorities and responsibilities, supported by formal, 'bureaucratic' authority; for Marx the division between detail, 'hand' employees who execute procedures designed, controlled and coordinated by management – the 'brain' workers) both theorists are not only emphasising common and striking features of modern employing organisations (albeit features which may, in fact, demonstrate some degree of variability): they are also isolating those elements of large-scale organisation which are *theoretically* significant, in terms of their theory of employing organisations in society. For both Marx and Weber their conceptualisation of organisation can only be understood in terms of their theoretical assessment of, and approach to, the nature and function of large-scale organisations in modern or capitalist society. To forget this leads to the sort of excessive, directionless empiricism which characterises much organisational analysis.

The second feature follows from the first. Both theorists sought to *understand* the major feature of organisational structures. Their explanations eschewed the available justifications and explanations of organisational analysis in terms of a neutral, apolitical conception of efficiency, and replaced rhetoric with analysis. For both Marx and Weber the major elements of the structure of modern large-scale organisations stem from the efforts of those who own, manage or design the organisation, to achieve control over the members. For both writers the structure of modern organisations can only be understood in terms of control for sectional interests. For Weber, bureaucracy, which is not restricted to government administration, but is a *type* of organisation which is 'in principle applicable with equal facility to a wide variety of different fields' (Weber, 1964, p.334), depends on, and reflects in its structure and its process, the acceptance of certain ideas about the legitimacy of rational–legal control and power. Bureaucracy must be seen in terms of the form of authority which prevails in it, and which determines, and is reflected in, bureaucratic structure. 'Experience tends universally to show', he writes, 'that the purely bureaucratic type of administrative organisation is . . . formally the most rational known means of carrying out *imperative control over human beings*' (Weber, 1964, p.337 my emphasis). Weber's analysis is useful for emphasising the centrality of control and the importance, to senior members, of achieving ideological justification for the structure and function of the organisation.

For Marx the structure of modern employing organisations, and the design of work within them, characterised by extremes of sub-division and specialisation – the creation of 'detail' work – must be seen as a result of the capitalist's efforts to direct and coordinate the labour power of his employees to achieve profit: 'Division of labour within the workshop implies the undisputed authority of the capitalist over men, that are but parts of a mechanism that belongs to him' (Marx, 1954, p.336).

Both writers insist, as noted, on the close relationship between 'efficiency' as defined by senior organisational members and processes of organisational control – an insistence which has been largely forgotten, but which is evident in their analyses of many aspects of organisational design, structure and activity. Marx points to the control implications of management structures, and of automation and technology. Weber notes the control functions of bureaucratic regulations, personnel and selection procedures, career structures, etc. Whereas many modern organisation analysts and re-searchers are prepared to regard these various aspects of organisa-tions as discrete processes or elements which coalesce in various patterned forms as a result of pressures for efficiency (a concept which most writers regard with insufficient scepticism), Marx and Weber in their delineation of a genuine sociology of organisations emphasised that *no* acceptable understanding of any feature of organisation – and especially those features which they saw as most typical and significant – could be achieved unless it proceeded from the realisation that organisations are, quintessentially, structures of control and domination. And that this control, and the goals it serves, are surrounded by ideological activity which strives to mask or neutralise the political nature of organisations by reference to generally acceptable values and ways of thinking – e.g. rationality, efficiency, etc.

But if organisations are structures of control, what is this control for? What interests or purposes are served by bureaucratisation, or minute sub-division and specialisation of work? And what efforts are made to legitimise these structures? It is a third common element in Marx's and Weber's sociology of organisations that they both emphasised the necessity to see organisational structure and activity in terms of their social context, or their relationship with society.

It is clear the two writers differed in their conception of the relationship with societal interests and values. For Marx large-scale employing organisations reflected capitalist priorities and sectional, class interests not merely in their activity, but in their structure. He was at pains to discuss the relationship between the division of labour within organisations, the nature, function and size of management, and the design and use of technology and capitalism. While conceding that some degree of division and specialisation of labour was evident in pre-capitalist societies he stressed that the extremes of specialisation and differentiation occurred under capitalism as a result of the priorities of the capitalist and the relationship with the employees: 'the most diverse division of labour in the workshop, as practised by manufacture, is a special creation of the capitalist mode of production alone' (Marx, 1954, p.339).

Weber, on the other hand, regarded the major element of bureaucracy as significantly influenced by capitalism, and notes that modern capitalism 'strongly tends to foster the development of bureaucracy' (Weber, 1964, p.338), but argued that both socialism and capitalism rely upon bureaucratic organisations in numerous spheres – armies, governments, administrative agencies, economic enterprises, etc. For Weber bureaucracy was not a feature of capitalism only, but was a key feature of the modern world dominated by rationality. It was in their emphasis on rationality that bureaucratic organisations reflected key features of modern (as against capitalist) society.

But if Marx and Weber differed in their assessment of the most significant feature of modern organisations, and their analysis of the societal roots and causation of such elements, they agreed in firmly locating their organisational analyses in terms of societal variables and the interests and purposes of those who own or run the organisations. 'The question is,' remarks Weber, 'who controls the existing bureaucratic machinery?' For 'the bureaucratic apparatus is driven to continue functioning by the most powerful interests which are material and objective but also ideal in character' (Weber, 1964, p.338). Similarly, their organisational analyses are firmly placed in their societal analyses, and their discussions of processes of legitimation and mystification, although their assessment of the pertinent societal features differs.

In short, despite their differences, both Marx and Weber in their sociology of organisations isolated and emphasised those key elements in the structure of large-scale organisations which were of most significance to their theoretical interest in processes of control and legitimation within organisations and the relationship between organisational structure and process and societal values and interests. Both stressed that organisational structure – the design of work and control – can only be seen in terms of general processes of organisational control initiated by, and in the interest of, those who ran or domiated the organisation. Both saw the purposes of organisations (or of those who dominated the organisation) and the structures of work and control to which they gave rise, as reflecting more general processes, cultures, interests and priorities, in the society at large. They firmly rejected the widely prevalent view that organisational structure follows from the application of neutral, apolitical priorities – such as efficiency, technology, etc. – and insisted that such concepts should be exposed for their political purposes and assumptions, and focus attention on the nature and function of organisational ideologies. These are the ingredients of a genuine sociology of organisations.

A sociological approach to organisations

There are welcome signs of a renaissance of interest in, and a re-utilisation of, the elements of a genuine sociology of organisations as shown in the works of Marx and Weber. This chapter is devoted to an exposition of this emergent sociology of organisations, as it is evident in recent publications. This chapter will, eclectically, select those arguments and insights which, together, can be seen to constitute a new and radical approach to organisations, for this approach supplies the background to the remainder of the book. Many of the points mentioned below will be discussed more fully later.

The approach has three major elements:

1. The politics of organisational structure

Conventional organisational sociology has shown a willingness to accept the inevitability of, and necessity for, current organisational structures. Such analysis accepts the ready emphasis that senior members of organisations and their spokesmen place on the role of efficiency as a determinant of organisational structures, failing to question the purposes and values that lie behind the notion, to note its sectional implications, or to consider the mechanisms whereby such structures were developed historically, or why alternative forms did not develop. Their analyses are vulnerable to such failures as a result of their use of the systems approach.

Thus in much conventional analysis of organisations the major elements of organisational structure – hierarchy, extreme division of labour – are presented as functional consequences of the imperatives of efficiency, of industrialisation and industrial technology. All that remains to explain is small-scale variations between organisations.

Blackburn has noted the deficiencies of such analyses:

This way of thinking . . . contains a large dose of technological determinism since it suggests that the industrial nature of technology dominates social organisation as a whole. . . . Thus the unavoidable concomitant of modern industry will be bureaucratic

*organisation. . . . By deducing social organisation from industrial
technology bourgeois sociology can portray capitalist society as void
of contradictions (Blackburn, 1972, p.42).*

The new approach to organisational structure is sceptical about
the universality, inevitability and neutrality of organisational structures, seeing them rather as reflecting societal structures of inequality, power and interests, within specific societal forms.

For, as Brown has remarked, arguments about the inevitability of
bureaucratic structures

*. . . in terms of functional necessity can be questioned on both
theoretical and empirical grounds. Two theoretical points
can . . . be stated very briefly. Firstly, to demonstrate the functional necessity of any particular element of social structure is not
to provide an adequate account of its origins; this requires
consideration of the actual pattern of actions and events which led
to its emergence in the first place. . . . Secondly, however clearly
any particular pattern of administration can be shown to contribute
to the maintenance and success of, for example, control and
coordination in large-scale complex industrial organisations, there is
always the possibility of functional alternatives (Brown, 1977,
p.197).*

If we are seriously to doubt the inevitability of current organisational structures alternative explanations must be considered.
Foremost among these is the possibility, increasingly suggested by a
number of writers, that organisational structures represent the
choices of senior organisational members. This suggestion is discussed at length in Section II. Basically, it argues that over time the
particular organisational forms which were utilized 'were chosen
because of their appropriateness in terms of values and interests of
those with power to decide rather than by reason of their functional
necessity' (Brown, 1977, p.191).

Once this possibility is conceded, all other aspects of organisational structure and functioning, previously regarded as inevitable,
sacrosanct features of modern organisation, become susceptible to a
more sceptical analysis. Two features which have attracted
particular attention – because of their central position within
organisational structures – are technology and the division of
labour itself. These are considered in detail in Section II. A number
of writers have argued for the political significance of technology
and division of labour within organisations. These features are seen
as functional only in terms of the typical problems and objectives
of orgaisations within class societies.

Any attempt to uncover the determinants of organisational structure must specify the organisational features which merit analysis.
It is one of the common elements of a number of recent analyses of

organisational structure that, following Marx and Weber, they attempt to focus on the major principles of modern organisational forms rather than on detailed empirical variations. Fox is one influential writer, for example, who has sought to 'explore fundamental principles implicitly informing the ways in which men organise, regulate, and reward themselves for the production and distribution of goods and services, and the significance of these principles for their wider social relations' (Fox, 1974, p.13). Not surprisingly, Fox, like Braverman, (1974) focusses attention on the distinction between 'hand' and 'brain' work – 'the division of labour between intellectual work and manual labour, the gulf between the organisers and the organised', which Deutsch has argued, 'is, in fact, the prologue to class society' (Deutsch, 1969, p.15).

A third important element of this view of the politics of organisational structure focuses on the *emergent* nature of organisational structures. Organisations are seen as being characterised by constant conflicts, negotiations, resistance or acquiescence. The 'given-ness' and fixity of organisational structure is replaced by an emphasis on the conditional, unstable nature of organisational reality as senior groups attempt to constrain and control subordinate groups, who resist, obstruct and avoid such efforts as they seek to defend or enlarge their areas of discretion, their share of organisational resources. This view of organisational structure will be discussed and presented in Section III. It is important to note, following Elger, that internal organisational negotiations and struggles must be seen in terms of the extra-organisational positions and resources of the participants – their class membership. He remarks, for example:

The manner in which such 'organisational objectives' as production plans or payment policies, designed by top management and mediated through the activities of middle-managers, are implemented on the shop-floor in an outcome of interaction between managers commanding resources buttressed by legal and customary prerogatives and workers commanding resources which flow from the character of their labour (Elger, 1975, p.12).

Just as the major features of organisational structures reflect not the inevitability of the demands of efficiency but class-based priorities and values, so this structure itself is the constant focus of conflict between organisational groups, in the course of which these groups demonstrate and employ their class memberships and resources.

2. Organisations and the social context

It will be clear that the approach to organisations under discussion in this chapter asserts the causal primacy of the relationship between organisational structure and process and the nature of the society within which they occur. As noted in Chapter 1, conventional organisational analysis takes a rather bland view of this relationship, if it discusses it at all. But a number of recent writers have made this relationship the cornerstone of their analysis, as noted above.

Benson, for example, has advanced a 'dialectical analysis' of organisations, which, like that of Elger, emphasises the processual aspect of organisational structure and functioning, and notes the significance of 'powerful forces which tend to occasion the reproduction of the existing social structure. These include . . . the interests of particular groups of people and their power to defend their interests within an established order' (Benson, 1977b, p.3).

As well as noting the manner in which organisational structures emerge from, or are constructed by, processes of negotiation and struggle within organisations, Benson notes three other features of the dialectical approach: *totality* which requires a focus on the whole organisation, and its constituent inter-connections; *contradiction* which refers to the inevitable strains and conflicts contained in, though they may be masked by, apparent organisational stability; and *praxis* which refers to the potential within organisational members actively to reconstruct their organisational experience and the structure of the organisation of which they are members.

Benson insists, sensibly, that a genuine sociology of organisations should reject the common assumption that an organisation can be abstracted from its relations with dominant groups, powerful resources, ideological structure etc., in the surrounding society and be viewed 'as if it were autonomous or at least capable of filtering the environment through its input – output orifices' (Benson, 1977b, p.12). On the contrary, organisations must be studied in terms of these relationships with their social contexts. Only then will it be possible for a dialectical approach to consider alternative forms of organisation, alternative designs of work and of control.

A broadly similar argument about the interrelationship between organisations and society has been advanced by Heydebrand in his article 'Organisational contradictions in public bureaucracies'. In this ambitious piece he argues that organisations must be studied in terms of the societal and historical forces that gave rise to them, for

Organisations, while they are themselves sites of developing contradictions, are always part of a larger political economy, a macrosocial and historical context, and particularly part of a sociohistorical formation in which a given mode of production is tending towards dominance over others. The basic contradictions within the political economy of advanced capitalism, e.g. those between state and economy or capital and labour or – within capital itself – those between capital accumulation and the realisation of surplus value, will be reflected in the formation and transformation of almost all types of organisations (Heydebrand, 1977, p.89–90).

The structure and process of modern large-scale organisations demonstrate these contradictions, one of which has been noted in a more detailed manner by Fox (1974): the contradiction is between controlling a potentially recalcitrant labour force, and maintaining the commitment of those so controlled. This is discussed in Section III.

Other writers, too, have usefully pointed to the importance of recognising that organisations are 'structurally embedded within the wider social context' (Clegg and Dunkerley, 1977, p.6, and see, for example, Allen, 1975.) Various linkages have been suggested which will be discussed more fully in subsequent chapters: that organisational structures reflect choices based on class values and interests; that they articulate class-based assumptions about members' reliability, value, abilities; that organisational conflicts reflect dissensions within society, and that inequalities within organisations are related to inequalities within the larger society.

3. Organisations and ideology

As noted in the previous chapter, both Marx and Weber saw modern organisations as articulating particular ideological, or cultural, forms. For both theorists organisations – or bureaucracy – represented the institutionalisation of socially located and specific systems of decision-making and assessment.

It is important to note, as these two theorists stressed, that the ways of thinking and evaluating characteristic of modern organisa-tions should not be accepted on their own terms. It is one of the major features of these ideational systems that they are presented as rational in the sense of sensible, or simply concerned with the most efficient means for achieving, chosen goals. Chapter 2 contained some reference to Marx's and Weber's claims for the ideological nature of these systems. (These questions are also discussed later, in Section IV.)

Drawing particularly on the Marxist tradition, recent writers have re-asserted the ideological nature of organisational rationality. This argument has two elements: that the logics of decision-making and evaluation upon which modern organisations are based are not neutral, merely technical systems, but contain implicit evaluative elements, and that these priorities and values which exist, masked, within organisational rationalities are socially located, and represent the interests of certain dominant groups.

A great deal of conventional organisational analysis accepts the 'rationality' of modern organisations. While being prepared to bemoan the 'human consequences' of such forms of organisation, they are seen as embodying inexorable and unavoidable and impartial constraints deriving from the basic processes of industrialisation – the application of technical rationality to work and organisation. Blau and Schoenherr have noted the ideological advantages – in terms of mystification and justification – of this sort of analysis: 'In as much as experts judge issues in terms of universal criteria of rationality and efficiency, they cannot be blamed for the conclusions they reach, even though these conclusions may lead to actions of powerful organisations that are contrary to the interests of most people' (Blau and Schoenherr, 1971, p.355). In much the same way, conventional organisation theory, by 'discovering' causal relationships which reveal the inevitability of current organisational forms, becomes so embedded within and celebratory of these forms as to be unable to envisage alternative structures. In this way, organisation theory has become, in many cases, part of the ideology of hierarchic organisations.

Writers who accept the rationality of organisations ignore the political, sectional, nature of apparently neutral procedures and technology. Like Mannheim's functionary, they transform problems of politics into problems of administration, failing to note that 'behind every law that there has ever been there lie the socially fasioned interests and *Weltanschauungen* of a specific group' (Mannheim, 1936, p.360).

Conventional organisational analysis accepts organisational definitions of organisational rationality (while conceding the possibility of some degree of irrationality due to informal organisation or human factors). In this way, the assumptions lying behind such rationality are overlooked, as is the relationship between 'rational' criteria and sectional or class advantage. In opposition to this, recent writers have noted that, for example, 'Bureaucratic organisation promotes efficiency or rationality only within the context of managerial control. Bureaucratic organisation, with its reliance on multiple levels of authority and supervision and its emphasis on discipline and predictability, is probably the only way of ensuring efficient production using alienated labour' (Edwards, 1972, p.118).

The point, of course, is not to reject the argument from efficiency out of hand, but to insist on asking whose interests are served by such efficiency and, as Brown noted above, how these 'efficient' organisational structures developed. For many writers the answers to these questions lie in the historical decisions of the owners and senior members of organisations as they sought to maximise their interests within a class structure – 'the capitalist division of labour is functional to a system that rests on forced labour and that therefore relies only on regimentation and hierarchical control, not on the workers' consent or cooperation' (Gorz, 1972, p.34).

The emphasis on organisational rationality as the determinant of organisations' structure removes organisations from the worlds of class interests or politics. The problems of organisational analysis – like the problems of organisations themselves – become technical ones. And, 'In so far as more spheres of decision-making are construed as "technical problems" requiring information and instrumental strategies produced by technical experts, they are removed from political debate.' The result is 'an infinitely flexible ideology which can be interpreted in ways that legitimate public or private policy adopted by established power and privilege groups' (Shroyer, 1970, p.212.)

These, then, are the three major elements of a new sociology of organisations. It is this approach which underpins the analysis presented in this book. This approach is not entirely new within organisational analysis, some of the elements having been suggested in the works of Gouldner (1954), Crozier (1964), and, more recently, Elger (1975), Collins (1975), Clegg and Dunkerley (1977), Benson 1977b). However, such works constitute the exception: conventional organisational theory, possibly because of its location within business schools, its close links with management consultancy (Brown, 1967); the nature of the audience it serves, or the groups and corporations that fund research (Silverman, 1970, p.68), has shown a marked indifference to a genuinely critical sociological approach to organisations, failing, as Benson notes, 'to deal with the production of organisational arrangements or to analyse the entanglements of theory in those arrangements' (Benson, 1977b, p.2).

It is, of course, true, as noted in Chapter 1, that the systems approach to organisations considers one of the features mentioned above: the relationship between the structure and activities of organisations and the society within which they occur. But within systems analysis this relationship is asserted rather than explored, an assertion which is based on the systems conceptualisation of the relationship between 'environment' and organisation in terms of 'inputs' and 'outputs' between the social system and the goal-oriented organisational system.

A genuinely sociological approach to organisations which investigates the relationship between societal forms and their attendant structures of interests, domination and values, and the design of work and control systems within large-scale employing organisations, has found little appeal within established organisation theory, for three main reasons.

Firstly, the popularity and pervasiveness of systems thinking – of various sorts – has resulted in a form of organisation theory, with its related concepts, which is at least indifferent, if not antithetical, to the approach under discussion. The deficiencies of the systems approach have been well rehearsed by Silverman (1970). The confusion between the prescriptive and descriptive is particularly important in this connection, since the prescriptive ingredient, coming, as it is likely to, from those who own or run the organisation, will minimise the approach discussed here, and exaggerate the role of societally necessary organisational goals in determining the internal structure and process of organisations. As Benson remarks 'the participants' explanations for the structure of the organisation have been formalised as scientific theories' (Benson, 1977b, p.1). The problems with the 'goal-oriented' approach have been reviewed elsewhere (Silverman, 1970; Albrow, 1968). Similarly, while it is true that the systems approach is not entirely blind to the existence of conflict within organisations, it exaggerates the degree of consensus, and conceptualises the origins of intra-organisational struggle in excessively parochial, i.e. internal, organisational terms.

Secondly, and relatedly, much thinking on organisations has employed not only as a desirable end-state but as an explanatory variable, the concept of *efficiency*. Clearly this concept is particularly appropriate within a systems setting. Frequently typologies of organisations employ, explicitly or implicitly, the concept of efficiency as a necessary causal link between a certain state of the postulated independent variable, and the related organisational type. It is because certain organisational forms are more *efficient* under the conditions in question, so the argument goes, that the observed or claimed variation in organisational structures occurs. The importance of efficiency in analyses of organisations has a number of drawbacks. Firstly, the concept of efficiency is insufficiently explained and defined – efficient for whom or for what? Secondly, it demonstrates too great a preoccupation with managerial issues and problems. As Benson notes,

According to this problematic, much of what occurs in the organisation is understood as a result of goal pursuit and/or need fulfilment. This view has been coupled with a methodological stance which accepts the conventionally understood components of the organisation as scientific categories. The combination has uncritically accepted existing organisational arrangements and adapted itself to the interests of administrative elites. As a consequence, organisational analysis has been dominated by issues of administrative concern (Benson, 1977b, p.2).

Thirdly, it reduces curiosity about the determinants of organisational structure, by assuming precisely what needs to be explained – the relationship between organisational forms and determinant variables, and by regarding as causal a connection which may merely be correlation. Rather than assuming such relationships as causal, the sociologist should analyse the nature and origins of such correlations.

The numerous classifications of organisations which demonstrate this reliance on the unexplored notion of organisational efficiency also demonstrate another obstacle to the development of a truly critical, sociological approach to organisations: their constant search for, and measurement of, organisational *variations*, distracts attention from the equally, if not more important, similarities between large-scale employing organisations. No doubt it is true that organisations whose prime beneficiaries are their owners and managers differ from organisations that exist to serve the public rather than to make a profit (Blau and Scott, 1963), or that organisations with a technology for processing oil differ from those making precision instruments. But how important are these differences? And what is gained (whose interests are served) by establishing and measuring these variations? It is not to be lost sight of that much as they may differ in detail, there are broad similarities between employing organisations within capitalism: similarities which can be related to their location within a capitalist economic system.

Fourthly, conventional organisational theory has been resistant to the sort of sociological analysis described here, paradoxically because of a preoccupation with organisations themselves. The society within which these organisations occur, and its relationship with these organisations, has been very little studied. To the extent that the outside world does impinge on the structure and functioning of organisations, it is conceptualised not as a source of interests, values, class loyalties, ideologies, market developments etc., but as the organisation's 'environment'. Environment is defined in terms of *senior members'* conceptions of their organisational environment, 'is to be considered only in as much as it affects the problems of the organisations, which is to say the problems of those with authority' (Silverman, 1970, p.39). Silverman argues for an approach more compatible with a sociological approach to organisational structure: 'it would be more fruitful to analyse organisations in terms of the different ends of their members and of their capacity to impose these ends on others – it suggests an analysis in terms of power and authority' (Silverman, 1970, p.39). (See also Elger, 1975; Collins, 1975; Allen, 1975; Benson, 1977a and b; Clegg and Dunkerley, 1977.) But conventional treatments of organisational environments, far from investigating the significance of class memberships, resources and interests in structuring organisational work and control systems – or resistance to them – prefer to restrict attention, at best, to the role of market demands, the behaviour of clients, customers, competitors. Again as Benson has remarked, the significance of extra-organisational interests and resources in affecting internal organisational structure and functioning has been largely overlooked by most conventional organisational analysis. Certainly some writers have noted that organisations are tools, that they must be analysed in terms of their prime beneficiary etc., but what is lacking is any serious effort to explain internal organisational structure and process in extra-organisational terms. Instead,

. . . the organisation is assumed to be an instrument designed for a purpose, and research focusses on the structural consequences flowing from that and on the technical adjustments necessary to enhance goal pursuit. The power base of the leadership is not examined; alternative systems based on different power bases are not considered. . . . An examination of the power bases of authority figures would generally extend beyond the boundaries of the organisation itself and this is perhaps why most organisation theorists have avoided the problem (Benson, 1977b, p.8).

Furthermore, a genuine sociology of organisations is not assisted by the efforts of some organisation analysts to develop hypotheses about organisations *in general*, lumping together such diverse examples as voluntary organisations, charities, political parties and employing organisations. (See for example Hyman and Fryer, 1975, and Clegg and Dunkerley, 1977, for support for this view.) Such an ambition results in generalisations of an extremely high level of abstraction. It also obstructs the analysis of those structural elements which are dramatically revealed in employing organisations (see above) but not necessarily in all forms of organisation. The search for general organisational laws reflects in its findings the bland assumptions from which it proceeds; that it is in the fact and the problems of organisation *per se* (regardless of context or location) that the structural and processual elements of organisations are based.

Allen has remarked on the extent to which models of organisations are underpinned by a 'static' version of reality. He writes: 'The aspect of reality in question, namely organisation activity, can, in consequence, be analysed without reference to any factor external to it' (Allen, 1975, p.89). Despite recent theoretical developments, Allen argues, the feature of organisational theory mentioned above persists: organisations are analysed independently of external environmental factors. The emphasis on efficiency as a causal link is an important part of this parochialism. But the conceptualisaton of the 'environment' is also crucial. (See also Elger, 1975.) Other writers have noticed the close links between much organisation theory, its concepts, interests, assumptions, and the interests and 'problems' of senior organisational members (e.g. Clegg and Dunkerley, 1977).

There are important exceptions to these remarks: some writers on organisations (particularly industrial sociologists) have shown an awareness of the significance of capitalist priorities and values in determining organisational structure and functioning (Gouldner, 1954); and some writers have distinguished themselves by recognising that 'lower level participants' in organisations are the same people who are known in other sociological specialities as employees or workers (Allen, 1975) – just as, occasionally, senior members of organisations, who play such a large part in structuring sociological interest in organisations, as well as the organisations themselves, are seen as the same people who are known elsewhere as members of the ruling class, or their agents (Child, 1973a). Of particular importance in reflecting a more conscious approach to organisations are two recent publications, Elger (1975) and Allen (1975), both of which have influenced this work.

Nevertheless, the main point remains: on the whole, conventional organisational analysis and theory has ignored the sorts of interests described earlier as constituting a genuinely sociological approach to the design of work and control in large-scale employing organisations, despite the useful and important contributions of the early theorists.

Capitalist and socialist societies

This book is concerned with the structure and process of organisations within capitalist societies. Throughout, it will be maintained that internal aspects of employing organisations can only be understood in terms of their location within capitalist societies. This conviction, which is explictly considered at numerous points in the argument, constitutes the backdrop to the book as a whole, as will be seen. To that extent the book offers a similar analysis to that outlined by Blackburn when he remarks of the ideal type bureaucracy described by Weber that it

is an institutionalisation of the imperatives of market society with its consequent alienations. The capitalist market reduces quality to quantity, makes human labour power a commodity and ensures that the exchange value of a commodity dominates its individual use value. In the same way, a bureaucracy reduces both its own workers and the public it administers to a set of abstract characteristics. . . . Just as the market organised human behaviour according to unquestionable economic laws, so bureaucracy imposes man-made rules as if they had some impersonal necessity. For Weber, all this was part of the formal abstract efficiency which bureaucracy provides. Such efficiency can only serve the powers that be; its formal rationality is dependent on the rationality of the capitalist system, of which it is a part (Blackburn, 1972, p.43).

Employing organisations within capitalism reveal, in broad terms, capitalist values, priorities and interests, and reflect class-based conflicts. The relationship between organisational structure and process and the existence of capitalism is, however, a subtle one. Within capitalism market forces encourage those who own or run organisations to install structures of work and control which management theory and practice has shown to be useful for maximising profit and control within a class society, and minimising, in the short term, the associated conflicts and contradictions.

Capitalist societies can be defined in terms of two interrelated features: private ownership of the means of production and the organisation of production around the pursuit of profit in the market. It is an important feature of capitalism that it results in the supremacy of the market and the search for profit. Under capitalism, labour becomes a commodity which is bought and sold on the market and used for the accumulation of (privately owned) profit. This fact determines the existence of, and structures the relationship between, owners and non-owners – 'Property relations constitute the axis of the dichotomous system: a minority of "non-producers" who control the means of production, are able to use this position of control to extract from the majority of "producers" the surplus product which is the source of their livelihood' (Giddens, 1973, p.28).

The implications of these relations of expropriation and conflict for work structures as described by Marx were noted earlier in this chapter. But to argue for a causal connection between capitalism and organisational structure necessarily occasions some consideration of the obvious fact that ostensibly socialist societies boast large-scale employing organisations apparently just as bureaucratic and hierarchic and using similar principles of work design as those in the West. Indeed, the presence of bureaucratic organisations in, for example, the USSR, has even raised the possibility that it represents the emergence of a new class based on the Party's monopolisation of bureaucratic power and control.

Not only are bureaucratic organisations to be found in many industrialised 'socialist' societies, but these societies often display the same explicit principles – and practices – of work design which characterise the capitalist West. As is well known, Lenin himself explicitly and energetically advocated the utilisation of Taylor's principles of work design: 'We must raise the question of applying much of what is scientific and progressive in the Taylor system; . . . We must organise in Russia the study and teaching of the Taylor system and systematically try it out and adapt it to our own ends' (Lenin, 1965b, pp.258–9).

It is necessary to add, however, as Szymanski (n.d.) has stressed, that to advocate the adoption of the work design principles of scientific management is not necessarily tantamount to installing capitalist forms of production. It is true that, within capitalism, Taylorism is an excellent way of achieving a concentration of control in managerial hands (a direct imperative of capitalist priorities) but Taylorism itself simply consists of a number of work principles (see Section II) which isolate and redistribute work skills. It would, hypothetically, be possible for a collective of workers to reorganise their work on a Taylorist basis, but retain control among themselves. It is, however, true, as Szymanski notes, that the principles of scientific management constitute a necessary basis for the development of capitalist control over a work force. But they do not, in themselves, constitute such an expropriation of control. Lenin himself separated two features of Taylorism which he noted combined 'the refined brutality of bourgeois exploitation and a number of the greatest scientific achievements in the field of analysing mechanical motions during work' (Lenin, 1965b, pp.258–9).

Such distinctions, however, although important conceptually and analytically, do nothing to alter the plain fact that in the USSR and other ostensibly socialist societies the methods, control systems and work principles evident in organisations in the West are used by large-scale employing organisations within very similar contexts of control and appropriation. This would seem, *a priori* to constitute a denial of the argument outlined by Blackburn and suggested above. However, there are a number of reasons why the existence of hierarchic, centralised, inegalitarian organisations within, say, the USSR need not cause any substantial modification of the basic thesis.

In the first place, as Braverman has recently noted, the utilisation, within the USSR, of capitalist work structures and organisations was the result, on the one hand, of the Marxists being 'impressed, perhaps even overawed' by the apparent efficiency and success of these principles as evident in American industry; and, on the other hand, of the very severe problems faced by the Soviet Communists in the early days of the revolution. 'The Soviet Union faced catastrophe unless it could develop production and replace the ingrained traditions of the Russian peasantry with systematic habits of social labour' (Braverman, 1974, p.11). Not surprisingly, under these pressures, the leaders of Soviet industry were attracted to what were seen as the highly efficient and rational principles used in the capitalist west. Over time, of course, these work practices became established within the USSR.

The difficulties of the early Soviet leaders were increased by virtue of the fact that by achieving a social revolution they had not achieved a revolution in 'automatic and immediate transformation of the mode of production' (Braverman, 1974, p.23). As a result, the only available model, as displayed self-consciously by the capitalist societies, assumed considerable significance. As Braverman remarks:

It took capitalism centuries to develop its own mode of production. . . . Socialism, as a mode of production does not grow 'automatically' in the way that capitalism grew in response to blind

*and organic market forces; it must be brought into being, on the
basis of an adequate technology, by the conscious and purposive
activity of collective humanity (Braverman, 1974, p.23, my
emphasis).*

This introduces the second argument about the relevance of the
Soviet example to the thesis under consideration. A number of
writers have argued that the USSR represents something less than a
fully-realised socialist society – a transitional or possibly mis-
directed form. Hyman, for example, remarks,

*Those who refer to Russia and other East European countries as
'State Capitalist' societies imply that, while the legal ownership of
industry may have been transformed, the system of management
and economic rationale adopted do not differ over much from
those in Britain or in the United States. It could be argued that a
privileged and self-perpetuating elite makes the crucial economic
decisions, and along basically capitalist lines, even in the so-called
'communist' countries. The irrational and often brutal consequences of a class-divided society cannot be expected to be overcome unless working people as a whole are able to take key decisions in the organisation and direction of production (Hyman,
1972, p.88).*

According to such writers, the formal abolition of private ownership of the means of production, while it creates significant
differences between the society and more overtly capitalist ones,
does not, in itself, produce socialism. It is a necessary, but not a
sufficient, factor in the emergence of socialism. Socialism also requires the genuine involvement of the people in the determination
of their destinies, including their work destinies. Clearly, the
relevance of the Soviet case to the argument under consideration (of
the close links between capitalism and hierarchic, inegalitarian,
organisational structures) is greatly reduced if the USSR is seen as
not being genuinely socialist.

This is the position adopted in this book. The pervasiveness and
persistence of capitalist organisation forms, even in State Socialist
societies, far from demonstrating the inevitability of such forms (as
necessary consequences of industrialisation) is in fact one index (but
by no means the only one) that the societies concerned have not
achieved socialism, which will bring about a genuine revolution in
the structure of control within production.

This is precisely why, within societies undergoing socialist revolu-
tions, or aspiring to genuine socialism, the question of appropriate
organisational forms becomes critical, as noted in Chapter 2. (It
also explains why Western intellectuals, disappointed with the
bureaucratic betrayal of socialism in the USSR, eagerly seize on
signs of anti-bureaucratic ideology and practice in countries such as

China.) In China, for example, as Yeo-chi King has noted, during and after the cultural revolution, Maoists articulated an anti-bureaucratic, voluntaristic conception of organisation. He remarks: 'Maoists seem to think that the touchstone of socialism is not the socialisation of the means of production, as such, but the domination and control by the producers over the conditions and products of their work' (Yeo-chi King, A., 1977, p.365). The organisational forms deriving from this conviction show, as Yeo-chi King mentions, a striking contrast to the major elements of Weber's ideal type: anti-hierarchic, anti-specialisation, anti-expert, anti-administrative professionalism and routinisation, in favour of role-shifting, or group-based decision-making.

It is not necessary to the argument of this book to claim that this Chinese form of organisation represents the only, or major, alternative to conventional hierarchical organizational forms. The point is simply that one would expect, within socialist societies (as opposed to State socialist societies which eagerly accept such organisational forms), considerable discussion or, in Braverman's words, 'conscious and purposive activity' concerning the best ways of translating socialism into appropriate organisational forms. Such discussions will find the pervasiveness (and, so it is claimed, mere neutrality of) the bureaucratic type a seductive, but in the long term destructive, model. To argue that established organisational forms articulate and reflect capitalist interests and values and that this accounts for their pervasiveness (rather than their instrumental efficiency) is not, unfortunately, the same as describing the structure and process of alternative organisational forms except negatively. That search continues. The absence of socialist organisational forms in Russia or elsewhere does not prove the impossibility of other forms.

Finally, one other issue must be clarifed: the way in which *organisation* and *bureaucracy* are used in this book. Bureaucracy has been – and still is – used in a variety of different ways. Two common uses are as a form of government administration, of rule by officials, and as a particularly rigid, formalised and rule-bound type of organisation. In this latter sense, which will be employed here, all bureaucracies are organisations but not all organisations are bureaucracies. Organisations are more or less bureaucratised depending on the extent of formalisation, standardisation, etc. they demonstrate. In fact, most organisations display a high level of bureaucratisation, but they need not.

But what do we mean by organisation? As with bureaucracy there is already a surplus of definitions, varying with their purposes. It is not obvious that it is possible to carve out one clear and unproblematic definition (see Eldridge and Crombie, 1974, p.22) but it is necessary to point out, as those authors do, that the OED in defining 'to organise' in terms of to 'form into an organic whole', 'give orderly structure to; frame and put into working order, make arrangements for or get up' (undertaking involving cooperation), certainly establishes the broad, basic features of a definition of an organisation. Eldridge and Crombie usefully point out that by 'organic' the OED refers to the fact of interdependence, and these two elements, of ordering or structuring, plus the interdependence of elements, constitute the essential features of organisation, with the addition of one further factor, which Albrow has pointed to: the fact that 'individuals are conscious of their membership and legitimize their co-operative activities primarily by reference to the attainment of impersonal goals rather than moral standards' (Albrow, 1970, p.162). It is in this sense that the concept organisation is used here.

Chapter 4

The experience of organisational membership

This book is primarily concerned with the structure of work organisations, and how this affects the employees' experience of organisational life and work.

But what is it like to work in an organisation? How can the sociologist 'understand' and describe such experiences? And how relevant and useful is organisation theory to the subjective aspect of organisational life? It might help answer these questions if we begin with some descriptive accounts.

First some excerpts from Beynon's *Working for Ford* (1973):

Working in a car plant involves coming to terms with the assembly line, 'The line never stops', you are told. Why not? . . . don't ask. 'It never stops.' The assembly plant itself is huge and on two levels, with the plant shop on the one floor and the trim and final assembly departments below. The car shell is painted in the paint shop and passed by lift and conveyor to the first station of the trim assembly department. From this point the body shell is carried up and down the 500-yard length of the plant until it is finally driven off, tested, and stored in the car park.

Few men see the cars being driven off the line. While an assembly worker is always dealing with a moving car, it is never moving under its own steam. The line – or the track as some managers who have been 'stateside' refer to it – stands two feet above floor level and moves the cars monotonously, easily along. Walking along the floor of the plant as a stranger you are deafened by the whine of the compressed air spanners, you step gingerly between and upon the knots of connecting air pipes which writhe like snakes in your path, and you stare at the moving cars on either side. This is the world of the operator. In and out of cars, up and over the line, check the line speed and model mix. Your mind restlessly alert, because there's no guarantee that the next car will be the same as the last, that a Thames van won't suddenly appear. But still a blank – you keep trying to blot out what's happening, 'When I'm here my mind's a blank. I make it go blank.'

They all say that . . . If you stand on the catwalk at the end of the plant you can look down over the whole assembly floor. Few people do, for to stand there and look at the endless, perpetual, tedium of it all is to be threatened by the overwhelming insanity of it. The sheer audacious madness of a system based upon men like those wishing their lives away (p.109).

On the assembly line each worker is termed an operator, he works at a particular station and work is allocated to him at that station. He is surrounded by stacks of components and maybe a man is sub-assembling these for him. His job is to attach his components to the body shells as they come to him. Obviously the faster the line runs, the less time he has on any particular body shell, and consequently the smaller the range of tasks that he is able to do. If the line is running, for example, at thirty cars an hour he is allocated two minutes' work on each car that passes him. The allocation of the two minutes' work is done on the basis of the times recorded for each operation by the Works Study Department of the Ford Motor Company (p.135).

We live in a world dominated by capital and capitalist rationality. In this world decisons are understood as 'investments', what makes a thing good or bad is the 'return' on it. Not it in itself. A good becomes a commodity valued not for what it can do, so much as the price it can be exchanged for. People too become commodities for the commodity world has men's labour at its centre. Spun around by capital and transformed into charts on office walls. 'Labour costs' – that sums it up. Production based upon the sale of labour power. By men putting themselves at the disposal of other men for over half their lives. In order to live they preserve capital and their bondage. It is not perversity that makes assembly-line workers claim that they are treated like numbers. In the production of motor cars they are numbers. Numbers to be manipulated by people who are trained and paid to do just that. To cut costs, increase output. And lay men off. As a commodity, so is their power to labour treated (p.159).

Now some remarks about the experience of managerial work from Sofer's *Men in Mid-Career* (1970).

We saw at Octane that one of the main concerns of the men was that their work was lacking in challenge. Nearly half our respondents felt that they had talents and abilities they were not called upon to exercise. They felt that the work was beneath them and that much of it was clerical and could easily be delegated to persons with less experience. They felt frustrated by the fact (or theory) that they had unnecessarily high qualifications for the duties they were in fact allocated. A high proportion complained that they did not receive adequate feedback on their performance or know their promotion prospects . . . the most interesting observation we were able to make was of the conflict between staying and leaving. The men felt that, despite their doubts, they were now reaping the benefit of years of investment. If they left, they would give up what

*they had but they could not be sure that they would really do better
elsewhere, and might in fact do worse (p.271).*

   *The Octane men had told us that young men were attracted to
the company in the hope of receiving rapid promotion while in fact
the firm needed only a proportion of effective people, and the
majority of those recruited would have to stay in fairly routine
work. They were saying, in effect, that unrealistic expectations had
been aroused in them by the company . . . It is certainly possible
that . . . those responsible for recruiting are unduly optimistic in
discussions with prospective recruits . . . Aspirations for mobility,
advancement, promotion may be said to be sustained and reinforced by the whole appraisal and management development
apparatus . . . the concept of being ambitious . . . is an important
part of the image of being a good salaried employee at both Autoline
and Novoplast. The men are expected to be ambitious; this is regarded as a virtue. Absence of ambition carries connotations of
being passive, indifferent, reluctant to learn and change . . .
(p.335–6).*

Sofer's account of management work and managers' anxieties
can be usefully supplemented by C.W. Mills' descriptions of the
experience of management, of what it is like to hold a managerial
job (Mills writes:)

*. . . seen from the middle ranks management is one-part people
who give you the nod, one-part system, one-part yourself. White-
collar people may be part of management, like they say, but
management is a lot of t/ings, not all of them managing. You carry
authority, but you are not its source. As one of the managed, you
are on view from above, and perhaps you are seen as a threat; as
one of the managers, you are seen from below, perhaps as a tool.
You are the cog and the beltline of the bureaucratic machinery itself; you are a link in the chains of commands, persuasions,
notices, bills, which bind together the men who make decisions and
the men who make things; without you the managerial demiurge
could not be. But your authority is confined strictly within a prescribed orbit of occupational actions, and such power as you wield
is a borrowed thing. Yours is the subordinate's mark, yours the
canned talk. The money you handle is somebody else's money; the
papers you sort and shuffle already bear somebody else's marks.
You are the servant of decision, the assistant of authority, the
minion of management. You are closer to management than the
wage earners are, but yours is seldom the last decision (Mills, 1956,
p.80).*

A large proportion of organisational employees work not as
manual, shop-floor workers, or as management, but as 'white-
collar' workers, office workers. What is their work like? There
aren't many first-hand reports, but one useful one has been

supplied by Elinor Langer. She describes what it is like to work for the New York Telephone Company. We begin with her account of the company training programme.

The representative's course is 'programmed'. It is apparent that the phone company has spent millions of dollars for high-class management consultation on the best way to train new employees. The two principal criteria are easily deduced. First, the course should be made so routine that any employee can teach it. . . . The second criterion is to assure the reproducibility of results, to guarantee that every part turned out by the system will be interchangeable with every other part. The system is to bureaucracy what Taylor was to the factory: it consists of breaking down every operation into discrete parts, then making verbal the discretions that are made . . .

The logic of training is to transform the trainees into machines. The basic method is to handle any customer request by extracting 'bits' of information; by translating the human problem he might have into bureaucratic language so that it can be processed by the right department. . . .

Daily life on the job at the New York Telephone Company . . . consists largely of pressure. To a casual observer it might appear that much of the activity on the floor is random, but in fact it is not. The women moving from desk to desk are on missions of retrieving and refiling customers' records; the tête-à-têtes that look so sociable are anxious conferences with a supervisor in which a representative is Thinking and Planning What to Do Next.

Given the pressure, it becomes natural to welcome the boring and routine – the simple suspensions or disconnections of service – and dread the unusual or complex. . . . (Langer 1970, p.16–19).

Elements of organisational experience

The experience of organisational membership contains three main elements: the organisation of work; the experience of hierarchy and control, and exposure to the ideas and values that exist within the organisation. These elements constitute the subject matter for the rest of the book.

The extracts given above illustrate these elements. First, they suggest some of the methods and principles of the organisation of work in organisations. The most important fact about employing organisations is that they are *places of work*. This work is designed in accordance with certain principles and priorities. These priorities and philosophies reflect the society within which they are developed and utilised. The organisation of work in capitalism reflects its social context, demonstrating, as it does, the importance of profit, 'efficiency' and productivty, and the irrelevance of the needs and aspirations of those involved in work. This subject constitutes the central issue of the next section.

Second, these brief excerpts show the critical importance of processes of *control* within organisations in capitalism. Organisations depend for their existence on control. These illustrations show some of the ways in which this is typically carried out: through technology and the automation of work (backed up, of course, by payment schemes and the 'neutral' rulings of the work study expert); through training and constant supervision and surveillance; through raising people's hopes for promotion, advancement, success. There are other ways of controlling members of organisations, many of them closely tied to the design of work. For an important consideration in the design of work in organisations in capitalism is not efficiency *per se*, but the elimination of the possibility of employee discretion. By designing work so that as far as possible the workers' commitment and judgement is unnecessary, the owners and controllers of the organisation can remove or reduce the costs of worker resistance to, or rejection of, the goals and priorities of the organisation. As Ure remarked, 'The grand object therefore of the modern manufacturer is, through the union of capital and science, to reduce the task of his work-people to the exercise of vigilance and dexterity' (Ure, quoted in Thompson, 1968, p.360). And Alan Fox has emphasised this point when he writes: 'The emergence of the factory system owed as much to the drive for closer co-ordination, discipline and control of the labour force as the pressures of technology' (Fox, 1974, p.179).

Methods and structures of control in employing organisations constitute the subject matter of Section III. It will be argued that a wide variety of control procedures are used, and that the particular method employed is related to the perceived trustworthiness of the personnel concerned, as well as to the nature of the task.

We must remember that the 'overall purpose of all administrative controls is, as is the case of production controls, the elimination of uncertainty and the exercise of constraint to achieve the desired result' (Braverman, 1974, p.265). Furthermore, we can only understand the need for these controls and constraints, and the ways in which work is designed and organised, if we bear in mind that in capitalism, 'Labour power has become a commodity. Its uses are no longer organised according to the needs and desires of those who sell it, but rather according to the needs of its purchasers, who are, primarily, employers seeking to expand the value of their capital. And it is the special and permanent interest of these purchasers to cheapen this commodity' (Braverman, 1974, p.82). As a result of this conflict of interest, and this cheapening of labour power by destroying skills and reducing jobs to tedious short-cycle tasks, control becomes ever more of a problem, as we shall see in Section III.

The third element of the experience of work in organisations is that, from the point of view of the individual, his employing organisation is *a world of meanings.* To enter an organisation is to enter an ideational and cultural world, a place fertile with specialised, idiosyncratic and esoteric vocabularies, values, ideas, knowledge, myths, heroes, villains and stories. These are interesting in themselves (see Turner, 1971) and clearly no worthwhile analysis of the elements of organisational experience could ignore this cultural aspect. But it is also significant because, as noted earlier, organisations typically *rely* upon ways of thinking and evaluating. This reliance has two features: within organisations a particular way of thinking tends to predominate, a 'rationality' which is oriented towards achieving certain goals 'efficiently'. This way of thinking, this method of decision-making, is presented as inherently neutral and heuristically unimpeachable, and is concerned with instrumental effectiveness and efficiency. But, as we argued earlier, such organisational rationalities must be regarded as beyond politics, or beyond criticism.

The rationality that characterises organisations flows from, and supports, the interests and values of those who own and control the organisations. As we have noted, organisational rationality must not be equated with a value-free, means–end logic, a way of thinking which is in some absolute sense efficient, but must be seen instead as a system of rules and procedures, which serves the interests of some, but by no means all, organisational members. The point about this prevalent form of organisational thinking is that it 'removes the total social framework of interests in which strategies are chosen, technologies applied, and systems established, from the scope of reflection and rational reconstruction. Moreover, this rationality extends only to relations of possible technical control and therefore requires a type of action that implies domination, whether of nature or of society' (Habermas, 1975, p.33).

Or to put it another way – for whom are organisational rules and procedures rational and efficient? For the employee, who suffers the deprivations of the assembly line, the anxieties of managerial failure and the pressure of constant surveillance, or for the senior organisational members who devise the procedures and design the organisation of work? As Gouldner put it: 'do bureaucratic rules provide equally efficient vehicles for realising the ends of all strata within an organisation? Do factory rules, for example, enable workers to predict things that are of most concern to them? It would seem that, under certain circumstances, it is normal for factory rules to make prediction difficult or impossible for lower strata personnel' (Gouldner, 1954, pp.26–7).

The second reason for the reliance of organisations on particular ideas and values follows from their concern for *legitimacy.* As Bendix has noted, 'Wherever enterprises are set up, a few command and many obey. The few, however, have seldom been satisfied to command without higher justification even when they have abjured

all interest in ideas, and the many have seldom been docile enough
not to provoke such justifications' (Bendix, 1963, p.1). Because of
the importance of achieving legitimacy within organisations (i.e. a
condition where organisational members regard the hierarchic structure of the organisation, the distribution of rewards, tasks and
power and pattern of domination, as necessary and right), these
devote considerable resources and time to trying to achieve
legitmacy. This will be discussed in Section IV. They are of course
assisted in this by the existence of supportive ideologies and
philosophies in the society outside the organisation. Such
philosophies stress an essential harmony of interests between
superiors and subordinates, the inevitability of hierarchy in
organisations (and society), the importance of managers' 'right to
manage', and so on.

The politics of organisational membership

It has been argued that organisations must be seen as playing a
political role, and that their activities, objectives, and philosophies
are not neutral and utilitarian, but politically significant and
committed. But this is not the only political aspect of organisations;
as noted, the structure of organisations, and nature of organisational membership, is also political.

The argument is as follows: organisations are hierarchic and
differentiated structures; their members differ widely in the extent
to which they control or are controlled, in the rewards and
deprivations they receive, in the content of the work they do. These
variations are related to the existence of conflict within
organisations. Organisations are regarded as arenas of conflict and
struggle. These struggles, reflecting class interest and resources, take
place within, and employ, the bodies of ideas which, within the
organisation, are regarded as having some legitimacy. (Remember
that Albrow regards the efforts of organisational members to
legitimate their activities by reference to 'the attainment of
impersonal goals' as a defining feature of organisations.) However,
the inequalities of organisational life are presented to organisational
members (and members of the society as a whole) as being so
irrevocable and inevitable as to be beyond human choice, interest or
criticism.

For many people, their organisational membership is a source of
deprivation and suffering. While the specialty known as industrial
sociology has for long concentrated attention on the nature of work
experience, and the relationship between these experiences and
'political' or class attitudes, organisational sociology has presented
a bland view of the organisation as a pyramidal structure consisting
of a series of gradations, or levels, organised around and oriented
to the attainment of organisational goals.

Organisational sociology largely ignores manual, shop-floor organisational members, or, if they are included in the analysis, its focus, and the conceptualisation of organisational members in terms of their *roles* distracts attention from the wide differences in treatment and rewards between these members and others, and ignores the need to see their behaviour in terms of their position within the *society*, not just their membership of the organisation. The behaviour of, say, the Ford workers described by Huw Beynon, cannot be understood as their fulfilment of senior members' expectations. It is clear that their work behaviour only makes sense in terms of their work experiences and expectations and position within the wider society. The men who speak in Beynon's book are not just Ford employees, they are first and foremost workers.

Organisations are, under capitalism, hierarchic and differentiated structures. While it is understandable that for some this fact has resulted in an interest in the relationship between the precise configuration of an organisation and various internal and external features, it is unfortunate that this concern to discover the ultimate cause of organisational variation has distracted attention from the more important question: what *principles* underly the inequalities of organisational life, and how are these experienced? But the content of organisational theory and its preoccupations have distracted attention from the nature and origin of members' experiences, as noted earlier.

Consider these descriptions of organisations: 'What they all have in common is that a number of men have become organised into a social unit – an organisation – that has been established for the explicit purpose of achieving certain goals' (Blau and Scott, 1963, p.1); or 'Formal organisations are established for certain purposes: men, in a more or less conscious way coordinate their activities in order to achieve certain goals. This coordination *necessitates* a system of purposive control. It usually consists of rules which define the tasks and responsibilities of each participant as well as the formal mechanisms which could permit the integration of these tasks' (Mouzelis, 1967, p.59). These definitions are misleading. Consider their relevance to, say, the Ford Motor Company. How far do the 'men' of the Ford Motor Company 'coordinate their activities in order to achieve certain goals'? Surely the obvious point is that some men are controlled by others, for goals and purposes which are not their own; and which, indeed, may be at odds with their own goals, might even be dangerous to them. And how far is it true that the goals give a method of work which necessitates control?

Is it not the case that the organisation of work, and control, reflects senior management's distrust of some of their employees, their determination to protect their interests and to minimise the re-

sources and discretion of 'untrustworthy' members? Of course their
experience of work designed in such terms serves to persuade the
members concerned that their interests are at odds with those of
management (Fox, 1974, p.26). And is it sensible to suggest that the
Ford Motor Company consists of men who have 'become *organised*
into a social unit . . . for the explicit purpose of achieving certain
goals'? Obviously workers' goals and interests are very different
from management's; obviously they didn't *become* organised: some
men organised the others. It wasn't a process of mutual decision
and organisation.

Similarly, it would seem likely that the structure and philosophy
of the Ford Motor Company owe as much to Henry Ford's conviction that the 'majority of men were well fitted to a life of drudgery.
They knew no better, nor were they capable of it' (Beynon, 1973,
p.24), as to some inevitable structural outcome of shared company
goals. Beynon suggests that an important element in the company's
goals might be the maintenance of the privileges, prestige and
power of the owners and senior managers. 'Throughout his (Ford's)
life, he maintained a single-minded, autocratic hold over his
company, entirely convinced of his right to run it as he saw fit.
This conviction outlived him, entrenched in the ideology of Ford
executives in the 1950s and 1960s. Every car plant was a hard place
to live in' (Beynon, 1973, p.18).

These examples could be continued, but the basic point has been
made: most conceptions of and approaches to organisations assume
an unjustifiable emphasis on cooperation, commitment and
harmony. They ignore the inequalities of organisational life – 'that
work has become increasingly subdivided into petty operations that
fail to sustain the interest or engage the capacities of humans with
current levels of education; that these petty operations demand ever
less skill and training; and that the modern trend of work by its
'mindlessness' and 'bureaucratisation' is 'alienating' ever larger
sections of the working population' (Braverman, 1974, p.4).

It is true that organisations display cooperation and coordination.
And the view of organisations as essentially cooperative has a
respectable pedigree. Perrow has described Barnard's influential
approach as follows:

The Barnardian model went beyond the pious statements that
labour and management should cooperate or that conflict would be
reduced or productivity raised by cooperation. Barnard was the first
to insist, at length, that organisations, by their very nature, *are*
cooperative systems and could not fail to be so.

In a sense that is true. Men do cooperate with one another in
organisations. . . . In organisations, the cooperation goes beyond
formal rules, is not precisely calculated to conform to the amount
of wages or salary, frequently is spontaneous and generous, and by

*and large, is in the interests of achieving the goals of the organisa-
tion. But in the Weberian view this is hardly the essence of
organisation since basically men are constrained to cooperate
because of hierarchy or authority, separation of office and person,
and so on (Perrow, 1972a, pp.75–6).*

But organisations contain both cooperation and antagonism.
While they are conspicuous for their coordination and interdependence, this is not the same as harmony of interests and consensus.
Just because members of an organisation are interdependent with
each other in the execution of their daily tasks this does not mean
that they regard this interdependence as unburdensome, or non-
coercive. Nor does it mean that the goals that are served by the
coordinated and interdependent tasks (for example the work of the
assembler on the assembly line described by Beynon) are equally
important to all concerned.

Beynon emphasises that the Halewood plant was characterised by
cooperation and conflict. As he puts it,

*It isn't an either–or question of being like a football team or like
two opposing camps. Factory production involves both. Because
production has a social basis the factory can obviously be seen, at
some levels, as a collectivity with management operating in a
coordinating role. The contradiction of factory production, and the
source of contradictory elements within class consciousness, is
rooted in the fact that the exploitation of workers is achieved
through collective, coordinated activities within both the factory
and society generally (Beynon, 1973, p.102).*

Organisations should not be seen solely as integrated, consensual
and cooperative phenomena. Nor should it be inferred that to the
extent that they do display coordination and interdependence these
demonstrate a general commitment to the goals of the organisation.

For many years, thinking on organisations was blighted by an
excessive and naive preoccupation with organisations as goal-
attaining phenomena. This perspective has many deficiencies. Consider, for example, how useful, and how limited, would be an
anlaysis of the Ford Motor Company that saw it only as a social
unit in which 'a number of men have become organised into a
social unit . . . that has been established for the explicit purpose of
achieving certain goals' (Blau and Scott, 1963, p.1). How would we
know what these goals were? Might they not change over the years?
Isn't it possible that the goals of some departments or levels might
conflict with those of others? Isn't it also obvious that a great deal
about the company is the result of outside pressures and restrictions
which have nothing to do with the goals that senior members
claim? Besides, organisations may pursue a number of different
goals, some of which they may prefer to disguise, or deny.

In another context, Mills has argued that goals, or motives, might be important not as causes of action, but as explanations for them – as 'vocabularies' which are accepted as *legitimating* behaviour. He writes, 'motives are the terms with which interpretations of social conduct by social actors proceed. This imputation and avowal of motives by actors are social phenomena to be explained' (Mills, 1940, p.904). Mills argues that particular epochs or institutions – including organisations – contain vocabularies of what are agreed (more or less) to be sensible and legitimate reasons and purposes. This means that what are presented as the goals of the organisation may actually be legitimating symbols.

It is not hard to think of a variety of organisational actions that are justified by reference to 'technological changes', 'modernisation' or 'rationalisation'. As we shall see, by presenting organisational decisions as inevitable, these sorts of 'motives' are not only symbolic, they are ideological.

But the most important effect of the preoccupation with organisational goals has been twofold: organisational structure is regarded as following automatically from the organisation's goals; and these goals are seen as producing cooperation and harmony within the organisation. The first of these points will be treated at length in the next section. The second has been lucidly discussed by Albrow, who argues that by seeing an organisation as goal-oriented, the impression is given that this goal is equally held by all members – indeed, that the organisation was formed by people with the same objective (say, making motor cars) getting together and sacrificing their freedom in exchange for a differentiated and hierarchic means of achieving their shared goal. This is obviously nonsense. As he says:

These accounts (of the origins of organisations) are altogether too like the social contract theory of the origins of the state and society. At some point of time, never specified, individuals conceive an objective with uncommon unanimity and clarity to live an organised social life . . . this account of the origins of organisations (must) be rejected. The . . . formulation of rules and goals is in fact a long and tortuous progress . . . to emphasise a common originating purpose blinds us to another important fact. This is that organisation may originate in the imposition of one group's purpose on another . . . . Workers in early factories scarcely 'got themselves organized'. The goal-attainment perspective persistently minimises conflict' (Albrow, 1968, p.160).

This is precisely the point. Conventional organisation theory is largely dominated by a perspective which ignores conflict, at least of a systematic kind. Organisations, as Albrow suggests, must be studied 'as societies' – i.e. as characterised by the same sorts of conflicts and struggles as occur within the larger society. Within organisations conflict – and therefore politics – is a routine feature of everyday life. Within organisations members are constantly trying to control each other, or to avoid such control. The main thrust of control comes from the senior and powerful groups within the organisation. But as we shall see in Section III, these groups by no means monopolise power, nor are the lower level members completely without the means of resistance. Furthermore, in these struggles and negotiations, the groups will attempt to employ organisational values and ideologies to demonstrate the organisational necessity and justice of their behaviour. And these struggles will employ and reflect the groups' interests and resources in the wider society, and their capacity – or inability – to achieve mass media, 'public opinion' or legal support. As Elger has put it:

any analysis of organisational relationship must attend to the ways in which actors protect or develop their positions within the enterprise. This requires consideration of, on the one hand, those overt strategies, involving explicit reference to some version of the organisational goal, by which members may defend or advance their interests in organisational bargaining; and on the other those less explicit manoeuvres which are also important in defining the position of members, but which avoid reference to the jurisdiction of organisational mandates. . . . The patterning of bargaining strategies can be considered in terms of the resources and alliances available to the various organisational members (Elger, 1975, p.101).

Organisations consist of men and groups seeking to impose their will and their purposes on the middle and junior members. The main mechanism for this control is through the design of the structure of the organisation. Organisational structure involves limits on members' decision-making. As such it is the essential form of control. Therefore it is not surprising that considerable effort has gone into showing that the hierarchic structures of organisations, and the constraints, limitations, deprivations, frustrations and pressures they involve, are necessary and inevitable results of the company goal, or the organisational technology. If this could only be believed, then the inequalities of organisation experience could be regarded as cruel but inevitable necessities, and, therefore, as beyond particular group's interests or choice. And beyond politics.

In fact it might be true that the organisational decision-makers cannot be blamed for a particular decision (a redundancy, a dangerous product or whatever) for this may be the logical outcome of a system which is inherently anarchic. But the point about this argument is that it disguises the fact that organisational structure is *changeable*. As Edwards has remarked:

Bureaucratic organisation of firms and other places of work . . . has become a pervasive characteristic of capitalist society . . . people often have difficulty imagining other forms of organisation. But the dominance of bureaucratic forms is not inevitable in an industrial society; it derives instead directly from capitalists' need to control production (Edwards, 1972, p.115).

Fox has expreesed this view neatly: 'technology and organisational work patterns take on the shape, values and assumptions central to the class structure, and consolidate that structure by sustaining and promoting the interests of the upper strata' (Fox, 1976, p.50).

This argument will be developed in the next section. It is not new, but it is necessary to give it emphasis, for the argument that organisations are determined by technology, rather than by choice, has proved most pervasive. One of the early critics of this view was Gouldner, who in an important paper attacked the view that 'those who want modern technology must be prepared to pay for it with a minute and even stultifying division of labour' (Gouldner, 1955, p.501), and argued that current organisational forms are not the logical, or even empirical, correlates of technology.

The form of organisations is not given by the technology that is employed, any more than the decisions and choices of senior organisational planners and executives follow the mere application of a value-free rationality. Both reflect the interests of the senior members and purposes the organisation plays in the larger society. The function of these explanations, these 'vocabularies of motives', is to de-politicize the organisation and the experience of its members. But this is misleading for, 'the productive enterprise cannot be considered in isolation from the economy or the policy, since it is essentially an organisation operating in an economic and political environment' (Haddon, 1973, p.15).

Work and organisational structure

Chapter 5

Organisational structure

This section will describe some of the ways in which work can be designed in organisations, will consider some explanations of these variations, and will advance its own explanation.

We must start with the fact of organisational *structure*. Organisations involve processes of control which affect and dominate the behaviour of organisational members. It is only because of this control that it is possible to speak of an organisation, instead of the individuals who comprise it.

Organisations, of course, consist of people, but they persist despite changes in personnel, because processes of control transform individual variations into organisational continuity. As Blau has remarked, 'formal organisations, as well as other social structures, exhibit regularities that can be analysed in their own right, independent of any knowledge about the individual behaviour of their members' (Blau and Schoenherr, 1971, p.viii). Any understanding of organisations must include reference to the structure of organisations. This will involve, as Hall remarks, an emphasis on the extra-individual processes of organisational control, supervision and surveillance, 'the very nature of organisations is such that they are intended to minimize the influence of individual variations. . . . Structural characteristics are an important consideration in understanding how an individual does react and behave in an organisation' (Hall, 1972a, p.10).

However, it is not only clear that organisations are structured, but also evident that they are structured in different ways. As Pugh and Hickson put it:

All organisations have to make provision for continuing activities towards the achievement of given aims. Regularities in activities such as task allocation, supervision, and co-ordination are developed. Such regularities constitute the organisation's structure, and the fact that these activities can be arranged in various ways means that organisations can have differing structures' (Pugh and Hickson, 1973, p.51).

However, if the structure of organisations is basic to our understanding them – and our experience of organisational membership, – it is also true that 'despite its importance it remains primitive in empirical applications' (Pugh and Hickson, 1973). These authors note that organisations differ in their structures but emphasise that the important question is 'exactly how much they differ. In what respects do they differ, and in each characteristic do they differ a very great deal, a lot, a fair amount, a little, or hardly at all?' (ibid).

Not surprisingly, organisational researchers have shown a great deal of interest in delineating how organisations differ with respect to their structures, and the factors which are responsible for these variations. Such concerns are evident in the abundance of organisational classifications that litter the field. Among organisational researchers the urge to classify is strong. This is hardly surprising. After all, 'Man must classify phenomena in order to be able to think about them' (Hall, 1972a, p.40). Nevertheless, the exercise is not without its problems.

Classifications of organisations

Academic interest in classifying organisations is basically similar to the layman's concern to establish similarities amongst, and differences between, them. When we talk of government bureaucracies, industrial companies, military organisations, charities, hospitals and so on, we are suggesting that each type has certain features which differentiate it from the others; and, furthermore, that the organisations in each classification have more features in common with each other than they do with members of other groups. The trouble is, as many organisational researchers have pointed out, that these 'common-sense' classifications tend to be confused and inconsistent. What are the differentiating characteristics of, say, industrial companies? That they make things? So do military organisations. Is it that they employ people? So do hospitals. Maybe the key feature is that they aim to make a profit. But so do charities. The difficulties are obvious. And it is exactly the pervasiveness and frequency of these confusions that have led many who study organisations to devise their own, more accurate and consistent classifications.

It might help illustrate the aspirations and weaknesses of these academic efforts to establish organisational classification if we consider a couple of famous examples.

We are already familiar with the suggestions of Blau and Scott. They argue that

Four basic categories of persons can be distinguished in relation to any given formal organisation: (1) the members or rank-and-file participants; (2) the owners or managers of the organisation; (3) the clients, or more generally, the 'public-in-contact', which means the people who are technically 'outside' the organisation yet have regular, direct contact with it, under whatever label – patient, customer, law violator, prisoner, enemy soldier, student; and (4) the public-at-large, that is the members of the society in which the organisation operates (Blau and Scott, 1963, p.42).

These authors suggest that organisations can be classified on the basis of which of these groups benefit from their operations. And, on this basis, they argue for four types of organisation –

(1) 'mutual-benefit associations', where the prime beneficiary is the membership; (2) 'business concerns', where the owners are prime beneficiary; (3) 'service organisations', where the client group is the prime beneficiary; and (4) 'commonwealth organisations', where the prime beneficiary is the public-at-large (p.43).

The authors suggest that special organisational problems are associated with each type. If an organisation is oriented towards a particular group, and operates to the benefit and advantage of this group, then it will attach particular importance to some issues and problems and be relatively indifferent to issues which preoccupy senior members of other types of organisation. For example, as they suggest, 'the crucial problem in mutual-benefit associations is that of maintaining internal democratic processes – providing for participation and control by the membership; the central problem for business concerns is that of maximising operating efficiency in a competitive situation' (Blau and Scott, 1963, p.43).

There can be little doubt of the neatness and elegance of Blau and Scott's typology. In arguing that the *cui bono* principle has greater predictive value than common-sense classifications, these authors are making a valuable contribution to the sociology of organisations. But the point with this, or any other, classification, is not simply its utility, but its *relevance*. While it may well be true that organisations with different beneficiaries are characterised by different 'organisational problems', or even that 'The characteristics of the (organisational) public have important implications for the organisation's structure and functioning' (Blau and Scott, 1963, p.58), it is not immediately clear why this matters. There is a risk with organisational typologies that they be true, but trivial, or tautologous.

But there are other difficulties with the Blau-Scott typology which are worth elucidating because they are common features of many such elegant typological exercises. Firstly, the typology is excessively concerned with efficiency. This is worrying not only because it suggests an ideological bias (efficient for whom, and for what?), but also because a reliance upon efficiency as a classificatory mechanism weakens the edifice itself.

Essentially, by noting that organisations are concerned with – or operate in the iterests of – different publics, Blau and Scott are simply breaking down the concept of efficiency into four varieties. They are specifying four major groups for whom organisations are efficient. But as we shall see, it is by no means clear that efficiency is a determinant of organisational structure, no matter who it is that supplies the measure, of the efficiency or benefits from it.

Furthermore, like Parsons, Blau and Scott's conception of organisations is naive. By focusing on the organisation, and its products and beneficiaries, they ignore the political role of organisations. They forget that no matter what 'public' the organisation 'serves' it may still be serving the dominant ruling groups within the society. To understand the political role of an organisation one must not restrict one's interest to those groups which are ostensibly served by the organisation or which have some say in its mode of operation. To understand the politics of an organisation it is necessary to understand what it does, and how it treats its members. Such things are not encouraged by this typology.

Finally, this typology is inadequate in its treatment of the relationship between the classificatory variable (in this case the *cui bono* principle) and the nature and structure of the organisation. Basically Blau and Scott are offering a disguised version of the goals-based type of classification. They are saying that if an organisation has a certain sort of public, or beneficiary, it will face certain sorts of prime problems. It is in attempting to resolve these problems that the structure of the organisation will be moulded. For problems, one can read goals. But how is it that the goals, or objectives, or 'problems' of an organisation might determine the structure of the organisation? A brief consideration of another famous exercise in organisational classification might help answer this question.

Etzioni's classification is even more elegant than Blau and Scott's. It is directly concerned with the relationship between the type of power that is operative within an organisation and other, structural and processual features of the organisation. He is scathing about 'common-sense' classifications:

The use of such common-sense classifications as labour unions and corporations to isolate the units of comparison creates considerable difficulty. This method of classification tends to attach the same label to organisations which differ considerably, and to assign different names to organisations which are analytically similar in many significant ways. (Etzioni, 1961, p.24).

Compliance refers to 'a relationship consisting of the power employed by superiors to control subordinates and the orientation of the subordinates to this power' (p.xv). And by classifying organisations in terms of their compliance type Etzioni attempts to combine and interrelate structural and motivational elements: the 'differential commitments of actors to organisations' (p.xv),and 'the kinds and distribution of power in organisations' (p.xv). Compliance refers to the relationship between power and actors' reactions to that power, within organisations. He suggests that three basic types of power exist: coercive, remunerative and normative. These types are differentiated in terms of the 'means employed to make the subjects comply. These means may be physical, material, or symbolic' (p.5). Although organisations use all three forms in varying degrees, Etzioni feels that 'Most organisations tend to emphasise only one means of power relying less on the other two' (p.7). This is because the use of a particular sanction or reward creates attitudes and reactions amongst the organisational members which make the utilisation of other sanctions inappropriate or inefficient.

The reactions of members to the type of power to which they are subject constitutes the other element in the organisation's compliance type. Etzioni lists three types of reaction or involvement – which he defines as 'the cathectic-evaluative orientation of an actor to an object' (Etzioni, 1961, p.9).

These are *'alienative*, for the high alienation zone; *moral* for the high commitment zone; and *calculative*, for the two mild zones' (pp.10–11).

The two elements – power types and involvement types – combine to produce the compliance types. But such a combination should, strictly speaking, produce nine options, whereas in fact Etzioni insists that three types of compliance *'are found more frequently than the other six types*. This seems to be true because these three types constitute congruent relationships, whereas the other six do not' (Etzioni, 1961, p.12, emphasis in the original).

The three congruent types result in three types of organisation, claims Etzioni: coercive, utilitarian and normative. These are characterised by the following combination of power and involvement types respectively: coercion and alienation; remuneration and calculative involvement; and normative power and moral commitment. The mechanism whereby these congruent types emerge more frequently than the other six types is interesting and will be considered later.

Etzioni argues that to categorise organisations in terms of this classification of three organisational types supplies useful predictions and insights into organisational structure and process. He writes, 'compliance patterns were chosen as the basis for our comparative study of organisations because compliance relations are a central element of organisational structure' (Etzioni, 1961, p.21).

He suggests, for example, that the sort of goal the organisation pursues is directly related to the compliance structure, and classifies three types of organisational goal: order, economic and culture goals. These will involve the following sorts of compliance structure, respectively: coercive, utilitarian and normative.

Etzioni continues his claim that compliance relates to other aspects of organisations by insisting that there is a close relationship between the 'compliance structure and the distribution of power in the organisations' (Etzioni, 1961, p.125). He argues that the relationship between the ruling organisational elite and other members of the organisation – i.e. the extent to which they are amalgamated or differentiated – also varies with the compliance structure. Numerous other variables are similarly associated: consensus, communication and socialisation, recruitment, scope and pervasiveness and others.

Etzioni's description of the mechanism whereby different compliance structures relate to the many associated variables is highly pertinent to the purpose of this book. Etzioni describes the nature of the relationship between organisational features and compliance types in terms of *effectiveness*. This argument is most clearly stated in his remarks on the relationship between organisational goals and compliance. He argues that it is quite *possible* that, say, an order goal could be pursued through normative compliance structure (an 'incongruent' match), but of this sort of combination he remarks, 'It is *feasible* but not effective' (Etzioni, 1961, p.77). Because of the seriousness and frequency of this argument it is important that it be presented and discussed in some detail.

Etzioni regards organisations as 'social units oriented to the realisation of specific goals' (p.79). He acknowledges that organisations may try to present accounts of their objectives which are at variance with their *actual* goals, a point which will be developed later, but he still regards orientation towards goal attainment as the defining characteristics of an organisation. As a result of this view of organisations, Etzioni is able to employ a somewhat unusual version of the functionalist conception of the relationship between the parts of an interrelated structure, or system. Etzioni does not argue that the relationship between organisational characteristics and compliance structure that he regards as 'congruent' is absolutely necessary for the *survival* or existence of the organisation (he regards this as the usual mechanism underlying functional inter-relationships) but he does insist that congruent relationships between features of the organisation and its compliance structure are more *effective*. He writes 'the *effectiveness* model defines a pattern of interrelations among the elements of the system which make it most effective in the service of a given goal' (Etzioni, 1961, p.78).

Furthermore Etzioni delineates the process whereby organisations develop congruent relationships between their various elements – i.e. move towards effective combinations of structure, process and goal. He writes of 'incongruent' combinations of goal and compliance type:

In the six effective types we would expect to find not only wasted means, psychological and social tension, lack of coordination, and other signs of ineffectiveness, but also a strain toward an effective type. We would expect to find some indication of pressure on goals, compliance, or both, to bring about an effective combination (Etzioni, 1961, p.87).

Etzioni supplies some plausible illustrations of these arguments, showing, he claims, that for example organisations that are committed to order goals, like prisons, would be ineffective if they relied upon the normative compliance of their inmates. And indeed Etzioni's suggestion that organisations – and groups within organisations – differ in the form of organisational power to which they are exposed and which is used to control them, and that this difference is directly related to variations in the members' reactions and attitudes towards their employing or membership organisation is a very useful one, and one that has attracted a great deal of attention lately (see Fox 1974). It is also true that the form of power not only develops related types of involvement but that the resulting compliance type is related to other organisational attributes of the sort Etzioni specifies.

But what is seriously wrong with the classification is the causal mechanism which Etzioni argues achieves these interrelationships. He argues that the clustering of organisational variables around a particular compliance type is the result of the strain towards effectiveness, and that it follows from the goals pursued by the organisation. We should by now be familiar with the difficulties that surround this assertion. Its main and basic drawback is that it removes observed features of organisations, and interrelationships between organisational attributes, from the realm of discussion and choice (and alteration) and presents them as universal laws, as 'functional imperatives'. Just because most manufacturing organisations, for example, employ largely remunerative-calculative forms of power and compliance, with strong inputs of coercion and alienation, Etzioni regards such a situation as an inevitable and unalterable result of the organisation's attempts to achieve certain goals efficiently. But why should this be so? Isn't it entirely possible that industrial organisations could be run on less conflict-arousing lines? Is there any necessity for the manufacture of goods and services to be so organised as to sacrifice the welfare, autonomy and individuality of the workers concerned for the sake of output and profit? And, besides, is it really proven that such methods of organising work and control *are* the most effective?

Many of these issues will be raised later in this section, and later in the book, but it must be remarked at this stage that Etzioni's ingenious classification is more successful as a *description* of common organisational *correlations* than it is as a statement of any necessary, causal relationship between organisational goals, compliance and structure. The main problem concerns this concept effectiveness, and Etzioni's apparent conviction that this mechanism operates independently of interests and choice. But as Tom Burns has said 'for whom and for what are organisations to be reckoned effective?' (Burns, 1967, p.121).

But even if the typologies of Blau and Scott and Etzioni reveal a misconceived view of the relationship between organisational goals – or problems – and the structure of organisations, they are surely correct in noting that organisations differ and it is this variation in organisational structure which they attempt to explain. But what exactly are these obvious, but elusive, differences in the ways in which organisations' structures differ? We all know and refer to the differences between, say, hospitals and factories, armies and research institutes, universities and government departments, but what are we talking about when we compare the structure of one organisation with another?

Organisational variation: the design of work and control

From our point of view, organisational structure can usefully be seen to consist of two interrelated elements: *the way in which work is organised and control exercised.* These two constitute the most obvious and significant features of organisational structure, and are responsible for the major distinctions between organisations. It is differences in the design of work activities, and the manner and methods of control, direction and surveillance which are of most significance in determining members' commitment to, or withdrawal and alienation from, the employing organisation. In his recent statement of the three components of organisational superstructures, Vic Allen (1975) notes that the major feature of organisations is the input and utilisation of members' skills and labour: 'skills constitute the prime activity in social activity and, hence, in organisations' (p.213). Allen remarks that skills themselves contain two relevant elements; some expertise or ability (which is required by the organisation) and 'an ability to control that action to some degree' (p.213). We shall see that both these elements are interrelated and that organisations' efforts to reduce the latter element – members' ability to control their skills and actions – frequently leads to forms of work design which purposely minimise the former element – level of skill involved. 'The second major component, Allen argues, is 'the ability to control action which is derived from skills, namely power' (p.213). Within organisations, skills are so deployed and differentiated as to wrest power from individuals and invest it in the hierarchy of the organisation. Organisations represent, in an extreme form, the separation of skill and control: the routinisation and de-skilling of work in organisations is directly associated with the centralisation of control. Allen notes the third component: 'the ideological setting within which the skills are used and the power exercised' (p.213). This is the subject matter of Section IV. At this stage we are concerned with the first two elements: work and control.

Support for the primacy of these elements comes from other writers. Fox notes that organisational roles include four elements, all of which are concerned with the specification of work tasks and responsibilities – some of which involve controlling the work behaviour and performance of others. For some organisational work concerns the managing, directing and monitoring of the work of others – or the design and installation of more 'effective' control, monitoring, accounting procedures. As well as norms governing and specifying the content of work, Fox notes that organisations contain a normative system through which 'subordinates seek to regulate and control the behaviour of superordinates (Fox, 1971, p.30).

Similarly, Katz and Kahn have noted the primacy of these two organisational features. They have suggested that organisational systems are characterised by two sub-systems – production and maintenance of working structure – and boundary systems (of three kinds) that support and feed these two major processes. By 'production or technical structures' they mean the organisation of people to do the organisation's work, and maintenance structures are concerned with maintaining stability, order and predictability in the organisation – i.e. control (Katz and Kahn, 1966, p.88). Hall's work on dimensions of organisational structure (1972a), which argues that organisational structure can be collapsed into four empirical dimensions, adds further support to the primacy of work and control structures. All four dimensions – structuring of activities, concentration of authority, line control of workflow and size of supportive component – can be seen as aspects of the main elements of organisational structure: the organisation of work or control. See also the classification of significant dimensions of organisational structure suggested by Pugh and Hickson (1973).

Employing organisations are based upon, and give expression to, two basic principles – the design and allocation of divided and specialised tasks, and the subsequent reintegration and coordination of these discreet activities. Both are basic, and both are essentially interdependent operations. But the manner in which work is organised and control exercised is open to considerable variation – more variation, indeed, than is empirically apparent.

The interdependence of these two structural elements will become increasingly obvious. Differentiated jobs require some degree of coordination and control in order to achieve integration; but we shall argue that frequently jobs are designed and fragmented in order to increase centralised and decrease subordinate control.

Similarly, changes in job design, which usually mean a reduction in personal judgement, skill and autonomy are frequently resisted by the employees concerned exactly because they appreciate the close links between job performance appraisal, output records, computer stock systems, new payment procedures, etc. and organisational control. The employees concerned attempt to deny and oppose the power of senior groups through various group and individual (or even organisational, i.e. union) reactions to ostensibly 'rational' organisational developments. Those on the receiving end of changes in work design realise only too well the close links between work structures and control processes.

Chapter 6

Organisational work

Consider the following accounts of work in organisations:

Try putting 13 little pins in 13 little holes 60 times an hour, eight hours a day. Spot-weld 67 steel plates an hour, then find yourself one day facing a new assembly-line needing 110 an hour. Fit 100 coils to 100 cars every hour; tighten seven bolts three times a minute. Do your work in noise 'at the safety limit', in a fine mist of oil, solvent and metal dust. Negotiate for the right to take a piss – or relieve yourself furtively behind a big press so that you don't break your rhythm and lose your bonus. Speed up to gain time to blow your nose or get a bit of grit out of your eye. Bolt your sandwich sitting in a pool of grease because the canteen is 10 minutes away and you've only got 40 for your lunchbreak. As you cross the factory threshold, lose the freedom of opinion, the freedom of speech, the right to meet and associate supposedly guaranteed under the constitution. Obey without arguing, suffer punishment without the right of appeal, get the worst jobs if the manager doesn't like your face. Try being an assembly-line worker.

Wonder how you'll make it to Saturday. Reach home without the strength to do anything but watch TV, telling yourself you'll surely die an idiot. Know at 22 that you'll still be an assembly-line worker at 60 unless you're killed or crippled first. Be as old biologically at 40 or even 35 as a woodcutter of 65. Long to smash everything up at least once a day; feel sick with yourself because you've traded your life for a living; fear more than anything the rage mounting within you will die down in the end, that in the final analysis people are right when they say: 'Aah, you can get used to anything. It's been like that for 50 years – why should it change now?'
(Bosquet, 1977, p.91).

The following accounts describe office work:

. . . standard data have been collected specifically for office pur-poses, in the form of studies of particularly common office motions that are offered as interchangeable parts from which office managers may assemble their own complete operations. . .

The clerical standards . . . begin with unit time values for the various elements of motion, . . . but they go on to agglomerate elemental motions into office tasks, and to offer the office manager the standards by which labour processes may be organised and calibrated. For example:

Open and close	Minutes
File drawer, open and close, no selection	0.04
Folder, open or close flaps	0.04
Desk drawer, open side drawer of standard desk	0.014
Open centre drawer	0.026
Close side	0.015
Close centre	0.027

Chair activity	
Get up from chair	0.033
Sit down in chair	0.033
Turn in swivel chair	0.009
Move in chair to adjoining desk (4ft maximum)	0.050

Walking time is tabulated for distances from one foot to a thousand feet, but since walking within the office requires many turns, 'Walking (confined)' adds 0.01 minute for each turn. The reading of a one- to three-digit number is presumed to take 0.005 minutes, and of a seven-to nine-digit number 0.015 minutes (Braverman, 1974, pp.320–21).

As office machinery is introduced, the number of routine jobs is increased, and consequently the proportion of 'position requiring initiative' is decreased. 'Mechanisation is resulting in a much clearer distinction between the managing staff and the operating staff', observed the War Manpower Commission. 'Finger dexterity is often more important than creative thinking. Promotions consequently become relatively rare. . . . Some large office managers actually prefer to hire girls who are content to remain simply clerks, who will attempt to rise no higher than their initial level.'

As we compare the personnel of the new office with that of the old, it is the mass of clerical machine-operatives that immediately strikes us. They are the most factory-like operatives in the white-collar worlds. The period of time required to learn their skills seems steadily to decline; it must, in fact, if the expenses of introducing machines and new standardised specialisation is to be justified. For the key advantages of most mechanical and centralising office devices are that, while they permit greater speed and accuracy, they also require cheaper labour per units, less training, simpler specilisation, and thus replaceable employees. (Mills, 1956, pp.205–6).

And what about expert, professional work? This is how one large company sets out the duties and objectives of librarians:

Major job objectives	Standards of performance	Relative importance
Filing	Timely filing of all new stock. Maintain current knowledge of branch office manual library filing procedures	1
Cost control	Awareness of use of relevant paperwork with elimination of unnecessary items where possible	4
Resources control	Keep stock current. Maintain recorder system. Control of visual aids, etc. Maintain neat and orderly facility	3
Communications	Disseminate information on all new items. Maintain personal knowledge of inventory necessary to assist library users	2

These accounts of types of organisation work establish the starting point of this chapter: that organisational work, as it occurs within modern, western work organisations, is, first and foremost, *differentiated*. There are no organisations where all the members carry out the same activities; in all cases, the organisational labour is divided. As Weber remarks of the institutional form of rational-legal authority, it contains 'A specified sphere of competence. This involves (a) a sphere of obligations to perform functions which has been marked off as part of a systematic division of labour' (Weber, 1964, p.330).

The differentiation of organisation work is obvious. In industrial organisations one finds various levels, or layers, of management, each with different functions and responsibilities – sales, production, management services, stocks, transport, safety, etc. There are also expert management functions where management *per se* may be less important than research and development work, the design of new accountancy or work systems, personnel matters, product development, product planning, marketing and so on. Work differentiation occurs both vertically, in terms of responsibilities for managing, directing and coordinating the work of others, and horizontally, in terms of specialist activities. Within bureaucracies, the same processes are evident.

Differentiation and specialisation of work is older than organisations, but modern organisations take functional differentiation a great deal further than ever before, at least for some members. Within work organisations there are employees who, despite some occupational and specialist specialisation, are still responsible for a considerable range of operations and decisions; who can see their job through from beginning to end, who can exercise skill, judgement and discretion in the performance of varied, demanding and complex work. The scientific researcher in an electronics company is decidedly limited by his educational and occupational background and specialisation – as the doctor or surgeon is – and by his career aspirations, his research budgets, the size of his staff, his equipment and his organisational objectives and policies. Nevertheless he has a range and number of freedoms denied to the lathe operator, or the assembler on a television assembly line. The same is true for any middle and upper level organisational members – managers, administrators, and experts, such as academics, personnel managers, accountants and others. And even when the range of freedoms is restricted, so that members are not free to choose their own work projects, they may still be free to select their own methods, timing, and priority, and to take responsibility for the completion of an entire cycle of operations – to see the whole job through – rather than merely be allocated one detailed operation.

For many members the extent of work differentiation or specialisation within organisations is extreme. Many organisations' jobs consist of frequently repeated *operations*, sometimes lasting only a few seconds. The punch clerk, the comptometer operator, the typist, office worker, factory worker, assembly worker and many others, are involved in jobs where the process of specialisation has deliberately reduced each job to a few operations. Frequently this specialisation is directly linked to the employee's operation of specially designed and set machines, or to their place within an automated or highly mechanised work system.

The degree of differentiation between these sorts of jobs and those of traditional, pre-industrial craftsmen, has been presented by Marx in the following terms: in pre-industrial society the various crafts and occupations are specialised and differentiated, *'for instance, the cattle-breeder produces hides, the tanner makes the hides into leather, and the shoe-maker the leather into boots. Here the thing produced by each of them is but a step towards the final form, which is the product of all their labours combined' (Marx, 1954, p.335).*

But such differentiation is very different from that evident in modern organisations. What is it, Marx asks, that forms the bond between the occupations involved in boot production? 'It is the fact that their respective products are commodities. What, on the other hand, characterises division of labour in manufactures? The fact that the detail labourer produces no commodities. It is only the common product of all the detail labourers that becomes a commodity' (Marx, 1954, p.335). And Marx continues to assert the relationship between the sort of extreme – 'detail labourer' – differentiation apparent in industrial, and other, organisations, with the concentration of power in the hands of the organisational

executive, a power which previously belonged to the independent
producers of commodities.

These suggestions are relevant to our understanding of processes
of differentiation within organisations. Many organisational jobs
are so specialised as to disguise the actual meaning of the operations concerned, or the nature of the final product; other jobs
involve whole cycles of operations culminating in the achievement
or production of some entire entity or service. The point about the
extremely differentiated jobs in organisations is that they are
restricted to just a few of the operations which, under previous
arrangements, would be a small part of a person's work activity.
The activities which once resided in one man are now divided
amongst many men, such that each employee performs a part of
the original operation: they are allocated extremely routine, short-
cycle work operations.

Organisational work also varies in its *variability*, a quality much
valued by organisation employees. Some jobs involve the very
frequent repetition of the same activity, others contain few activities
and decisions. But some contain a considerable range of activities.
Obviously variability and degree of differentiation are very closely
related, although they are not synonymous.

It also varies in its *complexity* or *simplicity*. The work of the
senior manager, the academic, the senior administrator, planner,
personnel expert involves considerable decision-making and judgement concerning complex problems. The work of the office worker,
or shop-floor members, is notable for its simplicity. Of course it is
true that not all low-level (shop-floor) organisational work is
undemanding, but the majority is, and the elimination of complexity and its replacement by simple, routine operations is not
simply an empirical trend, it is also a significant managerial
philosophy. Touraine has argued that 'The most obvious fact in the
evolution of skills is their massive downgrading in the factory. The
worker specialising in a few repetitive and highly simplified jobs re-
places the craftsman wherever mass production is installed'
(Touraine, 1972, p.52). And another writer in a consideration of
the 'human factor' in the design of work systems involving.
machinery records the argument that the best role of man in a
man–machine system is when the man is doing least, i.e. has the
least capacity to interfere with, or interrupt, the reliability of the
machine. From such principles derive the extreme simplification of
many organisations' jobs.

As noted above, organisational work also varies in the amount of
freedom permitted. Some members are free to choose their own
projects, materials, advice, tools, timing, priorities, even locations
(subject, of course, to their showing a sense of responsibility,
maturity, reliability and predictability). Such extremes of freedom
are rare. More commonly, senior and expert organisational roles

are hedged about with budgetary and policy constraints, and expectations concerning levels of performance and commitment, 'guidelines' and other limitations. The academic is probably one of the least constrained organisational employees – considerable free time is allowed, for study and holidays. Working hours are flexible and short. Levels of performance are, usually, not subject to inspection. Job security is high. Methods and topics of work are open to negotiation. The 'freedom' of the academic is a significant claim. But it is by no means unlimited. There are activities which are regarded as evidence of failure or misdemeanour (though such actions will probably be interpreted as indicative of psychological collapse rather than personal failings or incompetence) and there are constraints and sanctions even in the gentlemanly world of the common room and faculty.

Nevertheless, the relative differences in freedom *from* control and specification, and freedom *to* choose rates of work, work activities, priorities, and conditions are extremely significant distinctions between organisations and between employees. Just compare a senior or even middle manager with an audio-typist, or a hospital psychiatrist with a punch card operator. Blauner (1964) has suggested that the 'powerlessness' of the modern worker – or employee – contains a number of elements: separation of worker from ownership of product and means of production, inability to influence policy, lack of control over conditions of employment, and over the immediate work process. As we shall see in the next section, while organisational executives strive to increase the powerlessness of employees with respect to these factors, the employees themselves struggle to retain or achieve some areas of autonomy or control.

It is useful to see these aspects of organisational work: degree of differentiation, variability, complexity and freedom as various aspects of the same basic process: the *structuring* of work. In these terms organisational jobs show a greater or lesser degree of structuring, or specification. The majority of organisational jobs reveal high levels of structuring. This is deliberate policy, and follows from the application of the model of human behaviour within organisations which strives to separate the functions of 'brain' and 'hand', and to allocate decision-making and planning, to one group, and the execution of purposely simplified and repetitive tasks to others. Such practices follow a mechanical conception of organisational functioning, in which

. . . *man's role was conceived to be that of an element or cog in a complex production system dominated by costly equipment. In mechanical systems, elements must be completely designed if they are to function. When transposed to human effort, this requirement states that initiative and self-organisation are not acceptable, for*

they may increase system variability and the risk of failure. . . .
The result was rigidly specified task assignments and complete job
descriptions indicating the specific behaviours desired and their
organisational and temporal bounds' (Davis and Taylor 1976, p.93).

We shall see that just as organisational executives and experts have
based their coceptualisation of the organisation, and the design of
work, on mechanical engineering assumptions, so some sociologists
have argued that organisational structures and processes are the
result of technological factors. Thus they have failed to separate the
ideology of engineering and technology from the reality, and have
ignored the functions served by these work principles.

High and low discretion roles

Organisational jobs differ considerably in the extent to which they
are structured. Such differences are, empirically, differences of
degree. But in order to highlight the differences, and to maximise
the distinctive characteristics associated with differences in degree
of work structuring, we shall, following the example of a recent
publication on this topic (Fox, 1974), restrict our attention to high
and low extremes of work structuring.

The structuring of organisational work is synonymous with some
of the characteristics mentioned earlier – especially *freedom* – and
is closely allied to the others. It is *possible* for work to be highly
structured and specified, *and* variable, complex and undifferentiated. But it is easier to supply procedures and techniques when
jobs are simple, routine, differentiated and specialised. And the
close empirical links between the specification of work and the
other variables are reinforced by the fact that all these work
features derive from the same motive – the concentration of control
and the reduction of unpredictability. 'To the dozen or so men in
control,' write Berle and Means, 'there is room for such initiative.
For the tens and even hundreds of thousands of workers . . .
individual initiative no longer exists' (1932, p.157). The extreme
structuring of work, such as described by Beynon (1973), Blauner
(1964), Nichols and Armstrong (1976), Chinoy (1955), Walker and
Guest (1952), and many others is closely related to other efforts to
simplify and fragment work, and, together, these 'principles' constitute organisational efforts to define in ever more rigorous, precise,
and limited terms, the content of low-level organisational work
while concentrating decision-making in higher levels. The techniques
may vary, but the motive is the same.

The extent of prescription, specification, or structuring of
organisational positions – or the amount of discretion they permit –
is the most significant feature of the design of organisational work.
As Jaques remarks, 'The *prescribed* content of a job consisted of

those elements of the work about which the member was left no authorised choice. These prescribed elements were of two kinds: the results expected, and the limits set on the means by which the work could be done. The discretionary content of work consisted of all those elements in which choice of how to do a job well was left to the person doing it . . . the member doing the work was required, authorised and expected to use discretion or judgement as he proceeded with his work' (Jaques, 1972, pp.33–34).

David Hickson, in an important paper, has commented on the pervasiveness of this distinction in writings on organisations: 'it has been noted – in various terms and guises – by a large number of writers (Hickson, 1973). This not surprising, since this distinction is very clearly demonstrated in organisations.

Fox has enlarged and developed Jaques' concept of discretion, and used it as the basis of an ambitious and interesting analysis of organisational structure. Fox argues that the most significant feature of organisational structure is the distribution of discretion among organisational jobs, i.e. the extreme differences in the extent to which jobs are structured. Fox distinguishes three levels of discretion: low, middle and high. To emphasise the differences, we shall restrict our attention to the two extremes.

Low-discretion jobs contain a number of interrelated characteristics. First, and most important, these jobs are heavily prescribed, constrained, regulated and limited, in various ways and by various methods – supervision, rules, procedures, technology, work design, performance records, etc. Secondly, 'The role occupant perceives superordinates as behaving as if they believe he cannot be trusted, of his own volition, to deliver a work performance which fully accords with the goals they wish to see pursued, or the values they wish to see observed' (Fox, 1974, p.26). Fox regards this issue of trust, which tends to create the very reactions which it assumes, as basic to the existence and design of low-discretion work: it is because senior organisational members don't trust the low-level members that they design work structures which minimise discretion.

Low-discretion jobs are distinctive in other, related respects: for the way in which they are coordinated and integrated, in standardised, established ways; for official definitions of, and responses to, failure and error, which are seen as the result of carelessness, indifference, insubordination, negligence; and for the ways in which conflict is handled, through group bargaining.

High-discretion jobs, on the other hand, assume a high level of trustworthiness among incumbents. Jobs are not strictly and thoroughly defined, emphasis is placed on the incumbent's expert judgement and knowledge. Close supervision and surveillance are seen as irrelevant, inappropriate, possibly harmful. Coordination is left open to negotiation and mutual adjustment – in terms of what is necessary and sensible. And conflict and failure are regarded as the result of training problems, communication breakdown, and as best remedied through diagnosis and discussion, rather than punishment. As compared to low-discretion work, where skills are deliberately broken down into elements, are tightly prescribed and routinised, leaving a minimum of decision-making, high-discretion jobs require the exercise of 'responsible' expert judgement and initiative over a range of issues. Such work offers 'enriching experiences through which men can meet challenges and overcome obstacles, develop their aptitudes and abilities, and enjoy the satisfaction of achievement. In the course of these experiences men undergo psychological growth, realise themselves, and reach dual stature as full mature and autonomous moral agents.' But low-discretion work is work 'which offers no – or only the most trivial – opportunities for choice, decision, and the acceptance of responsibility and is therefore one which offers no opportunities for growth' (Fox, 1971, p.5).

Other writers have regarded the distinction between high and low discretion in organisational jobs as the key feature of organisational structure and the key basis of organisational types. As Hickson points out, the distinction has been conceptualised in a large number of ways – but the main elements remain the same: extreme variations in the structuring of organisational work (Hickson, 1973). Burns and Stalker, for example, in *The Management of Innovation* (1961), isolated two organisational types: the *mechanistic* and the *organic*. In the first, the problems and activities are fragmented into specialisms. Members work on their particular specialisation. Coordination is achieved by superordinates. Methods, authorities and responsibilities are defined and allocated. Instructions and regulations abound. Decision-making and knowledge is concentrated in the senior executives. Centralisation is marked. In the latter types, individuals are left to determine their work behaviour in the light of their judgement and knowledge. Formal definition of authority, activities, duties and responsibilities is relatively flexible and fluid, subject to constant negotiation and alteration. Centralisation is less: delegation occurs. The critical feature of the two types is their 'suitability', or appropriateness, in the face of routineness, or variability, of raw material, market, etc. (See also Perrow, 1972.)

Burns and Stalker's distinction is very similar to Fox's, and others. But one difference must be stressed, since it pervades and muddles the discussion of the organisational structures and the design of work: Burns and Stalker are talking about two different and divergent systems of *management practice*. Their classification, like many others, is restricted to management levels in organisations, despite the fact that the most striking and obvious difference *within* organisations is exactly the same as that on which they base

their inter-organisational classification – the degree of structuring
of work. Fox, on the other hand, applies his analysis to intra-
organisational differences, and in doing so rescues low-level
members from the oblivion into which they have been cast by the
majority of organisation theorists. Of course the analysis can also
be applied to inter-organisational comparisons, of the type conducted by Burns and Stalker, but it is not restricted to them. Unlike
so many organisation theorists Fox does not take for granted the
inevitability and obviousness of the extreme differences in levels of
discretion manifested within organisations. And his analysis raises
the question to what extent explanations of inter-organisational
variations in work structuring (as deriving from the routineness of
the materials, products, technologies and markets) can also be
applied to differences *within* organisations.

To return to Fox's classification. What are these low-specificity
organisations and organisational roles? The following are some
examples: senior managers in companies and factories and offices;
senior administrators and bureaucrats, university and polytechnic
teachers, scientists, doctors and other professionals and research
workers. The roles involve either a senior location within an
organisation or the application of expertise; in both cases the work
role requires

*. . . not trained obedience to specific external controls, but the
exercise of wisdom, judgement, expertise. The control comes from
within. . . . The occupant . . . must himself choose, judge, feel,
sense, consider, conclude what would be the best thing to do in the
circumstances, the best way of going about what he is doing (Fox,
1974, p.19).*

High-discretionary organisational roles are important to the
organisation, and to the society within which the organisation
exists. Not surprisingly, in view of the privileges associated with
high-discretionary roles, their incumbents tend to identify with the
objectives and philosophies of the organisation, and the dominant
interests and values of the society. But how are these jobs organisationally important? They are important in two main ways. The first
applies to professional jobs, roles and organisations which are
ostensibly neutral and far removed from industry, commerce and
business.

These high-discretionary organisational roles are those in which
professional expertise and judgement is developed and applied for
organisational purposes. As was pointed out earlier, this is a
political exercise, and it is largely because of its political importance
that this activity receives so many rewards and privileges. But what
does it mean to argue that high-discretionary roles involve the
political application and utilisation of professional knowledge? As
stressed earlier, knowledge or expertise is not neutral: it is em-

ployed, purchased and utilised because it is useful to the society within which it has been developed:

. . . the type of technical and scientific knowledge, competence and personnel, is to a large extent functional only to the particular orientation and priorites of monopolistic growth. To a large extent, this type of technical and scientific personnel would be of little use in a society bent on meeting the more basic social and cultural needs of the masses (Gorz, 1972, p.29).

There have been numerous statements of the way in which professional expertise and knowledge, which is developed and applied in high-discretion organisation roles, plays an implicit political role. The main point of these works is that the expertise and professional practice of those who are privileged enough to have well-rewarded, high-discretion organisational roles is: (*a*) not politically neutral but functional for the existing social and political structure; (*b*) excessively concerned with misleading and inaccurate definitions and diagnoses of the problems it handles; and (*c*) inherently alienating and elitist. As Douglas has remarked, 'The most basic and pervasive change in Western society over the last several centuries has been the development and increasing dominance of the scientific and technological world-view – a complex set of cognitive and normative criteria specifying the realm of 'reality' and the appropriate ways of knowing and dealing with that 'reality' (Douglas, 1970, p.5). But this dominant scientific-technological world view, despite the claims of those who produce and employ it, is not as value-free and inevitable as its advocates would have us believe. On the contrary:

. . . technical and scientific knowledge is not only to a large extent disconnected from the needs and the life of the masses; it is also culturally and semantically disconnected from the general comprehensive culture and common language. . . . Whether in architecture, medicine, biology or physics, chemistry, technology, etc. you can't make a successful career unless you put the interests of capital (or the company or corporation or the State) before the interest of the people and are not too concerned about the purposes which the 'advancement of Science and Technology' is to serve (Gorz, 1972, pp.31–2).

These are some of the people who occupy the low-specificity organisational roles. But there are others who are more directly and clearly associated with the interests and values of dominant social and organisational groups. These are the organisational members whose job is to manage, direct and coordinate the members with high-specificity roles, or to supply the managerial expertise, advice, specialist services and relevant 'scientific' knowledge – i.e.

managers and their specialists. Often the specialists are employed by industrial and commercial organisations. But sometimes they are located in specialist organisations whose sole rationale is to supply specialist assistance.

As we shall see, one of the prime elements in the design of high-specificity organisational work is what Braverman has called the 'separation of conception from execution'. The worker executes the work, but it is designed and planned by others, who fill the high-discretion roles.

The institutionalisation of capital and the vesting of control in a specialised stratum of the capitalist class corresponds chronologically to an immense growth in the scale of management operations. Not only is the size of enterprises growing at a great pace. . . . but at the same time the functions undertaken by management are broadening very rapidly. . . . When fully reorganised in the modern corporation, the producing activities are subdivided among functional departments, each having a specific aspect of the process for its domain: design, styling, research and development; planning; production control; inspection or quality control; manufacturing cost accounting; work study, methods study, and industrial engineering; routine and traffic; materials purchasing and control; maintenance of plant and machinery; and power; personnel management and training; and so on (Braverman, 1974, p.260).

These are the specialities that are most directly functional to a form of production which aims to use the worker as a tool of management's decisions and conceptions. There are also the more theoretical, but highly relevant, contributions from psychology, social science, statistics, computer sciences etc.

The common feature of all these activities is that they play an important, indeed central, part in designing, monitoring and controlling the work activities of those in the low-discretion roles or in the design of new methods of surveillance and control. It is because subordinate members have been stripped of challenge and autonomy that the specialists have been able to establish their esoteric, but highly useful, theoretical specialities. Their specialisation is at the expense of others' deprivation, just as the interest and responsibility of their work is a direct function of the repetition and boredom of the majority of the organisation's members. And their functions follow from the form of capitalist economy which de-skills, oppresses and exploits the subordinate members.

In short, in the vast majority of cases, it is possible to see that the high-discretion organisations, or organisational roles, play a critical role in buttressing, legitimating and expediting capitalist values and interests, and the design of work, and the structure of organisation that are associated with those values and interests.

This function can be achieved in a number of ways: by the production and utilisation of politically relevant professional knowledge; by supplying 'expert' management services concerning either organisational structure or process, or by the de-skilling of workers which results in the intellectual aspects of work being concentrated in management and managerial specialists whose

> *. . . role is to dequalify workers by monopolising the technical and intellectual skills required by the work process. They embody the dichotomy between manual and intellectual work, thought and execution. They hold significant financial, social and cultural privileges. They are the workers' most immediate enemy; they represent the skill, knowledge, and virtual power of which workers have been robbed (Gorz, 1972, p.24).*

Or by engaging in organisational processes of management – which are not restricted to industrial organisations – such as surveillance, supervision, coordination, measurement, planning.

At the other end of the scale we have those workers who inhabit the low-discretion organisational roles. The quotations given earlier from Beynon and from Bosquet illustrated how devoid of responsibility and challenge these jobs are. It is true that between high- and low-discretion organisational roles there are some which contain, to varying degrees, elements of both types. The two types are poles on a continuum; and there are jobs which fall between, e.g. some will approximate to the high-discretion end, others to the low. And precise locations on the continuum will fluctuate over time, with the strongest tendency being the reduction of discretion. For example, a great deal of modern clerical and office work is, increasingly, designed so as to permit little, if any, initiative from the workers. Nevertheless, there do remain some intermediate jobs, even if they are not of particular interest here where our concern is to establish, in very broad terms, the nature and determinants of the two opposed types of organisational roles: high- and low-discretion positions.

Some people have argued that low-specificity organisational roles are gradually disappearing, or, phrased somewhat differently, that the working class (and working-class jobs) is declining in size *vis-à-vis* the middle class (whose members hold jobs with greater responsibility, challenge and rewards).

This argument is sometimes expressed in terms of change in the demands for work skills. Kerr *et al.* for example suggest that

> *. . . the industrial order requires many new skills and ever-changing skills. There is a chronic shortage of skilled labour, or at least a relative scarcity. The levels of skill are gradually rising. The ever-shifting demands of skill – eliminating traditional occupations and*

*creating higher-skilled and more specialised workers – constitutes a
universal impact on the labour force (Kerr et al., 1973, pp.201–2).*

Other writers have pointed to the expansion of office or clerical
work as indicating a raising of the status and prestige levels of a
large section of the population and as resulting in a decrease in the
number of workers engaged in unskilled or semi-skilled work. Since
'blue-collar' production and manufacturing work is usually seen as
containing the least skilled work, the reduction of this category of
employment is regarded as implying a general raising of skill levels:
'As a share of total employment, the percentage of semi-skilled will
slide downward from 18.4 per cent in 1968 to 16.2 per cent in 1980
and will at that time be third in size ranking, outpaced by clerical,
which will be the largest, and by professional and technical
workers. Equally, the proportion of factory workers will probably
drop' (Bell, 1974, p.136).

Bell and others argue that the sort of organisational work which
we have here described as low-discretion is, gradually, on the
decline. But his assumption that clerical work is not semi-skilled
should warn us to approach his analysis and his classifications with
caution.

Levison has recently exposed some serious inadequacies in the
sort of classification employed by Bell and others. For one thing
the category 'blue-collar' (i.e. that group that contains most of un-
or semi-skilled work) is limited to production and distribution
workers, 'who are only a fragment of all the Americans who are
still employed in essentially rote, manual labour' (Levison, 1974,
p.22).

Service workers such as janitors, waiters, porters, etc. are not
included. But also 'the male clerical and sales category, considered
as part of the white-collar group, proves to have many working-
class jobs concealed within it. The postman is a clerical worker, so
is the young man in the supermarket who punches the prices on the
cans' (Levison, 1974, p.23).

But even more important as a counter to the decline of low-
skilled work argument is the fact that a great deal of office or
clerical work requires very little skill. Although office workers may
work in different and more pleasant locations, and although certain
features of their work situation may distinguish them from factory
workers, as far as the work itself is concerned it is often hard to see
the difference. The increasing use of office machinery and
computers, the application of scientific management principles to
office work, the expansion of office and clerical work which causes
problems of control, surveillance and assessment, have transformed
old-fashioned office work into a 'factory-like process in accordance
with the precepts of modern management and available technology'

(Braverman, 1974, p.347). So within the 'white-collar' category
there has grown a large aggregate of workers whose situation, with
respect to their work and their subordination, is that of wage
earners. The work of these people is hardly demanding or
challenging; it displays exactly the same principles and features of
un- or semi-skilled factory work. 'The apparent trend to a large
non-proletarian "middle-class" has resolved itself into the creation
of a large proletariat in a new form. In its conditions of employment, this working population has lost all former superiorities over
workers in industry' (Braverman, 1974, p.355).

Taylor and scientific management

It seems clear therefore that a predominant section of the working
population is involved in work of a 'proletarian', un- or semi-
skilled type. Such work is what we mean by low-discretion work –
where the worker is granted little or no autonomy or discretion,
and where the work is designed in accordance with Taylor's
principles of scientific management, which reduce discretion and
choice through specialisation and differentiation. Taylor's
philosophy is as follows: 'management must take over and perform
much of the work which is now left to the men', and 'The
managers assume, . . . the burden of gathering together all of the
traditional knowledge which in the past has been possessed by the
workmen and then of classifying, tabulating, and reducing this
knowledge to rules, laws and formulae which are immensely helpful
to the workmen in doing their daily work.' This 'burden' means
that 'management take over all work for which they are better
fitted than the workmen, while in the past almost all of the work
and the greater part of the responsibility were thrown upon the
men' (Taylor, 1972, pp.27–8).

But as Taylor remarks, the key idea in his philosophy is the task
idea – i.e. that a worker's work is planned and designed by
management, that management specify 'not only what is to be
done, but how it is to be done and the exact time allowed for doing
it' (p.28).

Finally, of course, management's plans, rules, procedures,
techniques and priorities must be *imposed* on the worker. If his
work involves no discretion (which has been appropriated by
management and their experts) then it is all the more important that
the discretionary, planning elements be enforced on the workers,
and that their separate activities be integrated into some complete
process. 'It is only through *enforced* standardisation of methods,
enforced adoption of the best implements and working conditions,
and *enforced* cooperation that this faster work can be assured. And
the duty of enforcing the adoption of standards and of enforcing

this cooperation rests with the management alone' (Taylor, 1972, p.29).

These are the main elements of a philosophy of work design which is absolutely central to the distinction between high- and low-discretion work which, it has been argued, characterises organisations and constitutes the central feature of their structure – and variations in inter- and intra-organisational structure. This method of work design, as Rose has remarked, reflects 'the unthinking application of engineering logic, to the detriment of both the worker and the output' (Rose, 1975, p.217).

Taylorism, or scientific management, is the philosophy which underlies the organisation and design of most work of subordinate members of the organisation and legitimises and makes possible the concentration of discretion and decision-making in the hands of senior members. It is this philosophy which has created the central axis of high- and low-discretion work which distinguishes and characterises organisations, and groups within organisations. In organisations which exist within capitalism, or which are operated in pursuance of capitalist goals, the design and organisation of work is based upon 'efficiency', output and profit rather than the needs of those employed in the work of production. Under these circumstances, it is in the interests of those who own or run the organisation to cheapen and reduce the labour of subordinate members.

Braverman has described the principles of scientific management as follows: '*the dissociation of the labour process from the skills of the workers*' (Braverman, 1974, p.113). This is evident in the quotations from Taylor above. The second principle is a particularly important one: '*the separation of conception from execution*' (p.114). It is the managers and their associated experts and professionals who do the work of conception; the workers perform the actual execution. The third principle is management's use of their monopoly of knowledge of the work, the technology, the elements in the labour process and so on to '*control each step of the labour process and its mode of execution*' (p.119). This is made possible by the utilisation of the first principle. It is important to realise that these principles, although they concern the design and structuring of non- or low-discretionary roles, are principles of *management*. These are the principles from which the content and power of management and expert roles derives. Modern management came into being on the basis of these principles.

There is research evidence, as well as strong impressionistic support, for the assertion that these principles determine the structuring of work for the majority of members of most organisations, not just industrial ones. A study by Davis *et al.* investigated the principles by which jobs were designed. The study 'was undertaken on the assumption that underlying principles for assignment or job design (or whatever kind) do in fact exist and are in use. The purpose of the study was to bring them to light' (Davis *et al.*, 1972, p.66). Some of the results are highly relevant. The first finding is that

Overwhelmingly influencing the design of industrial jobs is the criterion of minimizing immediate cost of producing, i.e. the costs of performing the required operations. The usual indicator of achievement is minimum unit operation time. Designers of jobs see the criterion as being satisfied by the application of the following principles or guides for specifying job content:

(a)   The content of individual jobs is specified:
    (i) *So as to achieve specialization of skill;*
    (ii) *So as to minimize skill requirements;*
    (iii) *So as to minimize learning time or operator training time.*
(b)   Individual tasks are combined into specific jobs so that:
    (i) *Specialization is achieved whenever possible by limiting the number of tasks in a job and limiting the variations in tasks or jobs;*
    (ii) *The content of the job is as repetitive as possible;*
    (iii) *Training time is minimized (Davis et al., 1972, p.79).*

This study makes for depressing reading. Over and over again the authors report that their respondents sought to minimise skill and duration of task, simplify jobs, reduce learning time, maximise control. In conclusion, they report that 'Current job design practices are consistent with the principles of rationalization or scientific management. They minimize the dependence of the organisation on the individual. At the same time they minimize the contribution of the individual to the organisation' (Davis *et al.*, 1972, p.80).

This chapter has been concerned with the design of work within modern organisations. It has argued despite the rich and complex variety of jobs and work specifications, one basic distinction emerges as having great importance and as being very widespread: the division between high- and low-discretion jobs. This empirical distinction is derived from, and informed by, classic, conventional ideas – or 'principles' – of work design and organisation structure as articulated by Taylor, among others. But the distinction itself is by no means restricted to industrial organisations; it is also applied in commercial, governmental and professional organisations.

Chapter 7

The determinants of organisational structure

It is clear that organisations differ structurally, and that one significant axis of differentiation consists in the extent to which organisational work is differentiated, specialised, specified or autonomous. What is responsible for this variation? Each effort at organisational classification involves some suggestion of the organisational variable which determines the shape or structure of the organisation.

Blau and Scott argue that different beneficiaries of organisations establish certain prime organisational problems which, if they are to be efficiently resolved by the organisation, *require* certain organisational structures, forms and processes. Etzioni isolates compliance types as the variable which establishes the structure of the organisation. If an organisation is oriented towards certain objectives, then a particular compliance type will be more *effective* than the others.

Parsons' model also asserts the explanatory and causal primacy of one variable: *'primacy of orientation to the attainment of a specific goal* is used as the defining characteristic of an organisation which distinguishes it from other types of social systems. This criterion has implications for both the external relations and the internal structure of the system referred to here as an organisation' (Parsons, 1970, p.75).

Burns and Stalker on the other hand maintain that the structural differences which they term the *organic* and *mechanistic* types are the result of organisational reactions to *environmental* factors: 'When novelty and unfamiliarity in both market situation and technical information become the accepted order of things, a fundamentally different kind of management system becomes appropriate from that which applies to a relatively stable commercial and technical environment' (Burns and Stalker, 1966, p.viii). Later these authors add that by 'environment' they mean 'the technological bases of production and'. . . the market situation' (Burns and Stalker, 1966, p.vii).

Other students of organisations have pointed to another prime variable in the structuring of organisations – the size of the organisation. The normal thesis with respect to this argument is that organisations grow in complexity and degree of differentiation as they grow in size – 'The size of (an organisation) exerts a predominant influence on its formal structure, its technology, and its administrative overhead' (Blau and Schoenherr, 1971, p.81).

Blau and Schoenherr argue for the importance, and irreducibility, of the structural level of analysis in organisational research. Organisations, they insist, display regularities, many of which they show to be related to the size of the organisation, which cannot be understood in terms of the personalities of the members. They are independent of particular people. This is a point worth making, and worth stressing. But it leaves us with a problem: how do we explain the regularities, the correlations between size and other organisational variables across a large number of organisations? What *factors or mechanisms* cause organisations to become more differentiated as they become bigger? Merely to assert the primacy of the structural approach does not absolve us from the responsibility to specify the causal mechanisms in what is otherwise mere correlation.

And the causal links are made. Consider this passage:

If an organisation is large, it cannot operate *unless responsibilities are sub-divided in various ways; if such differentiation into structural components occurs, increased structural complexity is implicit in it; and* utter confusion would reign *if management would fail to react to increased structural complexity by appointing more supervisors to effect coordination (Blau and Schoenherr, 1971, p.326, my emphasis).*

The emphasised passages show that Blau and Schoenherr, like all those who classify organisations according to some determinate variable, employ as a causal link some notion of efficiency, performance, achievement, adjustment. Note how often, in the passages from Parsons, Blau and Scott, Etzioni, Burns and Stalker, and Blau and Schoenherr quoted above the words 'must', 'appropriate', 'requires', 'effective' and so on occur. The use of such words should warn us that these writers are basing their classifications on the idea that organisations which do not adjust or react in 'normal' ways and common directions to the determinate variable – be it size, technology, goals or environment – will be less effective than the others. And this will occasion at least strain and inefficiency, if not failure. These classifications are based upon the performance of organisations. If the organisation does not react appropriately to the determinate variable then its effectiveness will be reduced. As Child has noted: 'A theory of organisational structure has . . . to take account of performance dimensions' (Child, 1973a, p.98). For, as Barnard and others have maintained, 'The continuance of an organisation depends upon its ability to carry out its purpose' (Barnard, 1970, p.69). We must however stress the difficulties and dangers that surround the use of organisational effectiveness as a factor responsible for linking the determinate organisational variable (whatever it is) with the structure of the organisation.

Firstly, it is not clear that efficiency or effectiveness operates as a link between some contextual factor and organisational structure. Child concludes, on the basis of his review of the evidence, for example, that

structural design is likely to have only a limited effect upon the level of organisational performance achieved, . . . the conclusion that the design of organisational structure may have a restricted influence upon performance levels, and that performance standards may themselves allow for some 'slack', weakens the general proposition that contextual factors will exert a high degree of constraint upon the choice of structural design. In practice, there does appear to be some variation in the structure of otherwise comparable organisations, a variation which is sustained over periods of time without much apparent effect on success or failure (Child, 1973a, p.100).

Secondly, even if, or to the extent that, effectiveness *is* relevant to the design and structure of the organisation we must remember to consider the questions: for *whom* is the organisation efficient? Which organisational groups are concerned with monitoring levels of efficiency and what knowledge and theory do they employ in adjusting the organisation to deteriorating standards? And how is effectiveness defined? For *what* is the organisation effective?

Most of these questions revolve around, or derive from, the idea that organisations are goal-attaining phenomena, and that organisational efficiency can be easily measured in terms of their achievement of these goals.

We should be familiar with the suggestion that organisations exist to achieve certain stated goals and that their efficiency can be measured in terms of these goals. After all, these are probably the terms in which we express our personal indignation at what we regard as organisational incompetence, or 'red tape'. Similarly, most organisations produce, from time to time, especially in their early days, authoritative statements of their goals and aims. For example, in his inaugural address, the Chancellor of the Open University, Lord Crowther, remarked that the University was

. . . open, first, to people. Not for us the carefully regulated escalation from one educational level to the next by which the traditional universities established their criteria . . . the first, and most urgent task before us is to cater for the many thousands of people, fully capable of a higher education, who, for one reason or another, do not get it. . . . Wherever there is an unprovided need for higher education, supplementing the existing provision, there is

our constituency. . . . We are open to places. *. . . We are open to methods. . . . We are open, finally, to* ideas *(Lord Crowther, 1969, quoted in Open University Prospectus, 1972).*

How useful or real are such statements? Clearly they have importance of a general sort, not least as a source of justifying and legitimating ideas. Most of the attacks and defences of the Open University, for example, have been couched in terms of the objectives set out by Lord Crowther. But how useful are such statements as a guide to concrete organisational *structure* or *activity?* The obvious and immediate problem is that despite such public statements it is hard to know just what an organisation's goals really are. We could of course remain with the grand, rhetorical pronouncements. But these are themselves generally rather abstract and vague, and besides they may be completely belied by organisational activity.

Organisations, per se, don't have goals. The goals belong to, and are sought after, by groups and individuals within the organisation. This means that it is necessary, firstly, to distinguish between what Cicourel calls the 'front' and the 'back' of an organisation, and between practices which outsiders consider legitimate, and which the organisation can therefore parade, and those which would be considered as illegitimate, which must be hidden (Cicourel, 1958). Perrow has made a similar distinction with respect to organisational goals when he differentiates between 'official' and 'operative' goals, the latter being those that can be inferred from actual organisational practices (Perrow, 1961).

Furthermore organisational goals can change over time, as Michels (1970), Sills (1970) and others have suggested. Thompson and McEwen write: 'It is possible, however, to view the setting of goals (i.e. major organisational purposes) not as a static element, but as a necessary and recurring problem facing any organisation' (Thompson and McEwen 1973).

If organisations can have a variety of goals, some overt, some disguised, and if these can change over time, then how can we tell just what an organisation's goals are? Are the goals those that are stated by the organisation's public spokesmen? Or their leaders? Are they to be inferred from actual organisational activity, or interpreted from research responses? The difficulties are enormous, and they are multiplied by the fact that different groups and factions will hold different goals and interests but will inevitably seek to advance them by relating them to the vague and abstract organisational goal.

Yet there are even more problems: how does the structure of the organisation relate to these multiple, confused, contradictory and abstract goals? It is obvious, as Albrow (1968) has remarked, that many other factors besides the organisation's goals play a part in determining the structure – for example, government policy, legislation, philosophies of management, etc.

Nevertheless there is some merit in the goal approach. Firstly, it is true that when they are founded, organisations are often equipped with authoritative, symbolic charters, or statements of goals, which are important not only as supplying a general focus for organisational activity (though even this can be 'displaced' over the years) but also for supplying a legitimating symbol (see Strauss *et al.*, 1973).

Secondly, although organisations are not consensual phenomena where all the members willingly and cooperatively engage in differential efforts to achieve some shared goal, they are phenomena where members and groups work together and against each other to achieve or protect their own goals by manipulating or controlling the activities of others. Such activities are frequently justified in terms of the symbolic organisational goal(s).

The problem with the 'goal-attainment' approach to organisations is not simply that it frequently ignores the difficulties spelt out above, but that it assumes an unrealistic degree of internal consensus; ignores the symbolic, legitimating function of goals; misses their variety and changeability; and suggests a naive, apolitical view of the relationship between an organisational goal and the structure and process of the organisation. If there is such a link it is because senior members of the organisation have more power and more resources to mobilize to ensure that their interests (i.e. their organisational goals) are achieved rather than those of other groups. Blau and Schoenherr (1971) stress the need, in analyses of organisations, to concentrate on the structural aspects and 'to push men finally out' of sociological explanations of organisational structure and activity. But by asserting a somewhat simple-minded and mechanical, unalterable and inexorable link between factors such as goals or size, and structure (a link which misses the stage of human, or group, mediation and involvement, but argues directly from one variable to another as though the linkage was beyond alteration or debate), these authors disguise the extent to which dominant organisational groups impose their sectional interests or goals, their conception of the 'organisational goal', and attempt to achieve it through their notion of proper, necessary and suitable procedures.

Organisational structure is what members of the organisation do and say with some regularity and continuity. These regularities are the result of senior members' efforts to regulate and structure the behaviour of other members so that they contribute to the achievement of senior members' priorities. However, we must remember that these other members have *their* priorities too, and that they are never the mere tools of senior managers. Consequently, structure will always involve some degree of bargaining and struggle. And the

fact that in these struggles some groups have much less organisational power than others is directly related to the fact of the
struggle and the conflict of interests. The interests which are
buttressed by the greatest resources (i.e. those of senior members)
will be presented as the *organisational* (*n.b.* not sectional) goal.
Thus, 'the patterns of social relationships which constitute organisational structure are ongoing products of processes of negotiation
and interpretation, through which participants with differential resources and discrepant interests construct organisational social
realities under the jurisdiction of organisational priorities and programmes' (Elger, 1975, p.102).

In these struggles and negotiations the 'operative' or real goals of
dominant members of the organisations will predominate, and their
conception of the proper and appropriate technology and organisational structure will exert considerable, probably overwhelming, influence.

It is in the design of work within organisations that the real goals
of those who own or dominate the organisation are apparent. These
may of course contradict official, public organisational statements.
And it is very usual for the purposes and priorities which are
apparent in the design of the work – the meaning of organisational
structure – to be denied by senior members, or to be defined as
being beyond, or indifferent to, goals and interests. Often the
technology and design of work of an organisation is presented as an
unavoidable and necessary *means* of attaining the organisation's
goals; a means which, as we shall see, carries considerable implications for the structure of the organisation. In this way, organisational structure (which entails severe differences in the distribution
of rewards, dangers, deprivations, delights, etc.) is de-politicised
and defined as an unfortunate necessity, a consequence of our
shared commitment to the organisation's goals. But we have
already stressed: organisations don't have goals. The dominant
goals served by the organisation of work and technology are those
of some organisational members, and not others.

Even if the purposes of the organisation's activity are partial and
sectional, as has been argued, it might still be maintained that the
design of work and the design and employment of technological
procedures, follows unavoidably from the commitment to achieve
these goals efficiently. Such a view would probably add that
subordinate members – i.e. those with low-discretion roles – even
if they were not committed to the organisation's goals, nevertheless
achieved their personal goals through organisational employment,
and compensated for their deprivations at work through their out-
of-work lives.

The obvious benefit of this argument is that, while conceding the
political nature of organisational goals (i.e. that they benefit some
organisational and social groups at the expense of others), it main-

tains the inevitability and inexorability of organisational structure and technology. It depoliticises organisational structure. The characteristics of organisational structure as they are experienced by most members are seen as an unavoidable cost in the efficient achievement of the organisation's output – a cruel necessity. We shall consider this argument.

It is an important argument, because there can be little doubt that technology does play a significant part in the structuring of the organisation. If, therefore, the technology can be convincingly shown to be unavoidable, because of its efficiency in doing what it is the organisation does, then all that has been said about the political nature of organisational membership will become irrelevant. There can be no politics without choice. The only 'political' issue will concern selection to the various types of organisational position – a selection which will be justified by reference to ideologies of personal achievement, ability and intelligence.

Technology and organisational structure

Organisations do things, they create products, services, news, knowledge and other commodities. And what they do, how they do it, and what they do it to, all have implications for the structure of the organisation. In carrying out organisational work on the organisation's raw materials, the members are forced into specific types of patterned interactions and activities which are what is meant by organisational structure. This structure is shaped by the need to execute and monitor and coordinate the organisation's work activities.

A famous research study by Joan Woodward which was concerned to investigate the applicability of various management principles, revealed considerable variation in the pattern of organisation of the firms studied. These differences, Woodward reported, could not be explained by reference to the size or success or type of industry. What caused them then? 'When the firms were grouped according to similarity of objectives and techniques of production, and classified in order of the technical complexity of their productions systems, each production system was found to be associated with a characteristic pattern of organisation' (Woodward, 1969, p.196). This author distinguishes three types of 'production system': small batch and unit production, large batch and mass production, and process production. These three types differ with respect to *technical complexity*, which is defined as 'the extent to which the production process is controllable and its results predictable' (Woodward, 1969, p.203). Various structural features are related to these three production types.

Hickson *et al.* have lent some support to Woodward's findings.

Using a more precise and specific definition of technology, these authors found that 'although a sweeping "technological imperative" hypothesis is not supported, a residual seven variables have been identified in the tests on manufacturing industry that do have associations with technology' (Hickson *et al.*, 1972, p.148). These features are those that are most directly concerned with the organisation's technology – proportion of personnel in maintenance or inspection, 'structural variables will be associated with operations technology only where they are centred on the workflow' (p.150).

Perrow has argued that technology contains two relevant features from the point of view of the shaping of organisational structure:

. . . the number of exceptional cases encountered in the work, that is the degree to which stimuli are perceived as familiar or unfamiliar. . . . The second is the nature of the search process that is undertaken by the individual when exceptions occur. We distinguish two types of search process. The first type involves a search which can be conducted on a logical, analytical basis. . . . The second type of search process occurs when the problem is so vague and poorly conceptualized as to make it virtually unanalysable. . . . In this case one draws upon the residue of unanalysable experience or intuition (Perrow, 1972, pp.49–50).

These aspects of technology are related to the way the organisation's raw material is defined. Raw material can be seen to vary with respect to its understandability, its stability and its variability. He notes that senior members of organisations attempt to reduce the variability of their raw material and to minimise exceptional situations. If they achieve this it will have direct implications for the technology and the structure of the organisations. Broadly speaking, when the raw material is regarded as stable and constant the organisation will be able to prescribe its members' activities to a much greater degree than when the variability of the raw material requires members' initiative and discretion.

Hage and Aiken report that Perrow's suggestion about the relationship between the routineness of technology and the structure of the organisation receive support: 'The more routine the organisation, the more centralized the decision-making about organisational policies, the more likely the presence of a rules manual and job descriptions and the more specified the job' (Hage and Aiken, 1972, p.70). Both Perrow and Woodward argue not only that technology relates to the structure of the organisation but that highly prescribed and structured organisational roles (i.e. low-discretion jobs, and many formalized rules and procedures) will be most efficient when the raw material is standardised and stable.

But if technology is now the determinate variable, then what determines the type and scale of technology that is employed? The answer is clear: for a given raw material or operation (or goal) available technologies are considered, selected and installed in terms of their *efficiency.* Woodward (1969, p.202). 'differences in objectives controlled and limited the techniques of production that could be employed'. According to this view organisational technologies, with all their implications for organisational structure, the design of work and the deprivations or privileges of organisational members follow very closely the organisation's efforts to install and use the most efficient means of attaining its goals. As Child has pointed out it is assumed that the sanctions and dangers that would come to bear on senior organisational efficiency act as a restraint on the 'indeterminateness' that can be allowed to exist in the relationship between technology and structure.

In this approach the technology of organisation, despite its unfortunate consequences for the design of work, is highly determined by the organisation's efforts to achieve its goals efficiently. So technology, and the design of work, are placed beyond debate or alteration, and are defined as the inevitable and inexorable consequences of the organisation's need for efficient production. Fox has stated this 'received interpretation' very clearly:

This conventional view sees the existing design of work and job patterns, along with their profound differences of discretion, autonomy, opportunities for personal growth and fulfilment, and all the associated class and status differences . . . as having been 'created' by the scientific, technological and organisational advances of the continuing Industrial Revolution. According to such a view, this technological and organisational thrust, developing in response to what was 'necessary' or 'appropriate' to the demands of the prevailing economic conditions, is in itself neutral. As such, the work designs and job arrangements 'required' by this technology have been simply responses to the unavoidable exigencies of industrialisation; responses to the constant search for increasing efficiency and productivity which (it would be pointed out) has benefited us all . . . . (Fox, 1976, p.48.)

The technology argument has two interrelated elements. Firstly, technology in the sense of methods and techniques of work – machinery, scientific processes etc. – are held to be responsible for the design of work processes and job specifications and particularly for the degree of differentiation, amount of discretion and so on. This stage of the argument is very evident when management explains why established, skilled work procedures are to make way for more machine dominated jobs, or when individual skill and judgement is centralised in computerised planning, or human skills are replaced by automated processes. The cause of these changes is usually held to be the urgent need to install the most modern and efficient technology. To oppose it is to oppose progress. The second element in the argument defines both the machinery, techniques, and instrument of work, and the forms of work organisation, the allocation of activities, and the division of labour, as technology, and relates these to the overall structure of the organisation, particularly the degree of centralisation, the incidence and frequency of rules, standardisation, etc. These two forms of technology (both of which are regarded as crucial for the structure of the organisation), have been distinguished by Fox (1974, p.1) as 'material' and 'social' technology; and by Perrow (1972, p.166): 'Technology' is not used here in its commonplace sense of machines or sophisticated devices for achieving high efficiency, . . . but in its generic sense of the study of techniques or tasks.'

This sense of technology, of course, includes, but is more than, mere machines, and it would subsume the explanatory variable employed by Burns and Stalker: the stability and predictability of organisational tasks and conditions. Both senses of technology apply, of course, to non-industrial organisations such as banks, offices, bureaucracies, etc. What is wrong with the view that major differences in organisational structure – especially those outlined earlier between high discretion, un-differentiated, non-fragmented work, and highly routine specialised, subdivided, low-discretion work – are primarily the result of different technologies employed by organisations?

First, although there does appear to be a definite relationship between technology and organisational structure, the relationship is not as close as many have argued. Blauner writes, 'The most important single factor that gives an industry a distinctive character is its *technology*. Technology refers to the complex of physical objects and technical operations (both manual and machine) regularly employed in turning out the goods and services produced by industry' (1967, p.6). The type of technology used is influenced, Blauner argues, by three factors: the available technical, scientific knowledge, the economic and engineering resources of firms, and the nature of the product manufactured.

The most important product variable is its degree of uniqueness, or standardisation, plus its structural character which also conditions the type of technology – i.e. machine-tending technology, assembly-line technology, continuous process and craft technologies.

But underlying the choice of technologies appropriate for different products, materials and operations is 'the norm of technological and economic rationality' (Blauner, 1964, p.7). However Blauner acknowledges that 'Whereas technology sets limits on the organisation of work it does not fully determine it, since a number of different organisations of work process may be possible in the same technological system.' (Blauner, 1964, p.9). This introduces an important possibility: that while technology *limits* the organisation of work and the structure of the organisation, it does not *determine* it. This possibility is supported by the work of the members of the Tavistock Institute of Human Relations. These authors have argued that within particular technological arrangements there is some degree of flexibility, or choice, of organisational design. They note: 'The choice made by management was seen as being dependent on certain assumptions as to what would prove most efficient' (Parker *et al.,* 1977, p.95). Usually such choices reflect 'conventional production-engineering assumptions – high degree of task specialisation, regard workers as isolated individuals, separate planning, coordinating and control functions from the work group' (ibid., p.95). But the Tavistock researchers suggest the creation of work groups, able to carry out several of these tasks, and so regain 'responsible autonomy'.

Recent writings by John Child (1973a) and Argyris (1973) have also argued that the relationship between technology and structure may be less direct than usually thought, and that existing relationships may be *correlational*, not *causal*. Blau and Schoenherr have argued that we must not attribute the nature and structure of organisations to the psychologies of their members, but must focus on the analysis of the relationship between different organisational characteristics. They advocate 'the systematic study of the formal structure of organisations. . . . Reducing living human beings to boxes on organisational charts and then further reducing these charts to quantitative variables may seem a strange procedure, but it is legitimate in as much as concern is with the formal structure in its own right rather than with the people in it' (Blau and Schoenherr, 1971, p.18).

Such an emphasis is entirely legitimate, but in emphasising the relationship between selected organisational characteristics, for example size and centralisation, these authors and others like them have unwittingly contributed to the de-politicisation of organisatonal analysis, as Argyris has observed. Their analysis, Argyris asserts, presents as *laws* of organisational structure what are mere *correlations*, correlations which are not the inevitable consequence of the organisation's search for maximum efficiency, but the result of *senior organisational members'* decisions. Organisational structure for Argyris is not a neutral product of organisational technologies, themselves selected to maximise efficiency, but of senior members' objectives and their conception of the nature of their subordinates: 'The formal organisation is a cognitive strategy about how the designers intend the role to be played, given the nature of human beings' (Argyris, 1973, p.79). In particular, Argyris attributes the inter-variable correlations discovered by Blau and Schoenherr to the fact that the senior members of the organisations concerned held similar philosophies, conceptions and objectives, and therefore reacted similarly to the same organisational changes or pressures.

Argyris, then, suggests that the relationship between organisational structure and some imputed determinant (for example technology) might be less direct than is usually thought: it may indeed be the result not of 'the norm of technological and economic rationality' (with its implied inevitability) but of *choice*. A choice determined and structured by sectional interests and conceptions of purpose and personnel.

Similarly, Child suggests that the 'dominant coalition' within an organisation has considerable leeway, within the constraints of technology, environment etc., to choose how to structure the organisation and design work. Furthermore the technology itself can be chosen. Child writes that the choices of the dominant coalition extends to 'the context within which the organisation is operating, to the standards of performance against which the pressure of economic constraints has to be evaluated, and to the design of the organisation's structure itself' (Child, 1973a, p.91). And he notes that 'when incorporating strategic choice in a theory of organisation one is recognising the operation of an essentially political process in which constraints and opportunities are functions of the power exercised by decision-makers in the light of ideological values' (Child, 1973a, p.104).

In short, it is entirely possible that mere correlation between technology and structure has been mistaken for causation. And that although a given technology does exercise some constraint, the extent has been over estimated: the relationship between performance and efficiency and organisational structure is not a clear one: there is 'slack', and organisations with different structures but many other features in common do not seem to vary with respect to efficiency (Child, 1973a, p.100). Technologies are chosen, not imposed by 'norms of efficiency': and the structure of an organisation may owe as much to managerial philosophies, conceptions of organisational purpose and views of the nature and capacities of personnel as to any immutable logic.

What conceptions and purposes other than the urge for efficiency could possibly influence the choice of an organisational technology, with all its constraining implications? Two factors are significant.

First we must remember that technologies themselves – in the 'material' sense – are not God-given. Some technological advances are eagerly accepted; others rejected, some possibilities are ignored, others exploited. It has been argued that a major purpose behind the design, selection and installation of technologies is not merely increased production *per se*, but increased control and discipline, the substitution of the manager's control over the worker for the worker's control over his work, or his product. Dickson, for example, has suggested that 'Technological innovation was one of the new management techniques. Economic factors, although of primary importance in the long run, often became subordinate to short-term needs for dealing with labour' (Dickson, 1974, p.79). And Braverman has maintained that

machinery offers to management to do by wholly mechanical means that which it had previously attempted to do by organisation and disciplinary means. The fact that many machines may be paced and controlled according to centralised decisions, and that these controls may thus be in the hands of management . . . are of just as great interest to management as the fact that the machines multiply the productivity of labour (Braverman, 1974, p.195).

However, such purposes are disguised. Technology is presented as neutral, apolitical, an integral part of human progress (albeit with occasional unfortunate side-effects). Organisational technology is defined in terms of what Dickson has described as the 'ideology of industrialisation', which stresses the benefits of machine technology and the irresistibility of technological 'advances' but which disguises the steady advance of oppressive forms of work organisation and class-based interests.

We must, therefore, be careful not to accept the existence and function of managers, technicians, administrators and experts as givens which owe their existence simply to the exigencies of modern industrialism and to their own intelligence and achievements (Offe, 1976), but must consider the following questions, listed by Gorz:

1 *(a) Is their function required by the process of material production as such or*
  (b) by capital's concern for ruling and for controlling the productive process from above?
2 *(a) Is their function required by the concern for the greatest possible efficiency in production technology? or*
  (b) does the concern for efficient production technology come second only to the concern for 'social technology', i.e. for keeping the labour force disciplined, hierarchically regimented and divided?
3 *(a) Is the present definition of technical skill and knowledge primarily required by the technical division of labour and thereby based upon scientific and ideologically neutral data? or*
  (b) is the definition of technical skill and knowledge primarily social and ideological, as an outgrowth of the social division of labour? (Gorz, 1972, p.28.)

Gorz himself argues that the function of technical workers is only explicable in terms of capitalist priorities, and that their role is basically technical and ideological, i.e. concerned with maintaining the hierarchical structure of capitalist organisations, and with ensuring that the maximum of surplus value is extracted, and that control is achieved.

Marglin has taken this argument a step further. While agreeing with this conception of technology he argues that the two decisive features of capitalist organisations: the development of the minute division of labour, and the development of the centralised organisation that characterises the factory system, were the result not of their technical superiority, but of the capitalist's efforts to design a form of organisation which established a crucial intermediary role for the owner or manager, who, having substituted his control for the workers, could exploit the potential of de-skilled, dependent and proletarianised employees (Marglin, 1976.)

Second, the choice of organisational technologies – in both the social and the material senses – can be seen as a reflection of class-based assumptions about the 'reliability' and capacities of the lower-level organisational members. While the sort of work structures described by Bosquet earlier may be justified by management in terms of the unfortunate exigencies of inevitable technological and organisational advances they are clear manifestations of assumptions about the importance and nature of subordinate organisational members.

Bosquet is clear about the implications of such work design:

. . . technological innovations have always had a double purpose: to make human labour as productive as possible, and also to force the worker to work to the limits of his capabilities. The need for this constraint goes without saying in the eyes of the classic boss. The worker is suspected of idleness by definition; how could it be otherwise? Neither the product itself nor the purpose of the manufacture has anything to do with him (Bosquet, 1977, p.8).

Other writers have suggested that modern organisational structures, technologies and work arrangements reveal strongly held assumptions about the laziness, intelligence and reliability of the employees (and, of course, serve to create the truth of these assumptions by their alienating consequences). The principles lying behind the sort of low-discretion, highly fragmented and specialised, routine organisational jobs discussed earlier are not those of efficiency and productivity alone, but of control, a control which is seen as necessary in the light of the nature of subordinate organisational members.

Davis and Taylor have conducted an extensive review of the evidence concerning 'structural and organisational behaviour concomitants of technology'. They conclude their assessment with the suggestion that 'there is considerable flexibility in the design of technology, which challenges the widely accepted notion of technological determinism' (Davis and Taylor, 1976, p.410). But their account has greater relevance; they argue that technology, and related work systems, are *chosen* by organisational members: 'there are choices available based on social system values and assumptions' (p.380), and that these choices reveal strongly held 'psycho-social assumptions': 'nearly all technology is designed by exercising certain assumptions about people and work' (p.411). Furthermore, these authors write,

Hypotheses held about the nature of man embedded within a technical system are operationalised in the design of the system. . . . When the assumptions are held that a system is comprised of reliable technical elements and unreliable social elements, then, in order to provide total system reliability, the technical design must call for parts of people as replaceable machine elements to be regulated by the technical system or by a superstructure of personal control (Davis and Taylor, 1976, p.412).

The assumptions inherent in modern organisational technology and work design are not hard to isolate: that workers are potentially rebellious, that managerial control is superior to worker self-control, that low-level members will 'take advantage' of any freedom they are allowed, that they are untrustworthy. Many writers have commented on the value assumptions implicit in the extreme routinisation and rationalisation of work (Lockwood, 1958; Gouldner, 1955). Fox argues that the increasing application of scientific management principles (low-discretion work) serves to increase the very opposition and resentment and withdrawal of cooperation that it is meant to overcome and resolve. Lower level organisational members realise the implications of this sort of work design, despite management's efforts to define it as inevitable and neutral. They react by reducing commitment, and through collective mobilisation and resistance. These reactions induce further management efforts to reduce the disruptive potential, the capacity for disturbance, of these organisational members.

The design of low-discretion, highly routinised, differentiated and specialised work in organisations – wherever it occurs, on the shop floor, in the clerical office, the mailing department, the computer section, the punchroom – cannot be explained simply in terms of technology or the exigencies of modern, advanced and efficient work design principles. It follows from the primacy of some interests over others, some groups over others. It reflects and reveals the nature of class. As Marx pointed out, when the organisation of work shows the concentration of 'intelligence in production' in one part of the organisation, 'it vanishes in many others'. 'What is lost by the detail labourers, is concentrated in the capital that employs them. It is as a result of the division of labour in manufactures, that the labourer is brought face-to-face with the intellectual potencies of the material process of production, as the property of another, and as a ruling power' (Marx, 1954, p.341).

Technology and work organisation as Fox has stressed (1976) take on and reveal the class values of capitalism while assisting the supremacy of class interests at work. This is quite basic to any understanding of the development of the highly centralised organisation and highly routinised work systems and associated technologies.

The design of high-discretion jobs

We are left, however, with a residual problem: why is it that some jobs are not defined and designed in this way? Why are some jobs heavily structured and routinised, while others – those involving high discretion – are left undifferentiated, unfragmented? How do we account for the differences between the design of academic work and car-assembly work, between management and clerical work?

Part of the answer has already been given. The sort of material technology applied does constrain the organisation of work, even though the design, selection and installation of the technology itself must be seen in terms of values and interests. Nevertheless, while the technology is based on assumptions and priorities and while the relationship between the instruments of work and the design of work is less direct and rigid than often suggested, it remains true that it is impossible to understand the differences between the work arrangements of academics and car-makers without considering the very different technological bases of the two types of work.

What factors determine the application of technology and forms of work which separate the 'labour of hand and head', and which, while investing all decision-making and control in the design of the machine, or the work-process, transform the organisational employee into a mere appendage of the machine?

Perrow argues that some raw materials and work operations are more amenable to fragmentation and differentiation than others. The critical factors, as we have seen, are the degree to which the raw material is variable and the routineness of the actual operations. The assembly of cars can be organised in highly repetitive, standardised and fragmented ways because the raw materials are very standardised and similar (i.e. the quality of the pressed steel doesn't vary from day to day), and the activities are highly predictable. On the other hand, the academic's raw material – students – varies enormously, and the complexity of the academic task – its various demands, the importance of the academic's judgement – make the design and imposition of specified procedures difficult if not impossible. Of course, one answer would be to reduce the academic role to much more limited and detailed tasks, and thus enable greater specification. Perrow has noted that differences in the actual aims of professional organisations will make a great deal of difference to the extent to which tasks can be routinised or not.

The custodial mental hospital can be routinised; the treatment-oriented one cannot . . . the advantages of bureaucracy can be realised in the routine situation; the non-routine organisation must pay the considerable price of long periods of personnel training, professional employees, confusion, wasted materials, hit-or-miss efforts, unpredictable outputs, and so on (Perrow, 1972, p.167).

However, this argument that variations in the complexity of tasks and operations and the variability of raw materials limit the possibility of establishing routine technologies and procedures is only part of the answer. It might help explain why some jobs are *not* routinised, but it is only a necessary and not a sufficient explanation of why senior management takes advantage of the vulnerability of some organisational tasks and their ability to routinise them. In doing so they are, as we have argued, demonstrating the essential conflict of interests within the organisation and their own class-based priorities and assumptions.

The same is true of high-discretion, non-fragmented jobs – managers, experts, scientists. To some extent, these jobs have these characteristics because of the tasks and operations – and knowledge and skills involved. But these characteristics themselves are a result of the split of hand and brain. As Braverman notes, the development of important, complex expertise within the organisation cannot be seen in isolation from the stripping of expertise from other jobs: 'the relatively few persons for whom special knowledge and training are reserved are freed so far as possible from the obligation of simple labour . . . a structure is given . . . that at its extreme polarises those whose time is infinitely valuable and those whose time is worth almost nothing' (Braverman, 1974, pp.82–3). This polarisation of activities which is directly related to the extent to which the job can be routinised or not, derives itself from the class nature of organisations.

Similarly the complexity and importance of high discretion work derives from the function managers and experts play in the coordination and control of de-skilled employees, or from the development of professional, expert systems of organisational control, work design, accountancy, welfare etc. which are critical to the success of organisations of this type, or from other expert, professional functions. These various forms of organisational function, which achieve a considerable salience and significance within organisations, are themselves not neutral. Like the structure of the organisations in which they are located, they are reflections of the basic class nature of hierarchic organisations.

When Braverman notes that within any organisation there are some members whose time is infinitely valuable and others whose time is worth almost nothing, he is pointing to another significant factor underlying the application of routinised technologies and work procedures: the importance of their organisational contribution, and therefore their commitment. If some crucial organisational roles are essentially complex, containing discretionary elements and requiring skill and judgement, then the commitment and 'trustworthiness' of these members is most important. These members' discretionary work roles endow them with considerable organisational power. As a result, senior management must ensure that they are treated and rewarded in such ways as to ensure their continuing identification with the organisation and its structure. 'When top management takes care to supply the rewards and privileges considered appropriate to the status of these roles, lest the occupants misuse their discretion or leave the organisation altogether,' writes Fox (1974, p.60), 'it is manifesting an awareness of a power relationship'. Occupants of these roles will assume and expect that their organisational importance will ensure that 'their rewards, privileges, and prospects are those appropriate to members of the high-trust fraternity'.

But if the non-routine nature of some organisational jobs follows from the nature of tasks involved and the importance of the function, which bestows discretion, and organisation power, it is also to some extent a result of the capacity of the members concerned to resist routinisation and bureaucratisation, based on their extra-organisational class resources and ideologies. Fox has noted that even when routinisation is possible, senior management may be deterred by fears of the possible alienating consequences of such changes, and of the disruptions caused by the resistance of these members. And Freidson has argued that a professional group is most likely to be able to resist external control and bureaucratisation when it has obtained 'a legal or political position of privilege that protects it from encroachment', 'a code of ethics or some other publicly waved banner of good intentions', and is able to 'control the production and particularly the application of knowledge and skill in the work it performs' (Freidson, 1970, pp.134–5). Similarly Elger has warned of the dangers of explaining the organisational power of various groups simply in terms of the 'resources inherent in technical competences or production contingencies, for these technical properties are themselves embedded in a matrix of social processes' (Elger, 1975, p.124).

Particularly important are the occupational institutions and traditions which can be mobilised, as Freidson confirms. But we must also consider the larger society, with its class-based evaluations and definitions of high-status and low-status work, definitions which are related to the functions of the occupation concerned. Finally, of course, organisational power reflects the class membership and resources of organisational employees. We must also consider the argument that the application of modern, routine work technologies and structures is a result of 'the norm of technological and economic rationality', i.e. is *efficient*. We must ask 'efficient for whom'? And for what? Such technologies and principles of work design are clearly not efficient for the employees concerned. For them they constitute a barrier to their freedom to realise their creative and intellectual capacities. Their efficiency lies, we have argued, in the reduction of *autonomy* and self-control and the substitution of centralised, managerial, expert control. Bosquet makes the point that technological innovations have always had a double purpose – to make labour as productive as possible and to force the employee to work to the limit of his capabilities. The efficiency of this system lies in its capacity to control and discipline a work force which is systematically alienated from the work processes and the product. As he remarks, it is impossible to relax this control, for under these work arrangements the extent of alienation is so great as to make the employee ever more recalcitrant and 'irresponsible'.

This argument is most clearly stated in Fox (1974). Fox notes how low-discretion work roles generate alienation and commitment among their incumbents, which lead to a confirmation of management's definitions and assumptions, a further tightening of control very often through the application of work study, more control and regulation, tighter discipline and supervision or other methods of reducing discretion. This leads to low-trust relations between superiors and subordinates. It is only in the context of alienated employees that these work practices and technologies can be regarded as technologically or economically 'rational'. It is the need to control an organisational work force which engaged in work which is against its interests, and from which it derives few benefits, that the practices of scientific management, bureaucratic centralisation and 'advanced' work technologies gain their 'efficiency' and rationality. The alienation which is inherent in this form of organisation occasions a structure of work design and control which exacerbates the recalcitrance of the employees. From management's point of view this results in the 'problem of motivation'.

Interestingly, many writers have recently remarked that these 'rational' principles and technologies might be less efficient than is claimed – the levels of alienation and resistance they rouse might well be so great as to make these methods inefficient even in their own terms (see Fox, 1974; Bosquet, 1977; Fox, 1976; Argyris, 1968; Blauner, 1964; Walker and Guest 1952). But to usurp these basic principles and structures and replace them with genuine participation and democratisation would result in the loss of management's 'right' to control and manage the work force, and in the development of the lower-level employees' insistence on playing their part in the determination of the organisation's goals, activities and the distribution of rewards and privileges. This risk is too great: as we shall see in Section III, recent efforts to 'enrich' work and gain the participation of employees must be seen in the context of the problem of controlling an alienated work force, not as efforts to replace managerial control by employee control.

The inefficiency and 'problems' of modern forms of work and organisational structure stems from the human consequences of specialisation and subdivision and extreme control, which are made necessary by an economic and political system which values and organises people not for their benefit or in terms of their needs, but in terms of the priorities and interests of employers and their executives. Under these conditions it is necessary to subdivide and separate execution from design, for in this way the individual contribution and significance of any one worker is greatly reduced – he becomes highly replaceable because he is de-skilled – and training time is reduced as discretion is eliminated, managerial control increased, and exploitation intensified.

Processes of control within organisations

Chapter 8

Types of organisational control 1

We start with these accounts of processes of control within organisations.

One of the jobs in the Zap plant requires a man to pick up a plastic bag, shake it open, fill it from the bottom of a spout with one hundredweight of ammonium nitrate pearls, and then pass it on to a roller conveyor system. Twist to one side – open bag – lift to spout – twist to the other side – all this once every three seconds, one ton a minute, sixty tons an hour. If you watch this operation being performed it appears that if the man didn't twist – open – lift – twist fast enough he would be deluged by tons of ammonium nitrate pearls. The product comes to him continuously and the Zap plant itself is linked to other continuously producing feeder plants. Technology looks the master and man – an 'operator' – its servant.

However, talk about technology with a capital 'T' is often deceiving. The ChemCo site exists to make profit. The technology was designed from the beginning to make fertilizer efficiently, for profit. It was designed by men for men, but not for men like the one on the spout. He is there because he is cheap; cheaper, that is, than a completely automated system. Moreover, if you watch very closely you will see he is not, as it first appears, a robot. Every three seconds, as he lifts the bag to the spout, a quick flick of his hand moves a lever which releases the product. Despite appearances he is, in this sense, still a free agent. He doesn't 'have to' any more – or any less – than he has to accept management's right to manage, or his 'share of the cake'. But, if he chooses not to do what management tells him (which he may be 'told' either directly and personally by managers, or through their impersonal rules and regulations about working practices, or indirectly through the technology which mediates the imperative to produce for profit) – if and when he chooses not to comply with these dictates, he will make explicit what otherwise can lie dormant, namely the question of control. Control is always a latent issue in factory production whether it be explicitly recognised as such or not' (Nichols and Armstrong, 1976, pp.24–5).

Next, an example of the sorts of control mechanisms that are used for office workers. This example is from a study of a department in the public employment agency of an American state.

This agency's 'major responsibility is to serve workers seeking employment and employers seeking workers' (Blau, 1963, p.19).

The preparation of periodic statistical reports constitutes a method for evaluating operations well suited to the administration of large organisations. Dehumanised lists of cold figures correspond to the abstract, impersonal criteria that govern bureaucratic activities. Statistical records provide precise and comparable information on operations quickly and in a concise form that is easily communicated. . . . Quantitative indices uniformly abstract predetermined information and thus facilitate the objective comparison of operations in different departments by eliminating the different biases that necessarily are reflected in descriptive reports written by various officials. Statistical records are also more economical, since they can be prepared by clerks. Finally, these records provide an objective basis for the periodic rating of the performance of officials. . . .

Quantitative records were used widely in the employment agency. They provided accurate information on various phases of operations, such as the number of requests for workers received from different branches of the industry and the number of placements made. This information enabled higher officials to take the actions they considered necessary to improve operations. Statistical reports were intended to facilitate the exercise of administrative control. However, the collection of data for these reports had consequences that transformed them from an indirect means for controlling operations into a direct mechanism of control. . . .

In (the) bureaucracy the collection of data on operations, such as the number of interviews each official held, also influenced the interviewer's conduct. The knowledge that his superior would learn how many clients he had interviewed and would evaluate him accordingly induced him to work faster. Far from being a disadvantage, this direct effect constituted the major function of performance records for bureaucratic operations. . . .

In March 1948, two months after Department Head Xavier was put in charge, she instituted new performance records. These were issued monthly and made available to all interviewers.

They contained the following eight indices for every interviewer and for each of the three sections in department X:

1. The number of interviews held.
2. The number of clients referred to a job.
3. The number of placements (referred client was hired) made.
4. The proportion of interviews resulting in referrals.
5. The proportion of referrals resulting in placements.

6. The proportion of interviews resulting in placements.
7. The number of notifications sent to the insurance office.
8. The number of application forms made out.

Statistical reports influenced operations by inducing interviewers to concentrate their efforts on factors that were measured and thus would affect their rating. . . .
As an effective control mechanism, performance records served several functions for operations. First, it has already been noted they increased productivity. Second, they facilitated hierarchical control over operating officials. . . . Third, these records enabled superiors to institute changes in operations quickly and effectively. . . . Fourth, use of performance records improved the relations between supervisors and interviewers. . . .
Interviewers had reacted to the introduction of performance records with hostility and continued to dislike them vehemently. Their negative attitudes were similar to those of manual workers towards production quotas, intensified by the fact that 'working on production like in a factory' has negative status implications for these white-collar workers. . . .
The statistical method of evaluating performance had serious dysfunctions in Department X. It engendered competitive behaviour that interfered with operating efficiency, thereby producing an organisational need for social mechanisms to combat competition (Blau, 1963, pp.36–40, 80).

Finally, an example from a professional organisational setting – a psychiatric hospital.

The rules that govern the actions of various professionals, as they perform their tasks, are far from extensive, or clearly stated or clearly binding. This fact leads to necessary and continual negotiation. . . . In Michael Reese [the psychiatric hospital], as unquestionably in most sizeable establishments, hardly anyone knows all the extant rules, much less exactly what situations they apply to, for whom, and with what sanctions. Also noticeable . . . was that some rules, once promulgated, would fall into disuse, or would periodically receive administrative reiteration after the staff had either ignored these rules or forgotten them. As one head nurse said, 'I wish they would write them all down sometimes' – but said so smilingly. . . . As in other establishments, personnel called upon certain rules to obtain what they themselves wished. Thus the nurses frequently acted as virtual guardians of the hospital against some of the demands of certain attending physicians, calling upon the resources of 'the rules of the hospital' in countering the physicians' demands. As in other hospital settings, the physicans were only too aware of this game, and accused the nurses from

*time to time of more interest in their own welfare than in that of
the patients. . . . In so dredging up the rules at convenient
moments, the staff of course is acting identically with personnel in
other kinds of institutions . . . the area of actions covered directly
by clearly enunciated rules is really very small . . . we discovered
that only a very few general rules obtained for the placement of
new patients within the hospital. Those rules, which are clearly
enunciated and generally followed, can, for our purposes, be
regarded as longstanding shared understandings among the
personnel. Except for a few legal rules, which stem from state and
professional prescriptions, and for some rulings pertaining to all of
Michael Reese hospital, almost all these house rules are much less
like commands, and much more like general understandings: not
even their punishments are spelled out; and mostly they can be
stretched, negotiated, argued, as well as ignored or applied at convenient moments. Hospital rules seem too frequently less explicit
than tacit, probably as much breached and stretched as honoured,
and administrative effort is made to keep their number small. In
addition, rules here as elsewhere fail to be universal prescriptions:
they always require judgement concerning their applicability to the
specific case. . . .*

*Negotiation and the division of labour are rendered all the more
complex because personnel in our hospital . . . share only a single,
vaguely ambitious goal. The goal is to return patients to the outside
world in better shape. This goal is the symbolic cement that,
metaphorically speaking, holds the organisation together . . .
although this symbol . . . masks a considerable measure of
disagreement and discrepant purpose, it represents a generalised
mandate under which the hospital can be run. . . . In addition [this
symbolic goal] can be used by any and all personnel as a
justificatory rationale for actions that are under attack . . .*

*The problem, of course, is that when the personnel confront a
specific patient and attempt to make him recover, then the disagree-
ments flare up . . . and a complicated process of negotiation, of
bargaining, of give-and-take necessarily begins. [For example] the
personnel may disagree over what is the proper placement within
the hospital for some patient; believing that, at any given time, he
is more likely to improve when placed in one ward than in another.
This issue is the source of considerable tension between physicians
and ward personnel. Again, what is meant by 'getting better' is
itself open to differential judgement when applied to the progress –
or retrogression – of a particular patient. . . .*

*The model presented has pictured the hospital as a locale where
personnel, mostly, but not exclusively, professionals, are enmeshed
in a complex negotiative process in order to accomplish their
individual purposes and to work – in an established division of
labour – toward clearly as well as vaguely phrased institutional*

objectives . . . differential professional training, ideology, career, and hierarchical position all affect the negotiation (Strauss et al., 1973, pp.306–9, 318).

These exerpts from three widely different studies of very different types of organisation are directly relevant to the concerns of this section for the following reasons.

1. They show how organisational control is achieved through a variety of methods, or mechanisms. The first excerpt shows the controlling function of modern factory technology; in this case the 'operative' is controlled through his location within an automated production system, which is designed to achieve the highest possible level of production with the minimum of operative intervention or interference. That is one way to control organisational members. The second excerpt from Blau's study of two government agencies illustrates another common mechanism – work measurement. As Blau remarks this was traditionally restricted to shop-floor organisational members. But lately, in the guise of performance appraisal, management development, management by objectives etc., it has been increasingly applied to middle management and staff experts. The essence of this sort of control is the well-known principle that to measure is to control. Once senior management – or supervision – has available quantified information on people's work performance they are able to relate this information to the distribution of organisational rewards and punishments. Finally, the third excerpt argues that, at least in the professional organisation, control is based to some extent upon shared, expert, or professional understandings and commitments, deriving from professional, extra-organisational socializations and involvements. The organisational rules were used largely to justify, or oppose, decisions and preferences which had their origins, elsewhere, in professional philosophies and practices. There are other forms of organisational control, but these are three important ones. Obviously the excerpts quoted at the beginning of Chapter 6 also illustrate these and other mechanisms of organisational control.

2. These excerpts show the importance of the concept of *legitimacy* in understanding organisational control, and the salience of achieving this legitimacy for senior members of the organisation. In the psychiatric hospital, members attempt to disguise their real interests and gain the agreement of real or potential opponents, by defining their preference in terms of widely held shared goals, or objectives. In short, they try to bestow legitimacy on their actions; they attempt to gain the commitment of others by demonstrating the moral propriety of their measures. The importance of legitimacy is also evident in the excerpts from Nichols and Armstrong. As these authors note, the technological process in which the workers are placed operates as a system of control but, like any other form

of organisational control, it depends on the operative 'playing his part'. Just because control is exercised through machinery rather than through rules, procedures or supervisors (though these may be important as well) does not mean that the acquiescence (if not involvement) of the worker isn't crucial. What it does mean is that it might be more difficult for workers to articulate and conceptualise their opposition to a massively buttressed – and seemingly inevitable and inexorable – process of automated control. To oppose, resist, sidestep or obstruct the automated forms of control is, in essence, to question the legitimacy of management's right to manage, to resist 'progress' and as such is clearly a difficult, and ultimately political, step.

3. These excerpts show some of the consequences of forms of organisational control. The Blau study demonstrates the important point that controls set up to achieve one effect often achieve others – many of them undesirable from the point of view of those who designed and installed the control. This study also demonstrates, as Blau mentions, that official procedures can produce informal developments and arrangements which may counter the overt objectives of the procedure. The role of informal groups and norms in resisting formal control and as alternative sources of authority will be discussed. The study by Strauss *et al.* of course goes even further in highlighting the actual ways in which organisational rules and controls may be used by members. The organisational members in that study attempt to sidestep the rules when they can and to use them to justify their own purposes and priorities. Such behaviour is not restricted to professionals. Both the studies by Blau and Nichols and Armstrong record the resentment of the members to the organisational control exercised over them. Members' reactions to, and resentment of, attempts to control them constitute topics of this section.

Organisations and control: an introduction

Organisations are, essentially, structures of control. The question is, how is this control exercised, by whom and for what purposes? This section will be devoted to these issues.

Numerous writers have remarked that organisations consist of two interrelated processes: differentiation and coordination. As we have seen in the previous chapters organisational differentiation concerns the design of work within organisations which is characterised by more or less specialisation, differentiation and subdivision. Even amongst departments or organisations where high-discretion work is permitted, considerable specialisation of activities occurs. And for shop-floor or 'lower-level' organisational members the degree of specialisation and differentiation is very considerable. Such differentiation is only possible within a context of control and coordination. Indeed, as argued earlier, such differentiation and concentration of organisational work has the consequence of making centralized control easier, more thorough, and more effective.

Consider a university. A university is made up of a variety of specialist groups: academics, administrators, personnel, technical services, library staff, maintenance staff, catering, cleaning, and so on. These specialities, which are arranged hierarchically in terms of status and authority (though it should be made clear that universities like other organisations employing large numbers of professionals have more than one hierarchy of authority) are themselves subdivided and specialised. This is especially true of the academic and administrative staff. The academics are divided into disciplines and/or faculties. These bodies are headed by discipline heads (professors) and faculty heads (deans). These people have some authority and control over other members. Furthermore even within disciplines and faculties there is differentiation of function: some teach one topic, some another; some are concerned with research supervision, others with admissions, or faculty administration.

In short, despite their apparently relatively unstructured nature, universities, as other organisations (but to a lesser degree), also require coordination, direction and control. To say this is not to argue that the forms of control apparent within universities are themselves functionally necessary and inevitable. But it is to argue that some sort of coordination and control is necessary. In fact as we shall see later in the section, processes of control within universities contain hierarchical and centralised and delegated elements. There are (at least) two control systems within universities – one based on faculty or discipline, the other on the administrative hierarchy. Examples of conflict between these two are not hard to find; though examples of real, continuing struggle between the two systems are rare. This point too will be considered later. At this stage the point to make is this: if (academic or university) work is differentiated and specialised then there must be control, direction and surveillance to ensure that all the functions and tasks are allocated and carried out – it wouldn't do to have all the academics concerned with one discipline, sub-speciality, or one administrative activity, or some important function (say admissions) not done at all – and that differentiated functions are coordinated, so that for example at the time of examinations the resources, rooms, personnel and exam papers are ready. Or to ensure that decisions taken by one group are taken in the knowledge of all the relevant constraints and are communicated to all the relevant departments and agencies.

These remarks are, clearly, even more applicable to commercial, production, civil service or armed forces organisations where the greater degree of differentiation requires (or justifies, see Marglin, 1976) a proportional investment in processes of coordination, surveillance and control. When a work force of many thousands is engaged in work activities, lasting, per item, no more than 30 seconds, and where the overall objective of the operation, or meaning of the item of the operation, is unclear, and where each operative is instructed simply to perform the operation as frequently as possible, then the importance of controlling these various operations, and of ensuring that, at the end of the day, the sum of these different specialisations is a certain number of marketable products, is enormous.

Furthermore, of course, organisational control is necessary to ensure that members perform their differentiated tasks, and that they operate at the organisationally adequate level of competence or quality. Once again, we have argued in the previous section that a highly specialised division of labour is designed precisely to achieve this sort of 'discipline' and quality control. Indeed it is the attainment of organisational regularity through the work-based control of the work force that some writers have seen as the essential achievement of modern organisation. Historically such organisational regularity was an innovation, as Ure remarks, 'It required, in fact, a man of Napoleon nerve and ambition to subdue the refractory tempers of work people accustomed to irregular paroxysms of diligence' (Ure, 1835, p.15, quoted in Marglin, 1976, p.85).

Such remarks are true not only of industrial organisation (though organisations of this type have been particularly well described in these terms). They are also applicable to the classic conception of bureaucratic organisations, where work is specialised and differentiated in such extreme ways as to make the ultimate coordination and integration of the diverse activities a major organisational activity.

In short, Baldamus's remarks about industrial organisations are true, we argue, of all sorts of organisations, though the manner in which this control is exercised differs. Baldamus remarks: 'the organisation of industry, with all its complexities and diversities, ultimately revolves on a single process: the administrative process through which the employee's effort is controlled by the employer. This means that the entire system of industrial production (is) viewed as a system of administrative controls which regulate quantity, quality, and distribution of human effort' (Baldamus, 1961, p.1, quoted in Allen, 1975, p.215).

The point is that just as organisations are, essentially, structures of control and power, so it is true that 'The behaviour and attitudes of people and groups within an organisation cannot be explained without reference to the power relationship existing among them' (Crozier, 1964, p.107).

But it no longer requires a 'man of Napoleon nerve' to 'subdue the refractory tempers of work people'; the processes of control within organisations, for all the resistance they might encounter, or alienation they might engender, are presented by senior members of the organisation – and frequently the agencies of education and cultural, mass-media dissemination – as normal, and as legitimate. It is time to turn briefly to the question of organisational legitimacy.

Organisational legitimacy

For Weber, bureaucracy was a form of administration which was based upon a particular form of legitimacy, based upon men believing that their rulers were acting in accordance with legal codes and rules – rather than respect for tradition, *qua* tradition, or the personal qualities of the rulers. Weber regarded bureaucracy as based upon this form of authority. Weber argues that the effectiveness of legal authority rests on the acceptance of the validity of a number of mutually interrelated ideas (see Weber, 1964, pp.329–330, and Albrow, 1970, p.43). These ideas or convictions constitute the necessary intellectual elements of any commitment to legal authority.

Weber related rational-legal authority to certain organisational forms: the design and control of bureaucratic administrative work, and the nature of bureaucratic appointments, promotions and personnel, for example, the fact that the members of the bureaucracy inhabit clearly defined offices arranged hierarchically. The officials are selected on merit, and enter a career structure and are incumbents, not owners, of their bureaucratic positions. Weber regarded this form of administrative structure as 'The purest type of exercise of legal authority' (Weber, 1964, p.333).

Weber's remarks on legitimacy and power within bureaucracy are relevant to this chapter in the following ways. Weber was concerned to analyse the links between certain ways of thinking or certain ideas which underpinned forms of legitimacy, and their articulation in organisational structures and processes. This interest in the origins and consequences of the ideas and philosophies which are revealed in organisations has recently been revived, as the discussion in Chapter 7 demonstrated. However, conventional interest in the legitimacy of organisational control and reward systems, although inspired by Weber's work, focuses on the relationship between systems of organisational control and members' reactions to, and perceptions of, these controls. Such work treats as problematic the granting of legitimacy to organisational controls by organisational members. Our interest in organisational legitimacy focuses on senior members' efforts to define their control over others as normal, proper and necessary. The frequent references to management's 'right to manage', or to a 'fair day's work for a fair day's pay' are part of such efforts. These will be discussed more fully in the next section. We shall also consider the ways in which organisational control and hierarchy are buttressed and supported by extra-organisational ideas and moralities which, by supporting the structure of organisations, play an ideological role.

Weber's remarks on the nature and structure of bureaucracy have a further relevance to our interests in the legitimation of organisational control mechanisms and hierarchy. The relevance derives from Weber's work on bureaucratic rationality. As was noted earlier, Weber did not regard rationality as synonymous with efficiency but as deriving from the application and utilisation of certain formal procedures of administration and organisational philosophy which derive from and are supported in the larger society. In short, Weber pointed to the 'rationality' of bureaucracy as a specialist form of ideology which serves a highly important legitimating function with respect to organisational hierarchy and control.

Yet although these various legitimating efforts, which will be described briefly in this chapter and more thoroughly in Section IV, are important, and have some success in reducing the level, or in structuring or diverting the *form*, of members' opposition and resistance to organisational control, they do not, as we shall see, by any means eliminate such resistance. It is important to bear in mind the conception of organisational life outlined earlier and illustrated by many of the empirical accounts at the beginning of this chapter: despite their apparent regularity, stability and permanence, organisations are in fact characterised by constant and continuing processes of struggle, resistance and domination. Very often the resistance and bargaining occur in subtle and disguised forms, and the process of control can be so routinised and impersonal as to be barely apparent. This should not be interpreted as implying that organisational life is anything other than a constant process of 'negotiation and interpretation through which participants with differential resources and discrepant interest construct organisational social realities under the jurisdiction of organisational priorities and programmes' (Elger, 1975, p.102). This section will consider some of the ways in which organisational members attempt to control others, or to avoid or resist such control. In these considerations it will become clear that, since organisations are hierarchical structures with most formal authority vested in the senior members, most but not all of these processes of struggle and resistance (however disguised and gentlemanly) tend to take place between senior and subordinate groups – i.e. on a vertical organisational axis.

Such a perspective leads directly to other questions: what are the resources employed by organisational members in these struggles? What rewards and sanctions can be deployed by senior members?

What bargaining counters and resources can subordinate members use when they attempt to resist hierarchical control, and to enlarge or retain their small areas of autonomy and self-control? We shall see that to some extent an understanding of these issues can be gained through investigating the organisational position and importance of individuals and groups: the greater the organisational significance and salience of a person or group, then the greater the likelihood of that group being able to protect and advance its interests – regardless of its formal organisational authority. But obviously the single most important determinant of organisational power – other things being equal – is location within the organisational hierarchy; for this hierarchy is, itself, a differential distribution of organisational power.

It is also important to remember that organisational power is related to power in the society as a whole. Earlier, in Chapter 2, it was emphasised that any proper sociological approach to organisations must analyse the relationship between organisational patterns of sub- and super-ordination, domination and oppression, in terms of the society within which the organisations occur.

Power within organisations is related to *the distribution of power outside the organisation.* The various features of processes of organisational control – sanctions, control mechanisms, legitimating ideologies, resources, justificatory assumptions about the qualities and intelligence of 'types' of personnel etc. – derive from, and only make sense (or could succeed) in terms of, their surrounding society. The inequalities of organisation reflect the inequalties of the host society.

Finally, this section will consider how these processes of organisational control are actually achieved. What are the mechanisms of organisational control? If organisations are structures of control then how is this control exercised? To return to the example of a university. It is obvious that different methods of control are used even within the same organisation – as the examples quoted earlier illustrate. It also seems that some members of organisations – for example academics – are less controlled than others – for example secretarial staff, or technical people. Is this in fact the case? And if so, why? One of the most striking and worrying differences between organisations (or between groups within organisations) is the difference in type and extent of control. One only has to compare the psychiatrists described by Strauss *et al.* at the beginning of this chapter with the worker described by Bosquet to see this difference. We must try to understand and assess this variation.

Chapter 9

Types of organisational control 2

If, as we have stressed, organisations are structures of control, then how exactly is this control exercised? This question, which is critical for any understanding of organisational structure and activity, or to any insight into the relationship between organisations and society, must be broken down into a number of separate but related issues. First, what rewards and sanctions are used within organisations? Second, what methods or mechanisms of control are used? And, third, how do we explain the observed variation in organisation rewards and sanctions and control mechanisms? This chapter will consider these issues.

One of the most striking differences between organisations – or between groups within organisations is in the rewards and sanctions that are employed. Consider the empirical examples quoted earlier; it is obvious that the workers described by Bosquet and the psychiatrists in Strauss *et al.* are controlled by very different sorts of rewards. It is useful to consider these differences.

Manual workers

For manual workers and low-level members, the reward of prime significance is the level of remuneration. It is true that the precise importance of this reward relative to other rewards – the nature of the work, working conditions, etc. – varies. And this variation is important in understanding workers' attitudes and reactions. Nevertheless, most 'blue-collar' workers find themselves involved in employment relationships where the organisation offers them few – if any – rewards apart from the financial, and where tight control over their performance, output and quality of work is directly tied to remunerative rewards. Fox has remarked that,

. . . insofar as managements have control over the supply of whatever men value, they are able to control and regulate behaviour by making a supply available under the threat of withdrawal if the required behaviour is not pursued. They can grant or deny men access to an income – and therefore livelihood. They can adjust the level of the livelihood and manipulate possibilties of promotional advancement. They can bestow or withdraw status. They can trans-

fer men to more or less satisfying work, and display signs of approval or disapproval as encouragement or threats (Fox, 1971, p.31).

For manual workers and low-level members of organisations it is 'access' to, and variations in the amount of, an income that constitutes the most important basis of organisational power.

To say, with Etzioni, that, in general, 'blue-collar' members of organisations are controlled through the manipulation of remunerative rewards, i.e. 'material resources and rewards, through allocation of salaries and wages, commissions and contributions, "fringe benefits", services and commodities' (Etzioni, 1961, p.5) is not to maintain that these members are, necessarily, only interested in such rewards, or that they are content to limit themselves to them. How far workers restrict their work aspiration to the financial aspects of the employment relationship will be considered later in this chapter. But it is to argue that for such members of organisations there are few, if any, rewards other than remunerative ones which are made available to them. For such employees the work itself is, on the whole, likely to be devoid of meaning, creativity, challenge, or autonomy. There will be few possibilities for pleasures; the nature and design of work, working conditions, the status of work, may be punishing and depriving, or, at least, without any positive, rewarding features. If, as is usually the case, such circumstances are allied with tight control, supervision and discipline, with the constant possibility of dismissal and redundancy, and with a massive organisational emphasis on financial forms of remuneration, then it is no surprise that the members themselves invest this form of reward with considerable importance.

Although the prime basis of the employment contract for blue-collar organisational members is remuneration, which, as Etzioni remarks, is the basis for a *calculative* employer–employee relationship, it is obvious that management tries hard to imbue this relationship with moral undertones. Efforts are made – within the organisation and outside it – to persuade the shop-floor members of the unity of worker–manager values and objectives, of the sacredness (and competence) of managerial decision-making and their 'right to manage', of the inevitability of technologically based innovations in control systems or work design, etc., of the crucial necessity for management–worker differentials in levels of pay, conditions, promotions, opportunities.

All these aspects of managerial ideology will be discussed later. The important point to emphasise at this stage is that although, as Etzioni emphasises, the control of shop-floor members of organisations is through the manipulation of financial rewards (for the work offers few, if any, other rewards), this should not blind us to the

ways in which this essentially calculative employment is surrounded
by ideological elements. These elements are very useful to those in
senior and privileged positions within organisations since they serve,
among other things, to legitimate the structure of organisations and
the distribution of rewards and benefits within them.

Finally, if, in Etzioni's terms, this primarily calculative relationship had ideological elements as management attempts to achieve
some moral commitment without altering the essential nature of the
relationship itself, so it also has elements of coercion. Behind the
calculation, the exchange of labour for money, there lies the threat
– indeed the possibility – of redundancy and dismissal. Sooner or
later, when other forms of control fail, these power bases are
introduced. Allied with the reward of financial remuneration is the
ever-constant possibility of lay-off, redundancy, and dismissal
(Martin and Fryer, 1973).

Senior members

Now what about the psychiatrists described by Strauss *et al.* What
rewards do they derive from their organisational membership?
Obviously remuneration is also important; but despite the fact that
their levels of financial remuneration (and associated benefits) are
much higher than for shop-floor organisational members,
professional and senior managerial members of organisations
receive many other rewards: most obvious of which is the intrinsic
satisfaction, challenge, and creativity of their jobs. They also
benefit from vastly superior working conditions, greater security
and job/career prospects, high status, more participation in
decision-making, freedom from supervison or onerous discipline
and so on. It is possible to conceptualise the control of such
organisational members as remunerative (in that these members
gain high levels of remunerative and associated rewards which are
obviously important to them) *and* as normative, in that to some
extent their work is controlled by 'the allocation and manipulation
of symbolic rewards and deprivations through . . . allocations of
esteem and prestige symbols, administration of rituals, and influence over the distribution of "acceptance" and "positive
response"' (Etzioni, 1961, p.5).

Professional members of organisations, and to a lesser extent
senior managerial members, are to some degree controlled through
their commitment to professional or organisational philosophies
and objectives. Senior members of organisations, especially
professional members, are likely to be so committed to philosophies
which emphasise the importance and value of a particular activity,
condition, practice or objective that to some considerable extent
they regulate their own work behaviour. Whether or not such self
regulation is adequate from the point of view of senior organisa-

tional members is, as we shall see, doubtful, But there can be no doubt that for such organisational members as academics, doctors, lawyers, personnel managers, technical specialists, senior bureaucrats, civil servants, officers in the services, or senior members of public corporations, their organisational control has a strong normative basis. The common feature of such organisational members is their conviction of the importance – indeed necessity – of their organisational activity, and of their personal responsibility to perform their part in the achievement of the desired goal with competence and diligence. Of course it is true that professionals and bureaucrats (or executives) may differ in the focus of their commitment; the one being more concerned with professional goals which may or may not be convergent with organisational practices, the other being concerned directly with his employing organisation, and its goals, authority and members. Nevertheless these groups are similar in that to a striking extent control is exercised through both commitment and personal monitoring.

To return to the example of the academic. The academic believes in the importance of higher education in general and of his specialist discipline in particular. In the execution of academic work – teaching, writing, assessing, researching, supervising etc. – the academic is committed to the importance of certain values and standards which he will strive to attain: honesty, thoroughness, clarity, objectivity, etc. To a very considerable extent in the execution of his work tasks – writing lectures, marking essays, assessing examination scripts, reviewing books and articles, selecting students etc. – the academic will be controlled by his own sense of the importance of these activities and his commitment to standards of fairness, thoroughness and impartiality, and by his consciousness of his colleagues' shared commitment to these.

Obviously one must be realistic: not all academics live up to these standards. The academic, like other professionals, is not immune to normal human failings, and it is worth emphasising that this sort of commitment to professional value systems can have extremely negative, elitist implications. For example, Freidson, in his study of doctors, has argued that, in 'the field of health, which is the most highly professionalised area of work to be found in our society . . . many of the rigid, mechanical, and authoritarian attributes, and much of the inadequate coordination said to characterise the health services, may stem more from their professional organization than from their bureaucratic characteristics' (Freidson, 1970, p.133). There will be more of this later. At this stage we're concerned to describe this sort of commitment and self-control, not to evaluate it.

The 'self-control' of the senior organization man – the bureaucrat, executive, civil servant, manager – is derived from his commitment to the organisation's goals rather than from a professional value system. And it is possible that differences between the two groups in patterns of selection and training result in less strongly held and internalised work-related standards and goals. But compared to lower-level organisational groups (especially shop-floor members) the 'normative' basis of the control of these members is striking. The origins of these attitudes are discussed later in this section.

How is this internalised, normative control achieved? How is it that these organisation members identify themselves so thoroughly with these professional and/or organisational values? We can deal with this issue only briefly. The answer must involve a consideration of the pre-organisational experiences of these members and the sorts of rewards, privileges and benefits they receive within the organisation.

The main feature of these organisational members is their socialisation into appropriate value and behaviour patterns. Their commitment is developed through processes of pre-organisational selection, recruitment, training and induction. The exact details of the organisational or specialist culture will vary with the discipline, profession, or specialism concerned. But they will be similar in the emphasis they place on accepting the existing structure of society (and organisation) and in the legitimacy and value they attach to the specialist function within this society (or organisation). Through their experience of pre-organisational selection and training the future organisational member identifies himself with the valued specialism, its goals, philosophies, members and practices; an identification which will later serve as the basis of his self-control in organisation settings.

Such members are attached to their employing organisations by their investment in careers. Because of the importance of this linking concept it is worth describing it at some length. As Wilensky remarks

Careers . . . are a major source of stability for modern society. . . . Every group must recruit and maintain its personnel and motivate role performance. Careers serve these functions for organisations, occupational groups and societies. At the same time they give continuity to the personal experience of the most able and skilled segments of the population – men who otherwise would produce a level of rebellion or withdrawal which would threaten the maintenance of the system. By holding out the prospect of continuous, predictable rewards, careers foster a willingness to train and achieve. . . . (Wilensky, 1968, p.4).

There is evidence of the role of organisational careers in attaching the commitment of senior organisational members. Sofer, for example, has studied the organisational careers of middle managers in two large British companies (1970 p.9). These high career expectations are not, of course, shared by low-level members.

Other factors which underlie the deployment of normatively based control over senior and specialist organisational members concern the organisation's efforts to attract, select and promote recruits with 'suitable', 'appropriate', 'reliable' and 'responsible' attitudes and features. Such efforts are especially evident during processes of selection, which is why an Open University course called *People and Organizations* devoted all its television programmes to filmed records of processes of selection and assessment in three organisations: the BBC, Ford Motor Company, and the British Army Officers Corps. An analysis of the selection and assessment procedure in the case of the British Army is contained in Salaman and Thompson (1978). Material from all three organisations is analysed in Salaman and Thompson, Media Booklets 1 and 2, 1974.

Overwhelmingly these filmed records make one major point: that despite the pervasiveness of modern personnel practices and systems derived from occupational psychology and psychometrics, the actual execution of the selection systems in all three organisations showed a marked concern for the candidates' attitudinal and cultural compatibility with the values of the relevant organisation. Each organisation stressed different values but were alike in the salience they attached to discovering candidates who showed sympathy with their philosophies and practices. (See also the discussion of the psychological basis of such personnel practices in Section IV.)

Once in the organisation the recruit finds himself exposed to further socialisation into 'appropriate' ways of thinking and reacting. Sofer, on the basis of his study, notes the efforts of senior management to

. . . *convince employees of the importance of what they are asked to do. . . . Identifications with one's task and employing organization are encouraged by formal induction and training procedures, by the personal sponsorship of seniors, by peer group sanctions and by assessment and counselling procedures. For his part, the person joining an organization and proposing to continue making his career in it is disposed to accept these influences (Sofer, 1970, p.325).*

The commitment of members of this sort to the moral basis of their employing organisation is also encouraged by the level of reward they obtain. There is a link between remunerative and moral rewards. High levels of remunerative rewards, such as are received by expert, professional and senior members of organisations, serve to encourage these members to regard the structure and objectives of these organisations as 'moral' and worth while just as less privileged treatment breeds alienation and resentment. Of course it is true, as Perrow has remarked, that 'lengthy training and specialised skills appear to be associated with higher morale and greater commitment to organisational goals . . .' (Perrow, 1970, p.61, quoted in Fox, 1974, p.30) *but* it seems unlikely that such trustworthiness, such reliability, would persist for long if these senior members were not granted levels of reward which they defined as 'appropriate' for their significant organisational contributions, their long and arduous periods of demanding training, their expertise, and so on.

And of course they *are* rewarded well. It is one of the most obvious features of organisations that as one rises in the formal hierarchy, not only the type of reward varies (i.e. a shift from the purely remunerative to the remunerative/normative) but the overall *amount* of reward increases enormously. The difference between the sorts of rewards of senior and shop-floor members of organisations are too apparent to require much discussion (though there has been remarkably little research done on this subject). Even excluding the sort of systematic, informal and unofficial rewards allocated to senior members (see Dalton, 1959), the level of benefits available to senior organisational members is striking. First there is the work itself. This tends to be intrinsically satisfying and challenging, less controlled and supervised, more demanding and interesting. Then there are conditions of work, security, work surroundings and support facilities, status and prestige, fringe benefits, pensions, career prospects, levels of pay, etc. etc. Although it might be too cynical to suggest that the normative commitment of senior and expert organisational members is *bought* by granting them high levels of remunerative rewards, it is undoubtedly important to note that this commitment is associated with privileged organisational positions. As Selznick has suggested:

The human tools of action come to an organization shaped in special but systematic ways. Levels of aspiration and training, social ideals, class interests – these and similar factors will have moulded the character of the personnel. This will make staff resistant to demands which are inconsistent with their accustomed views and habits; the freedom of choice of the employer will be restricted, and he will find it necessary in some measure to conform to the received views and habits of the personnel (Selznick, 1952, p.199).

And organizations themselves work hard to ensure that the incoming personnel are compatible; they also attempt to imbue them with appropriate attitudes and responses once they are in the organisation.

But this isn't the end of the story. It must be noted that there is a strong relationship between the sort of self-control imputedly practised by experts and professionals within organisations and the professional or occupational power of the occupation. This argument suggests that self-control is a result of colleague or occupational/professional control, and is therefore, potentially, at odds with bureaucratic authority. This issue is explored later in this section. It is true that such conflict is possible, but in practice bureaucratic and professional objectives have not been shown to be seriously at odds. What is worth emphasising however is that relative freedom from tight organisational control over work is a result of, among other factors, the ability of the people concerned to resist organisational attempts to reduce their 'control over uncertainty', their organisational and work autonomy. As such there is a link between normative control, occupational strength and work autonomy. But as was noted in the previous chapter, other factors too are important, such as the nature of the tasks involved, the 'trustworthiness' of the personnel, their ideological compatibility and commitment, and their qualities and attitudes.

White-collar workers

Finally, we must consider intermediate organisational groups, such as middle to lower managers, nurses, NCOs in the services, white-collar and office workers, secretarial workers, low-level administrators, clerks and the like. This intermediate organisational group or category is primarily rewarded with remunerative re-sources. But certain features of their organisational position and treatment have, traditionally, constituted the basis for the develop-ment of some normative involvement in the organisation, its objectives and structure.

One can overdo this argument. As we shall see: many commen-tators have noted that increasingly these intermediate organisational groups are subject to the same sort of controls, and have their work organised and designed along similar principles, to shop-floor members. (Remember the outraged reactions of the employment agency interviewers in Blau's study, quoted earlier.)

Nevertheless, in general, there are features of the organisational positions and rewards of these organisational groups which at least historically, and for some currently, encourage them to commit themselves more fully to their employer than lower-level members. These features have been studied by sociologists interested in the class consciousness of white-collar groups. The question addressed by such investigators is relevant to our discussion: how can we explain the white-collar workers' holding attitudes, identifications and aspirations which deliberately set them apart from (by stressing their superiority to) working-class cultures, communities and relationships? This question arises from the fact that white-collar workers are propertyless, like their shop-floor colleagues, and sell their labour (and are therefore in the same class position) but hold somewhat different class and political attitudes.

But as Lockwood and others have pointed out, it is only possible to understand the actual behaviour, identifications and attitudes of organisational employees by relating these to the features of the white-collar workers' organizational positon, and the rewards they receive. Lockwood suggests using the three concepts of 'market', 'work' and 'status' situation – which refer respectively to

. . . economic position narrowly conceived, consisting of source and size of income, degree of job-security, and opportunity for upward occupational mobility. Secondly, 'work situation' [is] the set of social relationships in which the individual is involved at work by virtue of his position in the division of labour. And . . . 'status situation', or the position of the individual in the hierarchy of prestige in the society at large (Lockwood, 1958, p.15).

Using these three sets of factors Lockwood concludes his investigation of the organisational origins of the attitudes of clerical workers by arguing that, historically, clerks have enjoyed superior material advantages, greater job security, greater opportunities for promotion, better working conditions, holiday allowances and other fringe benefits. Furthermore, historically, the clerk was not in-volved in the sort of social organisation of production to which the shop-floor member was exposed, and which encouraged a strong sense of shop-floor solidarity and antagonistic attitudes to manage-ment. Historically clerks were physically scattered about a number of small offices, working in contact with management, and fragmented by departmental or specialist distinctions. Finally, traditionally the clerks were able – with some success – to claim superiority, status and prestige.

Now the important point about Lockwood's analysis lies not in the current applicability of his discussion to present-day white-collar or clerical workers, but in the way in which he conceptualises the organisational features which make up 'class position'. The three sorts of situation – work, market and status – are of considerable use and applicability in understanding the greater involvement in, and identification with, their employing organisation demonstrated by the sorts of intermediate employees under consideration here. The fact that, to some extent, intermediate level employees such as nurses, technicians, secretarial staff, junior managers and bureau-crats, etc. differ from lower-level organisational members in their commitment to their employing organisation follows from variation in their location and treatment within their employing organisation which can be conceptualised and discovered through the use of the Lockwood analysis.

But is Lockwood's analysis currently applicable in practice? Are current white-collar workers still differentiated in the way he suggests from manual employees? And are these differences still to be found among all the intermediate category of organisational employees? The situation is ambiguous. It is true that increasingly some of these employees are subject to forms of work design and discipline and organisation which differ little from those apparent on the shop floor (see Braverman, 1974, and Levison, 1974, among others). And this is frequently associated with large offices and 'rationalised' procedures and systems. As Lockwood has noted:

In those bureaucracies, on the other hand, where larger office units, strict classification and grading, blocked upward mobility and unhindered horizontal mobility were the rule, there have been reproduced impersonal and standardised working relationships comparable with those created by the factory and labour market. It is here that the work situation of the clerk has been most favourable to the emergence of that feeling of collective interdependence among employees which is prerequisite to their concerted action. [But, he continues,] even where working conditions have fostered group action by clerks, the continuing physical and social division between clerks and manual workers has generally remained a barrier to the mutual identification of the two groups (Lockwood, 1958, p.207).

These remarks are applicable to many sorts of office workers – typists, clerical workers, computer operatives, comptometer operatives, etc. They are less applicable to other sorts of intermediate employees where efforts might have been made to impose factory-like discipline and rationalisation, but where the nature of the work, the strength of the occupation concerned and the survival of traditional expectations, have helped to preserve some genuine differences in terms of Lockwood's categories. Exactly how any intermediate group fares in these terms is an empirical matter – and one that is rapidly altering. But one point must be made: it is not uncommon to find some element of commitment and organisational identification within this group. To some extent this follows from genuine differences in organisational situation and treatment (differences which are being eroded in some cases), to some extent it is the result of the fact that such workers are 'subjected to ideological pressure designed to promote perception of shared goals with their superiors' (Fox, 1974, p.37). However, as Fox goes on to add, these ideological efforts are frequently (and increasingly) denied by the 'structure' of their work situation which often appears to reveal a conviction on the part of higher authority that they cannot wholly be trusted to behave in desired ways and must therefore be hedged about with rules, controls, checks, monitoring devices or discipline' (Fox, 1974, pp.37–8).

So much then for varieties of organisational reward, which as we have seen differ not only in type, but also in amount; such differences being arranged hierarchically. But what about methods of organisational control? How is organisational control actually exercised? We have already made a number of scattered remarks on this subject. Now it is time to pull these together.

Methods of organisational control

Just as organisational employees vary in type and amount of reward they receive, so they vary in the ways in which they are controlled. And as the examples from organisational studies quoted at the beginning of this and the previous chapter suggest, the way in which control is exercised is itself an organisational reward – or punishment.

We have already stressed that organisational members – and organisations – differ considerably in the amount of discretion accorded them in their work and in the degree of work fragmentation. This difference is related to variations in mechanisms of organisational control, because mechanisms of control vary in their tightness, stringency and rigidity. So, to suggest that jobs vary in their discretionary content and degree of specialisation and differentiation (for example, psychiatrists and the process worker) is also to argue that these jobs vary in the sorts of mechanisms of control involved. These variations are especially striking between shop-floor employees and senior management, expert or administrative members.

This issue is probably best approached through a consideration of a number of questions which can be asked of the senior and subordinate organisational groups. We shall see a considerable difference between manual and non-manual members.

1. How are the work activities themselves defined? For senior organisational jobs involving high discretion, work is defined by job descriptions of a more or less vague and general sort. A person's job might be to take responsibility for all the organisation's personnel activities: selection, recruitment, appraisal, dismissal, management development, etc. Or it might involve financial responsibility: preparing accounts, attending and advising at meetings, writing reports on the financial implications of various investments or projects. Whatever the details these jobs will inevitably be generally defined, and will involve complete projects and activities, not bits of jobs. The actual definition will come from senior members but will be subject to considerable day-by-day variation in the light of changing priorities and problems.

For subordinate members and especially shop-floor or clerical workers on the other hand, jobs are defined tightly, minutely and rigidly. There will be little room for alteration or variation, and the definition will consist not of whole activities, functions, responsibilities or projects for which the members take responsibility, but of closely specified specialised activities. Furthermore, while the senior job is defined by negotiation and agreement, and this definition is subject to constant alteration, the subordinate jobs are defined, very often, through automation, the flow of work, the assembly line, the machine or exact written formulations.

2. How is quality/quantity of work controlled? Again we find a striking difference. Senior members' work, since it is defined less strictly, is less amenable to measurement. Some senior jobs generate their own, measurable, output, and these can, with care, be used for assessing performance. But on the whole it is only extremes of performance that can be, or are, noticed. There is, however, increasing interest in both tightening the definition of senior members' jobs, and improving measurement techniques so as to be able to control performance. Such efforts at *appraisal* frequently encounter resistance, not surprisingly, as the excerpt from Blau's study illustrated. Despite the attractiveness of such work measurement to the organisation's hierarchy, it is frequently experienced as oppressive by those who have been taught to expect a high level of personal responsibility and control.

At the other end of the organisation, particularly in industrial and commercial organisations, there is considerable emphasis placed on constant measurement of work output, throughput, scrap rates, costs rates, etc. Remember the process worker described by Nichols and Armstrong. Such measurement is frequently easily taken; indeed it may, as argued earlier, constitute one of the main intentions behind the design of the machine, or work flow. The assembly line worker, the typist, the punch card operator, the check-out operator and many others spend their working time operating machines which, by their very nature, measure the quantity and standard of their work. Mechanisation means control, as Perrow says: 'Buying and installing machines . . . is one way of reducing the number of rules in an organization. The rules are built into the machine itself, and the organization pays for those rules in the price of the machine' (Perrow, 1972, p.27).

However, at this end of the organisation not all control is 'built into' machines; a great deal is also achieved through tightly specifying work routines and procedures, or through dividing work into various tasks which are distributed among the operatives in such a way that the mutual interdependence acts as a form of control.

3. How are *work practices* specifed? Once again we find significant variation between senior and junior organisational groups. As noted with senior organisational members, much greater reliance is placed on internalised standards and procedures, even

though these jobs are more complicated and demanding than lower level ones. Obviously some organisational structuring of how the work should be done occurs. Training and induction take place; juniors are advised to learn from their seniors; a great deal of instruction occurs informally. Furthermore, even at senior levels of the organisation there are rules and established procedures which govern work activities, and constraints, of budget, authority, or capacity, which limit the ambitious. But compared with subordinate groups the way in which work is done (like the way in which work, and standards, are defined) is left remarkably vague.

For subordinate groups – shop-floor workers, office workers, clerical and computer personnel, etc. – work practices are tightly controlled. Frequently this is done through machinery. As Perrow remarks, a typewriter establishes its own control over the shape, size, colour, etc. of written letters. It is also achieved through reducing the work activity to a minimum and therefore leaving the operative no choice about how to do the work – he or she must just 'work' the machine. There is no room, and no need, for variability. Both mechanisation and the establishment of tightly defined work procedures and regulations serve to specify the ways in which low-level organisational work is done to a very much greater extent than is true for more senior work.

4. How is supervision executed? The further up the organisation, the less reliance is placed on direct supervision. Whereas at lower levels differences in hierarchical position frequently consist solely of supervisory responsibility, at more senior levels differences in rank involve completely new work responsibilities.

These are the main differences in mechanisms of organisational control. We have seen that senior and junior groups vary in the tightness with which their work is defined; the stringency with which performance is measured; procedures and activities specified and supervision imposed. To these one could add that subordinate members are more tightly controlled overall than senior members – they are much more exposed to disciplinary regulations and control, covering such matters as punctuality, absenteeism, etc. An enquiry by Wedderburn and Craig into 'relative deprivation' at work discovered that:

. . . manual workers were in every case more closely bound by discipline than were staff. Sometimes this was because of the exigencies of the production system itself, but it also reflected a widespread belief among management that manual workers were less responsible than staff and less committed to the company. Discipline, therefore, tended to be stricter for manual workers than for staff, immediate penalties more severe, and the amount of discretion allowed both to the employees and their supervisors was much more limited. In the case of discipline there was a heavy

reliance upon the 'rules' to control manual workers; for staff, there was personal consideration, even in some cases counselling and guidance. Even where formal disciplinary agreements existed for all grades, they were more frequently invoked for manual workers and at earlier stages. Precisely because there was more flexibility and discretion for staff, recourse to formal procedures was less necessary (Wedderburn and Craig, 1975, pp.62–3).

These differences are especially apparent if one compares manual employees with others. Most organisational sociology prefers not to do this, choosing instead either to conceptualise *all* organisational sociology in terms of *roles* (a misleading enterprise, see below) or to restrict interest in variations in organisational control mechanisms to white-collar groups and above. Work of this latter sort has come up with some interesting suggestions and distinctions which are discussed later. But it would be a pity if these two traditions were allowed to pass into academic orthodoxy.

Explanations of differences in control

Finally, in this chapter on varieties of organisational control and rewards, one important question remains: why is it that different levels or grades of organisational employees are treated so very differently? Why is it that the sales manager or senior academic or Brigadier is allocated different types, and different levels, of reward from the council workman, the factory hand, the hospital porter or the punch card operator?

This might seem like a simple-minded enquiry. Some – possibly most – organisational researchers would regard this as a naive and irrelevant issue (an important exception being Alan Fox). Certainly it is a topic which gets very little academic attention – at least within this field of enquiry. Nevertheless it merits attention.

There are a number of possible answers. The most important and common one would be to refer to the design of work. The reason, such an explanation would argue, that some jobs are controlled much more tightly and rigidly than others, and are associated with much greater emphasis on discipline and punctuality, etc., is because of their highly differentiated and specialised nature. Such an explanation is most applicable to the shop floor, rationalised office work, or highly systematised and fragmented work. Such a view regards the tightness and closeness of organisational control of some (low-level) members as necessitated by the need to coordinate the discreet work process, and to ensure that, at any time, the highly interdependent work force is present and working at the required speeds and rates.

Such an explanation would maintain that 'Organization implies the coordination of diverse activities necessary for effective goal achievement. Such coordination requires some mode of control over these diverse activities' (Miller, 1970, p.508). And it would probably agree with Perrow that 'Given a routine (i.e. a few exceptional cases encountered) technology, the much maligned Weberian bureaucracy (high centralisation and control) probably constitutes the socially optimum form of organizational structure' (Perrow, 1972, p.61).

This approach would, predictably, explain the relative freedom from control and discretion of senior management and administrative, expert organisational members in terms of the inherent variability of their work tasks; the judgement required and knowledge and experience involved in complex and unpredictable decision-making. In short the sort of control exercised (in terms of the variations outlined above) follows from the way in which work is designed and organised and the nature and demands of the work itself.

There is something in this argument: the organisation of work *is* closely related to forms and stringency of control, but the key question remains – why is the work designed in such very different ways? Why are some tasks stripped of their discretionary content, and not others? The usual answer, as we have seen, is in terms of what is possible and what is efficient. It is not possible to break down, subdivide and routinise managerial, expert work; it *is* possible to do this to car making, office work, low-level administration, etc. When it is possible, it is done.

Once again there is plausibility in this argument: senior organisational jobs are, inherently, more resistant to this sort of 'rationalisation' than other jobs. But, as we have argued, their high level of decision-making and planning is only to the extent that other jobs have been stripped of such elements. A complete explanation of the extreme differences in types and levels of organisational control which are related to the discretionary content of organisational jobs requires reference to another crucial variable: the value or worth that is placed on different types of organisational personnel, and senior organisation members' definition of members' reliability, trustworthiness and importance. There is a close relationship between work design and control mechanisms and levels, in that methods of work design and organisation reflect the value that senior organisational members attach to low-level members; the organisation of work reflects the predominance of profit over people, and demonstrates, in engineering or work systems form, the consciousness of class conflict and class membership. Perrow, for example admits that his perspective (emphasising the determinate importance of the nature of the raw material and the organisation's technology) 'ignores the role of the cultural and social environment in making available definitions of raw material, providing technologies and restricting the range of feasible structures and goals' (Perrow, 1972, p.59). Exactly: and of course these cultural definitions, in this sort of society, stress the priority of profit and production over people, especially when the people concerned are working class. They also stress the inherent refractoriness of such organizational members, the need to control them closely, and to surround them with disciplinary measures. Such cultural definitions also carry an emphasis on the reliability and responsibility of educated, middle-class organisational recruits.

Such definitions are 'realistic', in the sense that the organisational and extra-organisational experiences of working-class and middle-class organisational members lead them, in general terms, to regard the existing order of society, and the usual structure of organisations, as supporting or opposing their interests. Beynon, in his *Working for Ford*, argues this point:

Too often it is assumed that if only the shop steward and his members had the 'right attitude', strikes and industrial conflict generally would be tremendously reduced. The only attitude that would ensure this is one of subservience and stupidity. For what the pundits fail to realise, or choose to ignore, is that we live in a world dominated by captial and capitalist rationality. (Beynon, 1973 p.159).

It is not adequate to explain varieties of organisational control in terms of the differential nature of senior and low-level organisational work because, despite the fact that organisational work does vary in its amenability to such control and 'rationalisation' – i.e. varies in its decision-making demands, variability, etc. – we must still consider the class-based definitions and interests (of the nature and value and trustworthiness of personnel) and priorities (profit and production over people) which encourage those who run and own organisations to take advantage of these variations in the nature of organisational work. Simply because some jobs are more easily and readily broken down than others doesn't explain why they are broken down, subdivided and fragmented. To understand this one must have recourse to capitalist values, definitions and interests. Even more basically, we must not take these original differences in work activities as inevitable and 'normal'. In the previous section we made much of the argument that the decision-making elements of senior organisational positions follows from the elimination of such elements in low-level jobs. It isn't possible to understand the existence of these specialised planning, research, technical, managerial, accounting, and coordinating functions except in terms of the interests and priorities whose natural organisational form is the hierarchical organisation which removes choice from some members only to concentrate it in others. To quote from an important article on the origins of this form of organisation:

The capitalist division of labour, typified by Adam Smith's famous example of pin manufacture, was the result of a search not for a technologically superior organization of work, but for an organization which guaranteed to the entrepreneur an essential role in the production process, as integrator of the separate efforts of his workers into a marketable product. . . . The origin and success of the factory lay not in technological superiority, but in the substitution of the capitalists' for the workers' control of the work process and the quantity of output . . . (Marglin, 1976, p.62).

The same analysis holds true for large non-production organisations: the activities of planners, administrators, coordinators, managers and experts must be seen in the context of the 'substitution' of their control for the workers – whether the 'worker' be concerned with production or not – or in the necessity, within a capitalist economy, to devote specialised resources to such functions as marketing, advertising, etc.

Finally, forms of control vary in their effects. Some are highly alienative; others actually encourage normative commitment. The reason for variation in the sorts of organisational control employed for various groups is not only that the sort of work is more or less amenable to this or that form of control. It is also because it would generally be regarded as inapplicable and dangerous to expose senior organisational members in the crucial, decision-making jobs to alienative forms of control, because of the importance of their normative involvement (see Fox, 1974). For this reason, as the next chapter discusses, these members are rarely exposed to explicit surveillance and discipline. Nevertheless, there are other ways of ensuring their 'responsibility' and 'reliability'.

Chapter 10

Alternative structures of organisational control

In section II it was noted that work within organisations is, for some members, deliberately designed to be specialised, differentiated and prescribed. The interrelationships between these features of some organisational work, and the intentions lying behind them, were considered. Now it is time to develop and expand our consideration of processes of organisational control. The application of scientific management principles and the reduction of discretion of low-level organisational jobs are clearly directly related to the *centralisation* of decision-making elsewhere in the organisation; but do all organisations display the same levels of centralisation? Are all members subject to these forms of control? How are the controllers controlled? What about the middle managers, experts, administrators – how are they controlled? To approach these questions we must return to the work of Max Weber.

A bureaucracy is the form of administration which best exemplifies the principles of rational-legal authority – i.e. it is based on rules; abstract rules which are applied, by the official, to particular cases. Bureaucratic positions are clearly defined with respect to authority and responsibilities, and are organised hierarchically, each layer being responsible for the control, supervision and direction of the subordinate office. The work of an office, or position, is regulated by rules; after all, rational-legal authority as represented in bureaucracy, involves 'A continuous organization of official functions bound by rules' (Weber, 1964, p.330). It is through the creation of these bureaucratic rules and their application by organisational members to their specified areas of activity, that bureaucracies achieve the precision, stability and reliability which Weber remarks on; and it is as the result of such rule-determined decisions and choices that the 'spirit of formalistic impersonality' achieves dominance.

So far, so good. Weber's description is clearly 'idealised' in the sense that it does not pretend to describe any particular bureaucracy but rather to gather together all those features which, in his view, represent the organisational manifestations of a particular way of thinking and believing. Even so, it is clearly recognisable to us all – at least those of us with any experience of government departments, military organisations and even some forms of industry and commerce. In organisations of this sort direction is applied through rules, norms and procedures applied to tightly prescribed work activities. Control is exercised through hierarchy whereby each position monitors and supervises the work of subordinate positions.

But elsewhere Weber suggests some other features of bureaucratic organisation and control which imply a somewhat different, and possibly alternative, basis and structure of authority. Weber remarks that

Bureaucratic administration means fundamentally the exercise of control on the basis of knowledge. . . . This consists on the one hand in technical knowledge. . . . But in addition to this, bureau-cratic organizations, or the holders of power who make use of them, have the tendency to increase their power still further by the knowledge growing out of experience in the service. For they acquire through the conduct of office a special knowledge of facts and have available a store of documentary material peculiar to themselves (Weber, 1964, p.339).

Earlier Weber has made a similar point about the rules which pre-dominate in bureaucratic activity: 'The rules which regulate the conduct of an office may be technical rules or norms. In both cases, if their application is to be fully rational, specialized training is necessary. It is thus normally true that only a person who has demonstrated an adequate technical training is qualified to be a member of the administrative staff of such an organised group. . . .' (p.331).

Once again these remarks ring true. We are probably aware of organisations where knowledge of the first, technical sort, and rules and procedures apparently deriving from such knowledge, seem to constitute the major determinant of members' behaviour, and where specialised knowledge acts as the basis of organisational con-trol and legitimacy. Think of the psychiatric hospital described by Strauss *et al.* in the excerpt quoted at the beginning of this section. Think also of other, similar organisations, universities, research establishments or departments, hospitals and so on.

It appears then that Weber's model of organisational control and authority contains two potentially conflicting, and certainly con-ceptually distinct, elements: one consisting of behaviour bound by rules and specifications backed up by hierarchical authority, the other involving expertise and technical knowledge as the basis of members' behaviour and authority. A number of writers have pointed to these two principles, and have considered their empirical manifestations and distinctiveness.

Parsons is usually considered to be the first writer to remark on these two different and possibly opposed principles, which are frequently characterised as professional (technical expertise) and

bureaucratic (rule-bound); but the distinction was first developed by Gouldner in his classic *Patterns of Industrial Bureaucracy.*
Gouldner argues for a distinction between two types of bureaucracy, one of which, the 'representative' form, is 'based on rules established by agreement, rules which are technically justified and administered by specially qualified personnel, and to which consent is given voluntarily'. The other is called 'punishment centred', and this 'is based on the imposition of rules, and on obedience for its own sake' (Gouldner, 1954, p.24). Gouldner emphasises that the crucial feature of any organisation is control, and he notes that it is only as a result of this control and discipline that organisations can be said to exist. Nevertheless what is interesting is the way – or ways – in which this control is exercised, and where it originates.

But this isn't the only distinction that can be discerned in Weber's writings on bureaucracy, although it is the most important one. It is possible to argue that Weber saw as compatible and similar two systems of bureaucratic control which in fact are alternatives, although they may serve the same purpose. Weber describes bureaucracy as containing tight specification of activities and procedures *and* hierarchical control and supervision. In more recent works these two organisational features are usually termed *formalisation* (the number and existence of rules) and *centralisation* of authority. It has been argued that, like the distinction between expert and bureaucratic control noted earlier, they tend to occur as distinct, and possibly functionally equivalent, bases and structures of control rather than as interrelated elements of one overall system of bureaucratic authority.

In short, it is being argued that Weber's model of bureaucratic forms and bases of control tends to lump together elements which seem, *a priori*, to be capable of operating as alternative, possibly opposing, principles. We must now turn to empirical accounts of control in organisations to discover how these principles occur in practice.

The first point to note has been made by Stanley Udy and by Richard Hall, among others: from the empirical point of view Weber's Ideal Type conception of bureaucracy represents a list of features which are claimed to interrelate and coexist, but which may, *in fact*, vary independently, act as substitutes, and occur in varying degree. Udy reformulated Weber's bureaucratic features as empirical dimensions and attempted to discover, through analysis of 150 organisations, the extent to which they occurred together. He distinguishes between what he calls the *bureaucratic* elements of the model – hierarchical authority structure, an administrative staff, and differential rewards according to office – and the *rational* elements: limited objectives, a performance emphasis, segmental participation, and compensatory rewards.

His investigations confirm the empirical clustering and distinctive-

ness of each of these two sets of characteristics: 'The three bureaucratic characteristics are all positively associated with one another.
The four rational characteristics are likewise all positively
associated. The general pattern of association between sets, however, is negative' (Udy, 1959, p.794).

These conclusions are echoed by Hall who argues that, far from
being a unitary entity, bureaucracy is 'a condition that exists along
a continuum, rather than being a condition that is either present or
absent . . . *bureaucracy is a form of organization which exists
along a number of continua or dimensions'* (Hall, 1963, p.33). Hall
delineates six bureaucratic dimensions, and his empirical investigations lead him to conclude that these 'dimensions are not
necessarily all present to the same degree in actual organization'
(p.38). In particular, Hall notes that one dimension seems to be
negatively related to the other more obviously bureaucratic features.
This is 'technical qualification'. As a result Hall remarks, 'This
finding . . . does raise the question of the appropriateness and
utility of the inclusion of the dimension in the bureaucratic
model. . . . In a highly bureaucratised situation the highly
competent person might not be able to exercise the full range of his
competence due to specific procedural specification, limited sphere
of activity, limited authority due to hierarchic demands, etc.'
(p.39). Furthermore, Hall attempts to explain the empirical
clustering he discovered. He suggests that different types of
bureaucracy might be related to the 'type of organizational
activity', and 'certain types of organizational goals'. These points
need some consideration.

The available empirical material, and various reworkings and
analyses of imputed dualities within Weber's model of bureaucracy,
suggest, in the main, two interrelated distinctions with respect to
the exercise of control within organisations; control, that is, over
expert, managerial and administrative organisational members.
These two distinctions are: control through centralisation and
hierarchy on the one hand and rules and procedures on the other,
and between bureaucratic and expert control. We shall consider
each of these. Empirical research suggests that modern organisations can be controlled through one or other of two alternative
principles: through direct or indirect control. Direct control means
the centralisation of decison-making. In highly centralised
organisation the senior member(s) keeps delegation to a minimum,
maintains close scrutiny and supervision, and monitors all activities.
Indeed the executive may even play a personal part in a large
proportion of the organisation's activities (see Salaman, 1977).
Centralisation refers to the concentration of organisational decision-
making in the chief executive(s) of the organisation.

We have seen in the previous section that some organisational
jobs are deliberately designed and structured so as to reduce

decision-making on the part of the incumbents and to concentrate and centralise it elsewhere, in the managerial, expert groups. To remove choice from one section of the organisation, as is achieved through the design of low-level, shop-floor work, does not necessarily imply that the administrative and managerial grades will also be controlled through centralisation. They may, as experts, be allowed some measure of self-control; or be permitted to act (within limits) on the basis of their professional, expert judgement and responsibility. These forms of control are considered later. When writers on bureaucracy discuss alternative types of control such as centralisation and formalisation, or bureaucracy and professionalism, they tend, implicitly, to restrict their discussion to managerial, administrative levels – i.e. to those levels which still retain some decision-making and have not had it systematically reduced by automation, work study, and technology, or which have some hierarchical, managerial authority. While this doesn't invalidate their generalisations about the functional equivalence of centralisation and formalisation, it does warn us that these analyses of aspects of bureaucratic control are not directly applicable to all levels of industrial and commercial organisations; for shop-floor, or lower-level members of such organisations are not controlled in these gentlemanly, bureaucratic ways, but are placed in jobs and subjected to processes of supervision and surveillance in order, deliberately and explicitly, to remove any possibility of judgement or any authority.

Indirect control is achieved mainly through rules. It is organisational rules which achieve the 'strict and systematic discipline and control in the conduct of the office' which Weber emphasises. It is through explicit elaborate and pervasive bodies of organisational rules that the remarkable standardisation typical of organisations is achieved; their extra-individual character. A number of writers have suggested that centralisation and formalisation might 'not be two expressions of the same underlying emphasis on strict discipline, but they may rather be alternative mechanisms for limiting the arbitrary exercise of discretion' (Blau, 1970, p.152). A parallel conclusion is presented by Meyer: 'Bureaucratic regulations can centralize authority in the managerial hierarchy; or rules can remove decisions from the hierarchy so that the regulations themselves exert authority' (Meyer, 1972, p.55). Empirical studies by Meyer and Blau, among others, support these conclusions. Child, too, has argued that two main strategies of administrative control exist: structuring of activities through rules and formalised procedures, and centralisation of decision-making (Child, 1973b).

Why is it that organisations employ one or another of these principles of control? Blau answers this question by reference to the *size* of the organisation. Centralisation of decision-making, in the managerial, expert, administrative levels, is most likely with small organisations. The growth of organisations is often accompanied by an increasing emphasis on control through formalisation. . . . 'large size creates conflicting pressure on top management's decision-making; it heightens the import of its decisions, which discourages delegation, and simultaneously expands the volume of its decisions, which exerts constraints to decentralize' (Blau, 1970, p.167). The point is that the main priority of the organisational executive is to retain control and achieve regularity, predictability, reliability. But organisational expansion and possibly, as we shall see, other factors like the nature and expectations of organizational personnel, makes explicit centralisation of decision-making difficult, for such expansion 'expands the volume of managerial decision beyond the capacity of the top executive and his deputy, and it thus exerts structural constraints that promote decentralization' (Blau, 1970, p.169).

Mansfield makes the same point. He argues that increasing size forces managers to construct rules to govern members' behaviour and thereby reduce the range of their discretion. Rules enable delegation to occur without the risk of any substantial loss of control to junior managers, because the delegated decision-making occurs within an established and secure framework of unalterable guidelines (Mansfield, 1973).

Of course the utilization of such control mechanisms as operate in large offices, on the shop floor, in factory-like clerical departments, etc. – i.e. control through the tight specification of work practices, often by machinery, and of repetitious, fragmented work activities – enables a high level of centralisation of such low-discretion work to occur within large-scale organisations. But Blau is thinking of managerial decision-making when he points to the significance of organisational size, not those jobs which have been designed specifically to achieve centralisation and standardisation which lack any authority over subordinate groups. Nevertheless, Blau's basic point remains valid: that centralisation and formalisation operate as functional substitutes.

But although formalisation and centralisation might be alternative control principles which are employed under various organisational circumstances, it must be stressed that the use of rules, or other mechanisms to ensure the reliability of organisational personnel, does not mean that senior executives lose control to their subordinates. The decisions that are delegated are inevitably the least important ones concerning the application of existing procedures, based upon established assumptions, and limited by various parameters and controls – budgetary, procedural, and formal authority, for example. The important decisions are still retained at the top of the organisation – as Blau nicely puts it:

'managerial decisions in organizations are either significant, in which case they are not delegated, or delegated, in which case they are not significant' (Blau, 1970, p.172).

Top management attempt to reduce the 'dangers' of necessarily decentralised control by establishing the bases of the delegated decision-making, and the final outcomes of subordinates' decisions, through established procedures and rules. But such reliability is achieved by other methods too, as Blau and Schoenherr remark. In a recent and important book these authors consider the various forms of 'insidious' power which serve to ensure the reliability of delegated decision-making. They consider such mechanisms as: automation, the use of computers, the installation of various personnel procedures concerning selection, promotion and appraisal, the recruitment of 'suitable', qualifed personnel, and so on. We shall have more to say about such control mechanisms later in this chapter. The point to stress here is this: although it is increasingly true that organisations appear to delegate decision-making to middle and lower levels of the administrative group, such delegation coexists with an increasing reliance on forms of control which buttress the control of the senior executives by ensuring the reliability and 'responsibility' of the subordinates' decision-making. It may seem that the academic, the middle manager, or the research worker have considerable work autonomy; but lying behind such apparent freedom there are constraints, limits, encouragements, sanctions and sources of direction, reward, and approval, which ensure that most instances of delegated or seemingly autonomous decision-making conform with senior executives' intentions. This is so even in the most autonomous organisations, like universities; it is certainly true of industrial and commercial organisations.

Another related and much discussed distinction between forms and bases of control within organisations is that between control based upon 'bureaucratic' and 'professional' or 'expert' procedures and commitments. This distinction is sometimes expressed in terms of organisations that rely on the 'skills and expertise' of their members and those that rely on rules, procedures and supervision. It has been noticed by a number of writers.

Stinchcombe, on the basis of empirical work, isolates two forms of organisation, in one of which members are controlled by training and socialisation into accepting the 'empirical lore that makes up craft principles', in the other by 'centralized planning of work' (Stinchcombe, 1970, pp.262–3). This distinction is, more frequently applied to expert and to managerial members of organisations. It is similar to Burns and Stalker's distinction between *mechanistic* and *organic* forms of organisation, the former relying on specialisation, differentiation and tight job prescription, the latter on negotiable and changing definition. See also Gouldner (1954) and Hage and Aiken (1967).

This claimed difference between bureaucratic and professional forms of control is usually attributed to the characteristics of the professional employees and the circumstances which necessitate their employment, i.e. professionals' reliance on self control deriving from their commitment to a shared body of knowledge and from membership of a significant colleague group. Such commitment necessarily leads to a reliance on individual professional practitioners making decisions with reference to their professional knowledge, experience and judgement. By their very nature such decisions, it is claimed, cannot be regulated and prescribed; they are too complex, variable, difficult, unpredictable. The nature of some organizational activities makes the employment of professionals necessary, and this results in the professionals *importing* their traditional decision-making procedures, which differ from conventional bureaucratic methods.

It is true that bureaucratic and professional forms of authority differ, although as Blau and Scott point out, the 'professional form of occupational life' and the 'bureaucratic form of organizational administration' are by no means incompatible with respect to all their elements. However,

A final characteristic of the professions is their distinctive control structure, which is fundamentally different from the hierarchical control exercised in bureaucratic organization. Professionals typically organize themselves into voluntary associations for the purpose of self control. . . . It is clear that this type of control structure differs greatly from that employed in bureaucratic organizations (Blau and Scott, 1963, pp.62–3).

Hall confirms these conclusions. He agrees that the gross polarisation of bureaucratic and professional forms of control is overstated, but maintains that 'a generally inverse relationship exists between the levels of bureaucratization and professionalization. Autonomy as an important professional attribute, is most strongly inversely related to bureaucratization' (Hall, 1973, p.132). There is also evidence that professionals who are employed by organisations and are subject to traditonal, bureaucratic forms of control find such methods particularly onerous and disturbing. When professionals cannot achieve a 'liberalisation' of bureaucratic practices – they experience, and articulate, a high degree of 'alienation'. For example, one survey of the work attitudes of scientists and engineers reported that, 'alienation from work is a consequence of the professional–bureaucratic dilemma for industrial scientists and engineers. Differences in type of supervision, freedom of research choice, professional climate, and company encouragement were associated with degree of work alienation in the expected manner' (Miller, 1970, p.514).

This debate about the forms and extent of control applied to

professional expert members of organisations has a special
importance because it introduces the possibility that some members
of organisations may be relatively autonomous within organisations, relatively free to pursue, in the light of their own judgement
and experience, goals which they personally and professionally find
sensible and meaningful. It introduces an optimistic conception of
the possible future of some large-scale organisations, which
increasingly employ large numbers of experts in relatively unstructured and even democratic ways – the substitution of
horizontal, peer and colleague control for hierarchical control.

Because of this significance we must investigate the reality of this
professional autonomy within organisations.

Professional autonomy

The first point to make is that although professionals working in
organisations eagerly express their alienation from, and dissatisfaction with, bureaucratic controls and objectives, there is singularly
little evidence of any large-scale or continuing opposition to the
interests and objectives of their organisational employers. Even with
their relative autonomy, and their untypically high amounts of discretion and decision-making responsibility, professionals in
organisations seem to toe the line. In section one we suggested some
of the ways in which organisations within capitalist societies play a
more or less explicit political role through the production and trans-
mission of expertise, ideology, education, through caring for the
'misfits' and those who will not or cannot accept the values and
priorities of such societies, by managing, coordinating and controlling the work of lower level members. Frequently the key
personnel in such organisations are those who, we have suggested
appear to be relatively autonomous. Yet their behaviour is usually
quite compatible with organisational requirements. How is this
strange paradox explained? How is it that those who are free
usually happen to be so 'responsible'?

To answer this question we must return to our earlier discussion
of the relationship between organisational control based on
centralisation and on formalisation. The significant thing about
these two alternatives, as Blau and Schoenherr emphasise, is that
the senior executives of organisations only permit delegation when
the recipient can be trusted to behave 'reliably'. The same can be
said for professionals and other experts who are allocated high-
discretion roles – it is ensured that they will perform these roles
responsibly. How can this be achieved?

A number of mechanisms can be discerned. When the professional, or expert, performs a professional type task – when a
university lecturer gives a lecture, or a psychiatrist carries out a
psychiatric therapy session – he operates in terms of an internalised

standard of workmanship and quality and reflects a strongly held body of professional knowledge. But it seems very likely that such standards and principles are by no means incompatible with the organisation's requirements. Indeed by restricting themselves to the expert solution to (organisational) problems but remaining indifferent to the wider, socio-political implications of the exercise, the professional is showing a highly congenial organisational attitude. The engineer engaged in designing ever more elaborate and thorough work procedures, the work-study expert devising a new structure of work fragmentation and operation, the psychologist working on improved selection methods, the sociologist studying morale, or the impact of improved canteen facilities, the accountant advising on the poor returns of some subsidiary, or of a long established department, and drafting new tax-proof company and financial structures, are supplying a much needed and very useful expertise to problems defined entirely by their employing organisation. Similarly the scientist working on a new drug, the designer considering the metallurgical or aerodynamic properties of a new plane, and the academic drawing up a research proposal to attract funds from government agencies, are using their autonomy, and their skills and expertise, with considerable and well rewarded 'responsibility'. From all their querulous complaining about obtrusive and unpleasant organisational restrictions and constraints the employed professional has yet to prove himself any more than the palace eunuch, well rewarded for important services, but unable and unwilling to question the real nature of his contribution or the real power behind his spurious freedom.

Blau and Schoenherr have noted this form of control: 'An organization can be controlled by recruiting anybody and everybody and then using a chain of command to rule them . . . or installing a technology that harnesses them to machines. But an organization can also be managed by recruiting selectively only those employees that have the technical qualifications and professional interest to perform on their own the various tasks for which the organization is responsible and then give them discretion to do what needs to be done within the broad framework of basic policies and administrative guidelines' (Blau and Schoenherr, 1971, p.350). In this way control is exercised through administration; control becomes in itself a *technical* issue – mainly a question of the administration of resources, the establishment of guidelines and budgetary and other controls, and the recruitment and selection of suitably, expert, staff.

Recruitment and selection are especially important under these conditions. As Perrow has put it, with characteristic vigour: 'one way of reducing overt control is . . . to 'buy' personnel who have complex rules built into them. We generally call these people pro-fessionals. Professionals . . . (have) a large number of rules . . . inculcated into them. They bring these into the organization and are expected to act upon them without further reference to their skills' (Perrow, 1972, p.27).

Because professionals are expensive, and the organisational problems they handle important, it is crucial that the experts who are chosen to join the organisation should be properly recruited, selected, inducted, and processed. Blau and Schoenherr point to the link between selection and control when they note that decentralisation was most likely to occur in the organisations they studied when it was accompanied by the installation of centralised selection procedures, and the use of 'qualified' personnel.

Thus the experts work to achieve ever more efficient and less obvious forms of control even over their fellows. Indeed, elsewhere Blau and another co-author have stressed that management's prime function – and that of their expert advisors – is to design appropriate impersonal mechanisms of organisational control (Blau and Scott, 1963, p.185; and see Baritz, 1975).

When this process is successful the recruited expert (or high-discretion manager or administrator) will be at the very least indifferent to the goals of the organisation, and entirely preoccupied with questions of technique and problem solving, or, at best, committed to the goals of the organisation as he sees them. Furthermore he will be able to monitor and direct his own behaviour in such a way as to avoid the need for much overt sanctioning or disciplining. In this way the appearance of autonomy is increased. Indeed he may even believe it himself and genuinely claim that his decision-making is entirely governed by common sense and 'reality' (see Stuart Hood's 1968 analysis of these processes in the BBC). The expert will be encouraged in this approach by various organisational personnel policies which attempt to relate work performance to promotion and rewards – procedures variously known as appraisal, management development, management by objectives, and so on. These procedures, which are designed by other, personnel experts, are intended to maximise the usefulness of organisational personnel by measuring their performance and relating such measures to organisational rewards and sanctions. From the point of view of the professional or managerial organisational member such schemes are significant because they are directly connected with that most crucial link between member and employer – the organizational career – the importance of which was noted earlier. Control through the manipulation of career chances is particularly insidious in that these formal schemes of appraisal rely for their impact not on directly related events and rewards, but on the member adjusting his own behaviour (with 'expert' guidance and help, when necessary) in the light of his demonstrated weaknesses and shortcomings. Self-control indeed, but when the self is so enmeshed within the organisation, the distinction between personal priorities and organisational goals becomes relatively meaningless, and self-control becomes little different from organisational regulation.

Personnel practices and the pre-programming of career orientated professionals are not the only methods of 'insidious' control apparent in organisations. Also important is the nature of decisions that are actually delegated to them. Fox has made an interesting distinction between substantive and procedural norms. Procedural norms are those which lie behind and govern 'the decision making methods by which norms are formulated'. Substantive norms 'emanating from these decison making procedures, cover every aspect of organization's activities' (Fox, 1971, p.322). Even when members are entrusted with decision-making, their decisions are more likely to concern substantive rather than procedural matters. But it is precisely these background issues and decisions that are of most significance. Fox notes what this means: 'decisions constantly have to be taken explicitly or implicitly, about what norms are to be used in dealing with a particular situation, problem or instance' (Fox, 1971, p.322). These remarks have relevance to the question of organisational control over members' decision-making. Organisational members may appear to be free to make decisions according to their assessments and judgement, but such freedom may be more apparent than real, because they are so hedged around with insidious controls and assumptions which limit resources and possibilities, establish basic parameters, vocabularies, communication channels and guidelines; and the members may be so well recruited, inducted, trained and appraised that when they make their decisions they adhere closely to the organisational priorities and practices. Such control over decisions also follows from the strict regulation of the amount and nature of information made available, the definition of normal behaviour, the limitation of choice and the setting of agenda and procedures.

A similar point has been made by Hage and Aiken when they note the limitations of decentralisation: 'Organizations vary in the extent to which members are assigned tasks and then provided with the freedom to implement them without interruption from superiors. . . . A second, and equally important, aspect of the distribution of power is the degree to which staff members *participate in setting the goals and policies of the entire organization'* (Hage and Aiken, 1967, p.518, my emphasis.) It is usually the case in large organisations employing apparently relatively autonomous experts and professionals that the reliability of such members is ensured by personnel practices, the professional training itself, with its inbuilt myopia, or by the organisation con-trolling the value and factual premises on which decisions are made. In the case of many of the professions that are relevant to organisa-tional functioning – personnel, accountancy, work study, engineering, etc. – the employing organisations certainly do not discourage processes of professionalisation, since this represents a guarantee of 'responsible' and well-qualified organisational personnel.

Finally, it isn't only professionals who are subject to this sort of insidious and impersonal control. As we have seen from the previous chapter it is also, and more evidently, true of shop-floor and lower level members.

The use of statistical records of performance is an impersonal means of control; mechanization, automation and computerisation are forms of control. Technology is a mechanism of control. These operate to constrain and direct employees' behaviour, limit or reduce their choices, determine the quality and quantity of their work activity, and all without the apparent involvement of management. These controls just become part of the context of everyday work, and as such hard to resist or oppose.

Even more closely analogous to the 'insidious' forms of control which ensure the reliability of organisational professionals is the increasing emphasis placed on job enrichment, work enlargement and participation and other similar schemes in modern organisations. No matter how substantial the actual changes initiated by such schemes, it is quite clear that their prime intention is to achieve a greater level of commitment on the part of the shop-floor and lower-level employees, to resolve the 'problem of motivation' by a more or less spurious enrichment or democratisation of work. As Nichols has put it: 'A capitalist mode of production is inherently authoritarian . . . substantial democratization (as opposed to 'propaganda') threatens its survival . . . managements and their social science advisers will be lacking in judgement if they ignore this. (And by and large they do not ignore this: not in practice.)' (Nichols, 1976, p.18).

Chapter 11

Struggle and resistance

Hyman has noted,

*Work within capitalism is at one and the same time an economic
and a political activity: it involves not only the production of goods
and services but also the exercise of power. Patterns of power in
relations of production reflect the differential distribution among
individuals and groups of the ability to control their physical and
social environment and, as part of this process, to influence the
decisions which are and are not taken by others. This ability is
typically founded on privileged access to or control over material
and ideological resources. Thus ownership and control over the
means of production involve immense power, since it carries the
ability to admit or exclude those who depend on employment for
their living (Hyman, 1976, p.88).*

This chapter will discuss these 'patterns of power' and resistance.
Many of these inherently political intra-organisational conflicts and
negotiations are mediated through, and institutionalised in, trade
union activity. Again, as noted by Hyman, the main significance of
trade unionism is 'that it formalises and generalises the processes of
worker resistance to, and negotiation with, the structure of
capitalist domination in the employment relationship' (Hyman,
1976, p.100). Hyman, and others, point out the political nature of
much union activity. He insists, with reason, that although the role
of trade unions as 'managers of discontent', involves a basic
ambiguity with respect of the issue of job control, it is not justified
to define trade unions' concern with economic issues as representing
an abdication of interest in control issues. Union officials are constantly concerned with procedural issues – all of which involve, in
the final analysis, issues of control; secondly, it is impossible for
workers successfully to define their employment relations solely in
economic terms since the essentially political nature of that relationship must, sooner or later, emerge in work-based conflicts of
various sorts; and thirdly, as many have noted, it is increasingly
likely that wage demands themselves ('pure' economism) can reflect
and create political conflicts, particularly with state intervention in
wage bargaining.

But if union activity can be regarded as, in one form or another,

political – i.e. having *some* concern for issues of control – this is
not to deny that a great deal of intra-organisational conflict occurs
outside the formal structure of union activity. Much organisational
conflict, after all, occurs on a horizontal axis, between specialisms
and departments. Usually such conflicts are not channelled through
union negotiations. Furthermore, not all conflicts between low-level
organisational employees and the owners and controllers of the
organisation occur within the union framework. The relationship
between formal union institutions and the concerns of organisational employees is by no means unproblematic, as Beynon (1973)
has shown.

Nevertheless, clearly a large proportion of intra-organisational
conflicts – especially those occurring on a vertical axis – are
mediated through formal union activity and organisation. Indeed it
could be said that all union activity reveals, in some degree, such
conflicts. However, we cannot, in this book, develop our consideration of processes of resistance and control within organisations to
include a proper discussion of the role and implications of trade
unions in these struggles. The issue can only be adequately dealt
with at length, and would require an analysis of the nature and
implications of unions within capitalism: a major issue. In this
chapter we shall focus on the organisational origins, and consequences of, processes of struggle and resistance within organisations.

The analysis in the first two sections implicitly presents the
organisational employee as a rather passive creature, controlled and
dominated by his employers, meekly subjecting him or her self to a
variety of organisational directions and sanctions. Clearly such a
view is quite erroneous: organisational employees actively strive to
avoid and divert control; they seek to maximise their own interests
which they may or may not see as coincident with the organisation's, and they attempt to resist the domination of others while
advancing or defending their own area of control and autonomy.
Consider these remarks by Crozier, in which he describes the
different preoccupations and strategies of varieties of organisational
personnel:

*Directors and assistant directors, socially conservative, fight with
great passion for technical change and modernisation. At the same
time, technical engineers, who would like to transform the present
social order, are very conservative about technical matters; they do
whatever they can to keep their skill a rule-of-thumb one and to
prevent efforts to rationalise it. This is the reason that they act as
trouble-shooters, even if it means always running to patch things
up, and that they oppose any kind of progress which could free
them from certain of their difficulties. Their only solution has
always been to ask for an assistant, and they are quite prepared to*

remain overworked if this demand cannot be met. What is the common thread among these diverse strategies? Each group fights to preserve and enlarge the area upon which it has discretion, attempts to limit its dependence upon other groups and to accept such dependence only insofar as it is a safeguard against another and more feared one, and finally prefers retreatism if there is no choice but submission. The group's freedom of action and the power structure appear to be clearly at the core of all these strategies (Crozier, 1964, p.156)

These suggestions of Crozier's raise the major points of this chapter: organisations are characterised by constant and continuing conflict. Despite the major efforts of senior executives to legitimise the activities, structure and inequalities of the organisation and to design and install 'foolproof' and reliable systems of surveillance and direction, there is always some dissension, some dissatisfaction, some effort to achieve a degree of freedom from hierarchical control – some resistance to the organisation's domination and direction. Frequently this struggle is muted, mainly defensive and reactive, often individualised, spasmodic, intermittent. Frequently it is defined and presented as the result of trouble-stirrers, laziness, bloody-mindedness, inflexibility, or stupidity, as the result of the psychological pathology or inadequacy of the members. But in fact it is the systematic response to a form of organisation which is designed to achieve hierarchical control and domination of members' activities for the pursuit of objectives and interests which are not theirs, and with which they may be in conflict. The inevitable result of such organisational forms, and the interests they serve, is the alienation and 'refractoriness' of members.

Secondly, Crozier's remarks (and the work from which they are selected), emphasise that such struggles, such resistance, usually centres around the very process which generates it: the efforts of senior groups to control the activities of subordinates. These struggles are not only *rooted* in conflicts over power, they are usually *expressed* in terms of efforts to regain, defend or achieve, control or autonomy. Thirdly, conflicts within organisations reflect internal inequalities and contradictions or organisational structure which in turn reveal class-based interests. 'Bureaucracies not only rest upon classes,' writes Mills,

they organise the power struggles of classes. Within the business firm, personnel administration regulate the terms of employment, just as would the labour union, should a union exist: these bureaucracies fight over who works at what and for how much . . . within the firm . . . and as part of the bureaucratic management of mass democracy, the graded hierarchy fragments class situations. . . . The traditional and often patriarchal ties of the old enterprise are replaced by rational and planned linkages in the new, and the rational systems unite their powers so that no one sees their source of authority or understands their calculations (Mills, 1956, p.111).

We can identify three bases of organisational conflict. The first is the result of 'distinctive functions' developing, or holding, their own culture, priorities and norms. The discussion below will consider examples of such conflicts, for example between academic and administrator, or sales and production departments. The second type of conflict occurs when organisational units have similar functions. In this case rivalry and competitiveness can develop. The third form of conflict is hierarchical conflict stemming from interest group struggles over the organisational rewards of status, prestige and monetary reward. Such conflict is particularly likely between lower-level personnel and their superiors, although such struggles are not confined to this group alone. In this chapter we shall encounter examples of all these types of organisational conflict.

We must remember that the final, demonstrated structure of an organisation is not the result of members' obedient execution of senior executives' (and their experts') directions as these are represented in bodies of rules, procedures and regulations, payment systems, budgetary limits, work design, technology, work flow, supervision etc. The actual structure of an organisation – i.e. its apparent regularity and predictability – is the result of members' reactions and resistance to, and interpretation and avoidance of, these formal limitations and restrictions. Many classic studies of the 'informal' side of organisations reveal the endless ways in which members *use* the formal organisational rules to produce results more to their own liking, and which demonstrate that *no* system of organisational control, however sophisticated and elaborate, can completely eliminate the discretion, however minimal, of the employee. In Crozier's terms, however thorough the organisation's effort to eliminate the discretion of the employee, some area of uncertainty will remain, and such uncertainty is the breeding ground for efforts to achieve some, however slight, self-control, some degree of autonomy. The final structure of an organisation – as compared to the mythical structure described so elegantly (and symbolically) on organisation charts – is the result of these negotiations, interpretations in which organisational members actively strive to resist some directions and controls while attempting to advance their own self-control. As Crouch has recently remarked of power relations within the labour contract:

The interest of the dominant role in such a relationship can be defined as the maximisation of control over labour, offset by the extent to which such maximisation will reduce the effectiveness, or incite the revolt, of that labour. The interest of subordinates consists in eroding, evading or replacing domination, offset by the extent to which attempts to do so will either incite coercive sanctions or involve destruction of existing means for securing subsistence (Crouch, 1977, p.6).

'Bureaucracy', remarks Gouldner, 'was man-made, and more powerful men had a greater hand in making it' (Gouldner, 1954, p.140). What's more, 'the degree of bureaucratisation is a function of human striving; it is the outcome of a contest between those who want it and those who do not' (p.237). Organisational rules and procedures and work design constitute efforts to resolve what senior executives regard as problems by achieving an increased degree of reliability. But the 'tools of action' retain their recalcitrance, and hierarchical intentions are seldom executed perfectly.

Blau's study of two government agencies shows some of the ways in which rules and procedures established by senior management to achieve a certain effect can produce unexpected consequences. He describes some of the consequences that followed the introduction of statistical records in an employment exchange. He notes how this procedure operated as a new form of control. And as such it created what he describes as a 'displacement' of goals. That is, it encouraged the members to orient their activities towards new priorities: 'An instrument intended to further the achievement of organisational objectives, statistical records constrained interviewers to think of maximising the indices as their major goal, sometimes at the expense of these very objectives' (Blau, 1963, p.46). Furthermore, Blau argues that the introduction of this sort of work measurement caused a reduction in cooperation and an increase in competitiveness within the work groups.

Blau regards bureaucratic rules as necessarily general and abstract: 'A bureaucratic procedure can be defined as a course of action prescribed by a set of rules designed to achieve a given uniformity. Agency-wide rules must be abstract in order to guide the different courses of action necessary for the accomplishment of an objective in diverse situations' (Blau, 1963, p.23). Because of this inherent generality rules must be interpreted, defined, and adjusted by the organisational member in the face of particular cases, clients, circumstances and situations.

Blau sees such modification as essentially functional, for otherwise the 'organisation could not have served the employment needs of the community' (Blau, 1963, p.35). This is a naive assumption. Organisational members use the inherent generality of organisational rules in exactly the same way as they exploit the inherent incompleteness of any structure of control and regulation – to achieve their own interests, advance their own self-control, defend themselves from what they regard as onerous, misguided or hostile constraints. They *might*, because of their commitment to their own conceptions of occupational, expert or organisational goals, merely *use* the rules to achieve with greater efficiency and speed, ends which are not incompatible with the formal objectives of the organisation (consider, for example, the psychiatric hospital described earlier) but this is simply a possibility, not an inevitability.

Gouldner has pointed out that one of the ironic characteristics of organisational rules is that although they stem from attempts to control and regulate the behaviour of employees, they can be used as bargaining resources in the interactions between superiors and subordinates. Rules tend to describe the preferred behaviour. *In so doing they also stipulate minimal behaviours.* 'The rules served as a specification of a minimum level of acceptable performance. It was, therefore, possible for the worker to remain apathetic, for he now knew just how little he could do and still remain secure' (Gouldner, 1954, pp.174–5). Similarly, supervisors could use the enforcement of the rules as a bargaining counter between superiors and subordinates. When things are going well various rules may not be enforced: *formal* control may be replaced by *informal* cooperation.

Conflict and negotiation over organisational rules, work methods, technology and procedures characterise all organisations, for such conflict is a 'normal' and endemic organisational feature. Even the rules themselves, introduced to reduce the recalcitrance of employees, are transformed, in organisational practice, into battle grounds of adjustment and bargaining.

There are numerous axes of conflict within organisations. Some conflicts are personal and individual, not only in *expression* (for this is true of many structural conflicts and divergences) but in origin.

Competitiveness is a natural product of a form of organisation that encourages ambition, rewards individual achievement, but offers progressively fewer promotion possibilities. However, such personal conflicts shall not concern us here. Our concern is with those conflicts which occur along socially structured differences and distinctions – of authority, prestige, culture and function.

One common ground for intra-organisational conflict is functional differentiation. Organisational employees engaged on different organisational or occupational tasks and specialities frequently develop, or maintain, distinctive work-based cultures and interests. A great deal of organisational conflict occurs between these specialist groups, as they attempt to advance their interests – enlarge their establishment, improve their facilities, raise their budgets, increase their voice in the senior councils and so on. At the Open University, for example, the various faculties compete for resources – especially personnel – and for influence, and the faculties as a whole come together, to some degree, to attempt to counter the growing power of the administrative bureaucracy and the regional structure. At the same time the administrators attempt to achieve greater regularity, predictability and standardisation of *operations* – i.e. the production, by the academics, of teaching materials by developing procedures and rules, limiting 'arbitrary' decision-making, regulating and monitoring expenditure, devising standard forms and establishing specialist *administrative* departments and sub-groups to take over and dominate areas of activity previously handled by academics. In this way, control becomes a question of administration, of deadlines, procedures, differentiated functions and 'operational' constraints.

Within industry, such conflict frequently occurs between sales and production, with production planning playing an intermediate, conciliatory role. Production's efforts to make life predictable and satisfactory by ensuring long stable production runs, are likely to be at odds with sales' efforts to please customers by promising quick delivery, and a front place in the work queue. Each department is likely to regard itself as the key one, and will seek to maximise its interests, which are defined as coincident with the 'real' interest of the organisation as a whole.

As noted earlier, these efforts to legitimise sectional interest and advantage will involve reference to general organisational objectives or symbols. So all departments within manufacturing industry show the importance of their departmental expansion or primacy by reference to general organisational efficiency, or customer demands. Within the Open University no faculty or department achieves a more than proportional share of resources (staff, broadcasts, budgets) without demonstrating, at least publicly, that these are necessary for the students. To be able to define sectional interests as coincident with the general organisational interest is not only a reflection of the power of the section concerned; it is also a useful and plausible strategy in intra-organisational conflicts.

Conflicts of this sort are obvious features of most organisations (Zald, 1970; Perrow, 1970). There are well documented accounts of inter-departmental conflicts in the armed services, and the civil service. The analysis of conflict between professionals with different theoretical and therapeutic orientations by Strauss *et al.* furnishes another example.

It must be noted that conflicts between departments and specialities within organisations can, like conflicts between ambitious individuals, actually serve the interests of the owners and controllers of the organisations. Firstly, such conflicts often centre around – however rhetorically – the over-arching organisational goal. More importantly, they distract attention from more basic conflicts between senior and junior levels within the organisation and divide and divert the work force. The advantages of this are most obvious with shop-floor, low-level organisational members. But there is no reason why this argument cannot also be applied to management levels, within which sectional, departmental and specialist conflicts proliferate.

Elliott's account of conflicting occupational ideologies ('therapy', 'basic science' and 'early diagnosis') held by doctors and scientists in a hospital specialising in the treatment of cancer patients, and an associated cancer research institute, explores the relationship between specialist ideology and work experience and pressures. The therapy and basic science ideologies, Elliott notes, 'supported a tendency towards separation and polarization between the two groups (doctors and researchers)' (Elliott, 1975, p.280). Elliott discusses the origins of these ideologies in the organisational settings and histories, the work practices (especially the variable of patient contact) and occupational/professional memberships, cultures and careers of the two groups. He notes the potential for conflict inherent in these ideological differences and remarks: 'One importance of these ideologies is the part they play in deciding the distribution of resources and reflecting the interests of those concerned. . . . ' (Elliott, 1975, p.286).

Pettigrew's analysis of relationships between specialist computer personnel furthers our understanding of the ideological and functional bases of intra-organisational, inter-specialist (or departmental) conflict. It concerns the efforts of a new speciality to define its task, protect its identity, develop a legitimating world view and occupational ideology, and expand its activities. These efforts are likely to produce a defensive reaction, from established, threatened specialities: 'As a defensive reaction, the more established group may accuse the expansionist one of incompetence and encroachment. The older group may also attempt to invoke a set of fictions about itself to protect the core of its expertise' (Pettigrew, 1975, p.260).

The temporal dimension to Pettigrew's analysis is particularly useful: his study of the expansion strategies of the new speciality, and the defensive reactions of established experts, each allied with particular patterns of belief and attitudes, is especially relevant to an understanding of intra-organisational conflict relations.

Even more frequent than conflicts between different specialities as they struggle for dominance, are conflicts between experts and bureaucrats, or staff and line. These conflicts, which have been discussed earlier, are often sharpened by the existence of associated differences and distinctions – of dress, age, cultural preferences, leisure habits, etc. It is true, as Elliott suggests, that 'organisation is not necessarily the bogyman of professional independence and autonomy as it has generally been cast. . . . Some of the studies of professional practice . . . suggest various ways in which independent practice is itself structured by the situation in which it occurs. Some organisations can be seen as insulating professionals from pressures they would face in private practice and providing them

with the means to perform their professional tasks in relative
security' (Elliott, 1972, p.99).

But if the degree of opposition and conflict between bureaucratic
and professional organisation and control has been overstated, and
if the extent of employed professionals' 'alienation' and dissatisfaction has been exaggerated (Perrow, 1972, pp.52–8), it is
nevertheless true that professionals in organisations attempt to
defend their autonomy, resist the imposition of bureaucratic control
and work patterns, and secure their own interests. These efforts
normally centre around the definition of professional, expert work
as inherently opposed to 'rationalised', specialised, fragmented and
differentiated work processes, and the definition of professional
work as innately resistant to external control, direction and
surveillance. Conflict around these principles is common in
organisations that employ professionals; even if, as noted earlier,
the fact of such conflict should not be interpreted as implying a
serious divergence between professionals' activities and senior
executives' objectives, for other 'insidious' forms of control and
training operate to minimise such divergence, such 'irresponsibility'

Professionals justify their opposition to centralised control and
bureaucratic work practices on the grounds of the efficiency and
necessity of self-control, and the complexity and mysteriousness of
the work tasks and skills. It is, however, possible to see such arguments as ideological, and as protecting professionals' privileged
position and treatment. Some writers have argued that bureaucratic
forms of control actually assist the achievement of the stated goals
of the profession by substituting more reliable explicit and
accessible forms of control. Of doctors, Freidson has argued: 'The
present need is for a variety of administrative mechanisms that can
temper the arbitrary exercise of professional authority by the
medical staff and institute procedures that give better assurance
than exists at present that the quality of medical care is adequate'
(Freidson, 1970, p.182).

Control and resistance of subordinates

The most common basis of intra-organisational conflict is that
between superiors and their subordinates over issues of domination
and the distribution of rewards. These conflicts are usually
mediated by trade unions. The most common and pervasive conflict
of this sort is between shop-floor members and their superiors, and
between those with the poorest share of the organisation's rewards,
the most fragmented and specialised and least autonomous jobs,
and the more privileged members who control, manage and
coordinate them.

Clearly, such conflicts can be revealed in a number of ways:
formal and informal, organised and unorganised, group or indivi-

dual. For example, Scheff's article, 'Control over policy by attendants in a mental hospital', shows some of the ways in which lower
level organisational members can influence, avoid and determine
policy decisions and organisational practice. The study documents
the ways in which a vigorous and ambitious programme of reform
in the hospital was launched by the administration and 'largely
frustrated' by the attendants. First the subordinate group had to be
able to maintain solidarity and discipline among its own ranks.
Such control is a frequent consequence of informal work groups.
Secondly, they must achieve some control over senior organisational members, and thirdly they must use their informal power to
achieve their conception of desirable and proper organisational
practice. Typically, whatever its real nature, this conception will be
firmly related to over-arching organisational or professional
rhetorics.

The attendants gained their power through explicit techniques
and sanctions (common among subordinate organisational groups,
in industry as well as in professional organisations), and as a result
of the structured vulnerability of the senior members and the
solidarity of the subordinate groups. The vulnerability of the senior
members – the physicians – followed from their *reliance,* or
dependence, on the cooperation of the attendants. 'Typically,'
Scheff writes, 'the doctor facing the ward staff was in a weak position, relative to the staff, because of his short tenure on the ward
and his lack of training in administration . . . the typical ward
physician was a newcomer. The ward staff, in contrast, was all but
rooted to the ward' (Scheff, 1970, p.331). The physicians were not
only new to the wards, and therefore dependent on the knowledge
of the attendants (knowledge which was framed in terms of
attendants' definitions and philosophies), but were unprepared for
the roles of leader and administrator rather than doctor and un-
interested in, and unenthusiastic about, their administrative duties.

The discrepancy between the formal authority of the physician
and the real power of his subordinates on whom he depended constituted a significant objective basis for lower-level control. The
subordinates employed a variety of sanctions: withholding
information; the manipulation of patients, so that the attendants
withheld their 'gate-keeper' role and encouraged the patients to
question and accost the medical staff; outright disobedience; and
the withholding of cooperation. Variants of these techniques are
extremely common in organisations. The latter, withholding of
cooperation, is possible because of an essential and basic dilemma
inherent in hierarchical organisations involving an elaborate division
of labour: although the rationale of such structures is the
separation of execution and conception – or manual work and
brain work – such that the lower levels of the organisations take on
the menial, routine and undemanding tasks, leaving the middle and

upper levels free for more complex tasks such as policy design, project planning, professional activities, etc. In fact each level of the organisation is always dependent on the cooperation of the subordinate level, for all jobs, however routine, require some 'common sense', some understanding of and commitment to, the organisation's objectives. No system of work design, or technology, or structure of rules and procedures, can achieve the transformation of man into a machine. But if cooperation is always required, it can always be withheld, even if this is achieved by liberal interpretation of, and compliance with, the rules.

Organisations as we know them are inherently inegalitarian structures involving, as basic elements, processes of superordination and subordination. These two features serve as the basis for conflict between the least advantaged and most controlled and the more advantaged controllers. It is true that some of the advantaged controllers are themselves controlled, as we have seen earlier in this chapter. But this control is itself less onerous and frustrating, and is accompanied by a much larger share of the organisation's rewards. But for our purposes the distinction between lower-level organisational members – with no managerial or supervisory responsibility – and the controllers *en masse* is the critical one.

'The reason why hierarchy is so crucial for the organisation's leaders', writes Fox, 'is that it facilitates the making of decisions over which they can hope to exercise some control. Acceptance of the norms covering these relationships is therefore the key to the acceptance of all other norms' (Fox, 1971, p.34). This is why management invests so much energy in trying to establish the legitimacy of the hierarchic structure of the organisation, trying to obtain lower-level members' consent to the norms covering the hierarchical relationships of superiority and subordination. The methods and values by which management seeks to legitimise the structure of organisation, and the place of individuals within it, are discussed in Chapter 4. The significant issue here is how far these efforts are successful.

The degree to which lower-level organisational members are incorporated into and committed to an ideology which justifies the structure of the employing organisation and their place within it, varies. Such commitment is more likely with middle-level members who have some degree of normative commitment. However, we shall limit our attention to white-collar and manual worker organisational employees, since it is they who are most likely to resent the structure of their employing organisation and their position in it.

How do these members react to their situation? We must remember that bureaucracy is instituted so that owners and managers can retain overall control. But the control of the executive is less than perfect since 'workers in the pyramid have some power as well (for example, they can withhold information or simply 'work to rule', thus diminishing efficiency). But the workers' power is mainly defensive and open opposition always brings into play the most basic power relation: the capitalist's legal right to fire the worker' (Edwards, 1972, p.116). Workers' resistance and opposition to their organisational situation and treatment follows from the obvious disparity between their levels of reward and status and the privileged treatment and prestige meted out to managers, administrators, etc., inequalities which reflect and make up societal differences in income and wealth (see Hyman, 1972, pp.89–94) and which include the nature of the work itself, conditions, promotion chances, etc. It is also a result of their status as employees, as people who sell their labour as a commodity to organisations which utilise their labour for their purposes. But it must be remembered that such an arrangement is inherently insecure – within industrial concerns in particular, but increasingly also within hospitals, universities, training colleges, the armed services, government departments, etc. This insecurity is the result of the basic feature of organisational work – that it is constantly subject to the vagaries of market and economic forces which make it profitable or unprofitable, possible or impossible to hire or retain labour.

Finally, their resistance is a result of the way in which they are controlled. It seems likely that different types and levels of control produce different types and levels of opposition (Mackenzie, 1975).

From the point of view of the senior executives of organisations, lower-level members never conform and comply completely. They never entirely lose their potential for recalcitrance. This is a major managerial problem. Recent interest in the 'problem of motivation' reflects an increasing concern for the efficiency of organisational control. As Henry Ford admitted – 'Machines alone do not give us mass production. Mass production is achieved by both machines *and* men. And while we have gone a long way toward perfecting our mechanical operations, we have not successfully written into our equation whatever complex factors represent man, the human element' (Ford, quoted in Walker and Guest, 1952, p.249). It is not for want of trying.

It is dangerous to generalise about the orientations and work aspirations and attitudes of all lower-level employees. There are bound to be substantial exceptions to any assertion. Nevertheless, some remarks can usefully be made. First, it is undoubtedly the case that the vast majority of lower-level members comply, in general, with organisational directions (though such compliance will possibly be perfunctory, partial, and unwilling); second, they do not *continually* oppose the hierarchical structure of their employing organisation, nor the principles which lie behind the design of their work, nor those which determine and justify their relatively low level of rewards, their working conditions, promotion opportunities, etc. Numerous surveys of work satisfaction have argued for a surprisingly high level of acceptance of these aspects of work. Such surveys are suspect, primarily because, as Fox has suggested, workers have 'high' and 'low' priority aspiration:

Men questioned about their response to work may respond on either of two levels: in terms of how far they have adjusted to work as it is, and in terms of how far they have any picture of work as it might be . . . men can at one and the same time
   (i) expect work to be largely instrumental in nature,
   (ii) become 'satisfied with' (i.e. resigned to) this situation, and
   (iii) wish that it could be otherwise (Fox, 1971, p.22).

Numerous accounts of low-level organisational work have confirmed this mixture of acceptance, fatalism, resentment and despair, which follow from and are results of the inequalities and oppressions of organisational life and the fact that organisations are also cooperative phenomena, where interdependence *is* important, and where the inequalities and hierarchy are heavily buttressed by supporting ideology. Probably Fox is right when he argues that such efforts to legitimate the organisation's structure and activity achieve a low-key acquiescence among the subordinates, nothing more: an acquiescence born as much of resignation as of commitment.

This low-key, begrudging acquiescence, however, is a long way from full-blooded resistance and opposition. Such reactions are the infrequent symptoms of a generalised malaise; less dramatic and explicit demonstrations of resentment are more common. Most accounts of organisational life contain descriptions of the various ways in which members attempt to circumvent the official rules and regulations, seek to interrupt the organised flow of work, or avoid obtrusive procedures and systems. Sometimes these efforts are organised and explicit; more frequently they are based on group reactions and norms which justify and impose the alternative behaviours in the light of the agreed injustice and unreasonableness of the official procedure. Occasionally such responses are spontaneous, or individual.

Fox has suggested that organisational members may respond in two distinct ways to the perception of a divergence between their interests and the organisation's treatment of them: withdrawal and positive efforts to change the organisation, or their position and treatment within it. Withdrawal would include such reactions as absenteeism, labour turnover, sickness rates, maybe even accidents. Withdrawal may just involve the withdrawal of attention, interest and commitment. The more definite form of response may be individual or group, or organisational, with union involvement (see Fox's application of Merton's classification of responses in Fox, 1971, pp.82–100).

Hyman notes the importance of the distinction between 'organised' and 'unorganised' conflict. In unorganised conflict, Hyman writes,

the worker typically responds to the oppressive situation in the only way open to him as an individual: by withdrawal from the source of discontent, or in the case of certain forms of individual sabotage or indiscipline, by reacting against the immediate manifestations of his oppression. Such reactions rarely derive from any calculative strategy. . . . Organised conflict, on the other hand, is far more likely to form part of a conscious strategy to change the situation which is identified as the source of change (Hyman, 1972, p.53).

However, it is also important to distinguish between varieties of organised conflict – not all group-based conflict and resistance is *organised*. Some group responses are firmly founded in informal group cultures, of which more below; others are displayed in, and mediated by, formal union activity. As noted earlier, we must leave such official responses to the consideration of others (see Hyman, 1975, and Fox, 1971, for particularly cogent analyses of the bases and forms of union activity). In this book our attention is restricted to less official forms of resistance.

How is it that low-level organisational employees show acceptance of their organisational position and treatment? Or to put it another way, why is it that the disadvantaged, subordinate members of organisations do not attempt more effectively to organise, collectively, radically to improve their locations, or to alter the structure of the organisation, and the distributions of rewards within it? Various factors are relevant, the most important of which, ideology, will be treated in the next section.

It must be noted that members of organisations, through their membership of, and support for, their trade unions, do actively attempt to resist their domination by senior organisational members and to improve their position within their employing organisations. Nevertheless, it remains true that such efforts are largely defensive in nature; often apparently concerned with conditions and rewards rather than control and structure; and trade unions can be seen to hold a rather ambivalent position with respect to such issues – seeking improvements, but rarely going beyond the bounds of established and accepted notions of proper and responsible union activities. Established relations between unions and employers; the very success of unions in winning improvements in employees' conditions; union representatives' exposure to ideological, political and organisational pressures, all serve to make union pursuit of increased employee control over organisation structure and process ambivalent at best. However, in this study we cannot include an anlaysis of the various factors which structure the nature and form of union concern with issues of employee control, since this discussion of union activity and function within capitalism necessarily lies outside the scope of this book. (For a good analysis, see Hyman, 1976.) We must content ourselves with an analysis of such features of organisations themselves which serve to obstruct or transform employees' interest in changing, or capacity to change, the structure of their employing organisation, and their location within it.

1. The fragmentation of the work force. As Hyman has remarked: 'While class opposition forms the basis of work relations in capitalist society, this is overlaid and often concealed by the immense variety of specific work contexts and distinctive group interests' (Hyman, 1976, p.94). The very fact of extreme differentiation of jobs and activities, and the associated variation in the distribution of rewards, status, working conditions, discipline, payment methods, holiday allowances and so on, noted earlier, also serves to fragment the theoretical unity of subordinate employees. This fragmentation has horizontal and vertical elements. Vertically, organisational employees are differentiated by various aspects of privilege. It is true that middle managers too are controlled: but their control is less onerous, and their share of the rewards greater. Such privilege serves to attract the individual loyalty of the manager, especially when it is allied with a strong emphasis on individual success and career development. Organisational employees who apparently share the same, low, level within the organisation also demonstrate a marked awareness of distinctiveness, even of opposition. Partly this follows from differences within the organisation – of activity, department, function, shift. Frequently it is based on extra-organisational differences – of sex, race, locality, or age. Often these two types of factor are compounded (see Nichols and Armstrong, 1976, pp.85–97, 'The case of six women').

Organisational differentiation – the fragmentation of the work force – is presented as an inevitable consequence of organisational technology (in the widest sense) and the search for greater efficiency. In fact, however, it is also – possibly primarily – ideological. This follows from two interconnected processes: the splitting of basically similar employees into differentiated, often competitive, groupings; and the construction of a finely graded hierarchy of small differences in privilege and position which acts to distinguish one employee from another and to raise his commitment to the beneficial organisation, through bestowing differential degrees of prestige, organisational rewards and career opportunities. To quote Dreyfuss:

If he (the organisational employee) holds a position which at least affords him the illusion of superiority to some of his co-workers, the employee is enabled to attain a degree of social recognition

*within the organisation as compensation for economic need and
social oppression outside it. Such a position is seemingly of higher
rank, and in the detailed organism of the artificial set-up it stands,
in fact, somewhat apart from other positions. . . . Jealousy and
envy among employees of the same rank or among those just one
step higher or lower in rank are incited and inflamed by the continuous struggle for promotion due to the employer ideologies of
employee (Dreyfuss, 1952, pp.260–61).*

It should be remembered that Lockwood has supplied a useful
method for understanding the exact elements of these positions
which generate such attitudes. It shouldn't be assumed that the
incorporation of organisational employees is easily achieved: it rests
on the utilisation of a number of subtle distinctions in working
conditions, payment systems, supervision methods, etc. Nevertheless
the main point is made: organisational differentiation and
graduation of status, conditions, rewards etc., serve to disturb
members' solidarity and to create an impression of superiority and
success among those in the organisational hierarchy, by enabling
some employees to see themselves as holding superior positions, and
by granting differential career opportunities.

Such processes of differentiation also occur among organisational
employees at the same level. Again to quote Dreyfuss, 'The
employer is fundamentally interested in preventing the employees of
his enterprise from confronting him as a homogeneous group. He
attempts to undermine and split their strength through minute sub-
division and differentiation' (Dreyfuss, 1952, p.259). This occurs
through the differentiation of functions, the use of payment
schemes, the division of employees into shifts and departments, and
the use of competitive procedures. Within organisations it is not
difficult to find employees who reserve most of their complaints for
some basically rather similar group who supply them with parts, or
perform some prior function to the product, or prepare the paper-
work they must process, or whatever. So biscuit packers complain
about the girls who process the biscuits from the ovens and check
their quality, and the bakers complain about the quality of the
flour, and personnel complain about the quality of the recruits sent
by the employment agency, and the safety officer maintains that the
worst problem is the 'apathy' of the other employees, and so on.
Undoubtedly there is some basis for these complaints, but they
don't go far enough. What is always forgotten is that the
development of conflict between basically similar organisational
groups is not the result of the innate contrariness, selfishness or
bloody-mindedness of the department in question, but follows from
the overall structure and nature of the organisation. Of course on a
day-to-day basis it is maddening for the biscuit packers to lose
earnings because the biscuits are crumbly and break, just as it is

frustrating for the salesmen to lose orders because of poor deliveries. But the problem must be seen in terms of a form of organisation which, having divided and differentiated the employees, puts pressure on all of them to achieve payment-related production quotas. As Nichols and Armstrong remark in their analysis of the conflict between night and day men – 'as the day men sit through yet another wasted half-hour, it is easy to see how the part played by management escapes their notice – the rules governing overtime having been laid down, the management retired from the active stage and seem to be uninvolved' (Nichols and Armstrong, 1976, p.96).

Beynon makes the same point in his *Working for Ford.* In the competitive and often bitter struggle for overtime it is easy to forget that the real 'opponent' is not the other claimants, but the organisation's executives who have devised such a system of payment, and a type of economy which produces built-in variations in demand.

2. The use of impersonal and insidious forms of control. This is closely related to the first mechanism, since conflict between groups and departments not only masks the ways in which both are constrained by hierarchical control, but is a function of it, as the remarks about overtime illustrate. This is a highly divisive form of control, through payment. By disguising control, or by making it appear as either inevitable and inexorable or a neutral function of extra-organisational constraints – technology, 'progress' or the market –, organisational employees must find it hard to locate the forms of control, understand their origin and articulate their opposition. It is a brave man who opposes 'progress', for all the harm it does him.

The forms of control discussed earlier – through technology, work design, regulations, personnel procedures and other insidious methods – not only achieve regularity, they disguise their own nature and origins, thus making resistance all the more difficult.

3. Ideology. These difficulties are compounded by the ideological underpinnings of modern forms of organisational control, which define the nature of the employment contract, the nature of the organisation, the necessity for organisational hierarchy, the neutrality of the organisation's objectives and activities, the justice and legitimacy of any individual's location within the system, and the benefits which all derive from organisational life.

Frequently these ideological efforts are sustained and buttressed outside the organisation. Individuals are prepared for their organisational roles by education and educational selection. 'Inappropriate' aspirations are 'cooled out'; excessively academic, or non-job-related schools or academic enterprises are disciplined; the shared benefits of consumerism and materialism (claimed products of organisational structure and process) are proclaimed; the individual achievements and superiority of managers, experts and executives are lauded; technology itself is worshipped and mystified. 'The prevailing forms of social control are technological in a new sense' writes Marcuse:

> . . . *in the contemporary period, the technological controls appear to be the very embodiment of Reason for the benefit of all social groups and interests – to such an extent that all contradiction seems irrational and all counteraction impossible. . . . The intellectual and emotional refusal 'to go along' appears neurotic and impotent. . . . The impact of progress turns Reason into submission to the facts of life, and to the dynamic capability of producing more and bigger facts of the same sort of life (Marcuse, 1972, p.23).*

It is thus that the 'sheer madness' of forms of work organisation that result in employees wishing their lives away in the endless repetition of moronic activities becomes, miraculously, *reasonable*. We must insist on the unreasonableness of such reason.

Within the organisation members' ability to articulate their feelings of frustration and oppression is further obstructed by the contradictory nature of organisational life: that it involves both conflict *and* cooperation: differentiation and coordination. It is difficult to define as entirely external and oppressive a system of work which is highly interdependent and where the 'victim' of individual recalcitrance is frequently a fellow member of the organisation – the salesman who finds his customer disappointed, the manager who has worked nights to put the finishing touches to some planned reorganisation, the fellow Open University academic who is urgently demanding the completion of some material for *his* course. In this way, by establishing the social nature of organisational life, resistance is made all the more difficult, more costly, more 'irrational'.

Furthermore, it is also, in a sense, true that there is some area of common interest between all levels of the organisation – from the executives and owners, to the lowest level employees. If the organisation ceases to function all will be out of work. This will probably hurt some more than others, but it will have its impact on them all. But this is not the same as saying that the organisation is a cooperative enterprise in which all pull together for the shared good, because the very social system within which they operate, and which they serve to sustain, is based upon a basic conflict of interest, and work and control arrangements, and the distribution of rewards, within organisations reflect this basic conflict.

Nevertheless, 'Sheer force of habit also makes at least a minimum of day-to-day co-operation between employers and workers seem the norm. So for workers to break out of their everyday routine and engage in some form of overt conflict, a specific incident or grievance must usually generate the necessary momentum' (Hyman, 1972, p.103). This habitual cooperativeness, allied with the employees' unwillingness to obstruct the flow, the momentum, of production, deliberately to stand there and watch things going wrong (see Nichols, 1975) must be seen in the context of the ultimate constraints of the market, financial viability and possibility, which are themselves defined as neutral and God-given. As something you can't do anything about – like the weather – and which cause an increase in work pressures within the organisation. As Marcuse says, you have to submit to the 'facts' of life, and in so submitting the facts are made more onerous, more oppressive more powerful.

4. The employment contract. This is frequently presented as a fair, equal and free arrangement whereby employees agree to sell their labour power to the employers. The employee is protected in this exchange by his trade union. Therefore, this argument runs, within work it is immoral and unprincipled for employees not to abide by their contract, and to resist management's 'right to manage', to question the reasonableness of management decisions, oppose innovations, or alterations. The weakness of this view is well rehearsed in Fox, 1971; Hyman, 1972; Beynon, 1973; and others. The employment contract is neither equal nor free, and the power of the parties to it are far from equivalent; there are numerous and massive obstacles to the employees gaining equal, legal, bargaining power; and the frequent restriction of bargaining to the financial aspect of the relationship is a reflection of its inherent imbalance.

Is this emphasis also evident among the work force? Are they prepared to sacrifice any interest in the nature of work, or in autonomy, for financial rewards? It is clear that organisational members vary in the emphasis they attach to various organisational elements and rewards (see Goldthorpe *et al.,* 1968; Ingham, 1970; Argyris, 1968; and others). And if people expect different things from their employer then it is clear that as long as the prime aspiraton is met, they might be prepared to put up with otherwise highly depriving work experiences. They might develop their 'central life interest' outside of work, and tolerate the sort of work activities and conditions described by Bosquet earlier in exchange for the reward they most value – money. In this way they could be 'bought off' from any interest in altering the structure of the organisation, their subordinate status, or the design of their work.

There are a number of problems here. First, what is the *salience* of the workers' claimed instrumentality? (Remember Fox's distinctions between high- and low-priority aspirations.) Second, how stable is this priority? Isn't it entirely possible that the frustration and dissatisfaction these instrumental workers experience (for their instrumentality doesn't reduce their dissatisfaction, just establishes a price for it) might suddenly explode into action? And even if it is true that instrumentality is so deeply held that it 'operates like a local anaesthetic' (Daniel, 1969), then it is quite likely it will result in ever larger claims for the valued reward. As Fox has remarked, simply because employment relations are increasingly characterised by an emphasis on financial remuneration does not mean the incorporation of the working class:

Insofar as subordinates are – or can be brought to be – strongly committed to the value of a continuously rising material standard of life, managers may hope to strengthen their legitimacy by trying to meet subordinates' aspirations in respect of material rewards, welfare and fringe benefits. Since this is one of the appetites that grow by what they feed upon, it is apt to prove an unstable basis for authority (Fox, 1971, p.41).

Has this apparent instrumentalism resulted in a loss of interest in struggles over control at work? Some have thought so:

The almost exclusive preoccupation of trade unions with economism is not a mere case of 'betrayal' by their leadership: it is rooted in the workers' very experience, and reinforces the union's positon. Normally confronted by an employer who will budge on economic but not on control issues, the worker takes what he can easily get and attempts to reduce the salience of what is denied him (Mann, 1973, p.32).

It would, however, be a mistake to regard such 'economism' as indicative of evidence of a loss of interest in control issues, as Hyman remarks, (Hyman 1976). Even when organisational members restrict their aspirations to the financial aspects of their work they need not, by virtue of this alone, lose interest in control issues. Goodrich has noted that discipline and management – aspects of any organisation – are expressive of control, and of the 'frontier of control', that 'shifting line in a great mass of regulations'. Goodrich points out how a great many taken-for-granted union issues and concerns are directly to do with control – for example over dismissal, hours of work, demarcation, apprenticeship, craft regulations, hours of work, working conditions, methods of payment, and so on. Even accepting the distinction between economic struggles (economism) and struggles over control, it is clear, as Goodrich remarks, that 'quarrels over methods of payment cannot be completely disentangled from the general question of the control of industry' (Goodrich, 1975, p.164).

It is of course true that much resistance to organisational control takes place in the general area of *conditions of employment,* rather than over *methods of production.* But it is not rare to find examples of opposition even in this latter sphere, albeit they be defensive and couched in financial terms. As Goodrich remarks, the famous – or infamous – restriction of output can be seen as an example of this latter type. Goodrich suggests a fourfold classification of the worker's interest in, and feelings about, industry: '(1) How much he gets – wages, etc. (2) What it's for – The Object of the Work. (3) How he's treated – Freedom and Authority. (4) What he actually does – Workmanship' (Goodrich, 1975, p.19). This is a useful classification, and can be applied to all levels of organisational membership and all types of organisation. Goodrich notes that the last two classes are most concerned with control, but emphasises that it is impossible to ignore the interrelationships between all four. He remarks on the current view (in 1920!) that the average workman is interested in nothing but wages and cares nothing about control, doesn't want to run things, and argues that long-run economic demands

may . . . be found greatly strengthening the demand for workers' control. . . . The demand for his pay may strengthen the demand for control. The desire for sure pay – for security against unemployment – is even nearer the surface of control schemes. . . . What starts as a wage demand may easily – often unconsciously – be coloured by an admixture of other motives (Goodrich, 1975, p.22–4).

Organisational members are enormously strengthened in their resistance to organisational control, and in their concern about the four aspects of employment set out by Goodrich, by the frequent existence of informal work groups which transform and inspire individual reactions to frustration and oppression. These groups may demonstrate one or other, or all, of the three types of employee resistance to control suggested by Goodrich: 'the demand not to be controlled disagreeably, the demand not to be controlled at all, and the demand to take a hand in controlling' (Goodrich, 1975, p.37). Informal work groups can be regarded as informal – but highly significant – efforts by organisational employees at all levels to pursue some or one of these goals.

Informal work groups represent a 'considerable structuring of the work situation . . . done by the worker themselves' (Katz, 1973, p.199). In many organisational situations, even where members are exposed to highly specific and detailed constraints, some unofficial culture will develop, with norms and expectations through which members carve out some area of autonomy and freedom. It has been argued that these informal cultures serve the purpose of supplying satisfactions denied by the formal organisation. Katz maintains that informal cultures and groups promote the affiliation of organisational members who are denied many or any areas of satisfaction in their work. Informal culture, he argues, 'permits continuation of working class style of life and provides ties of sociability' (Katz, 1973, p.191).

This is a rather naive, functionalist view: informal work groups are more likely to develop and support anti-organisational sentiments and behaviour than to strengthen members' commitment to the organisation through serving as an outlet for sociability and joking. Informal work groups – which means any organisational grouping which is not specified by senior members, and which contains its own distinctive culture – are always potentially active in their efforts to structure the work situation, the flow of work, the quantity of work and level of supervision, etc. Selznick has argued that (1) Every organisation creates an informal structure. (2) In every organisation, the goals of the organisation are modified (abandoned, deflected, or elaborated) by processes within it. Later Selznick emphasises that relationships between the official hierarchy and informal work groups are relationships of power, oriented towards attempts to control, and efforts to avoid such control.

The most famous study of an informal working group is that of workers in the Bank Wiring Room investigated by Roethlisberger and Dickson. These authors noted that the workers were subject to informal norms and expectations backed up by group membership and support. This informal control achieved internal similarity of levels of output, and protected them from external interference. The authors discuss the causes of the workers' restriction of output. They note that the workers explained it in terms of insecurity and anxiety: 'if output were too high something might happen – the "bogey" might be raised, the "rate" might be lowered, someone be laid off, hours might be reduced, or supervisors might reprimand the slower workers' (Roethlisberger and Dickson, 1964, p.532).

Roethlisberger and Dickson reject such explanations as based on confused, contradictory and groundless anxieties, but are prepared to grant that the workers are not simply 'ungrateful', or plain lazy, or deliberately and maliciously opposing management. They explain these sentiments as based on the workers' *ideology,* not on any *real* grounds (sic).

Although these authors deny that the behaviour of the workers they studied was a manifestation of any 'real' conflict between management and workers, other writers have been more prepared to see the origins and consequences of unofficial norms in terms of conflict of interest within the organisation. A recent example is Beynon (1973, p.188). Roy, in a fascinating paper, reports that workers co-operated with each other as fellow-members of a combat team at war with management, in ways which were completely at variance with the carefully prepared designs of staff experts and in flagrant violation of basic principles of shop-floor behaviour (Roy, 1954). His account of informal culture is particularly interesting for the emphasis it places on the constant, shifting 'frontier of control' between workers and time and motion men – each group attempting to outwit the other and to achieve, or circumvent, control.

Informal work groups and their associated cultures of resistance are by no means limited to shop-floor organisational groups. Blau's study of a government agency shows that the government agents developed their own strongly held group norms which directly contravened formal agency rulings – for example, the agents, whose job was to investigate business for violations of federal laws, were strictly instructed to report all cases of bribery, or attempted bribery. But they didn't, and they regarded any agent who did conform with this agency ruling as breaking an important moral norm. Zimmerman's study, 'The practicalities of rule use' (1973), supplies further evidence of the existence and significance of informal work norms among white-collar and managerial organisational employees. Zimmerman argues, sensibly, that it is *never* justified to assume actual behaviour from mere knowledge of organisational rules; it is always necessary to know what rules mean to, and how they are used by, organisational employees in their organisational work. In particular, Zimmerman stresses the importance of understanding the variety of circumstances, constraints, meanings, taken-for-granted definitions and stereotypes which members typically consider in using organisational rules. For example, one major determining feature is members' own assessment of the real objectives of their work (which will usually be different from formal organisational statements of objectives). Organisational members frequently bend, ignore or re-interpret organisational procedures and authority in order to achieve the real object of their work. This process frequently relies upon the member's extensive knowledge of his clients, patients, or cases. (See, for example, Sudnow, 1973, and Bittner, 1973.) Becoming a competent organisational member means becoming familiar with and committed to these shared conceptions of work priorities, the meaning of rules and procedures, and the varying significance and salience of typical organisational problems. It means learning the informal interpretation of organisational procedures and applying them to group conceptions of purpose and group definitions of the organisation, its work, and its reality. Such conceptions are, explictly or implicitly, in conflict with formal organisational structure and process. As Crozier remarks of the workers' subculture in the Industrial Monopoly:

There seems to exist among workers a set of attitudes and beliefs that cannot be explained as a collection of individual responses to a similar situation, but that suggests an autonomous group development. . . . The content of this subculture is in opposition to the goals of the organisation and the aims of management. It implies

*an idealisation of the past, some pessimism about the present,
devaluation of the future and distrust of management. The group's
demand for autonomy, and its affirmation of independence, are
directed primarily against the organisation to which it belongs
(Crozier, 1964, p.80).*

It is obvious from any study of informal organisational groups and
cultures that the power of individuals and groups within organisations is not restricted to their official authority. Officially, 'power
or authority would tend to be hierarchic; each level would have just
that amount of power necessary to carry out its responsibilities;
ascendant levels in the hierarchy would have increasing power based
on broader knowledge about the organisation and/or greater task
expertise' (Wamsley, 1970, p.53, quoted in Hall, 1972a, p.205). But
reality isn't as neat as this; actual power within organisations is not
simply the result of amounts of job-related authority allocated by
the organisational executive. Certainly most of the power of
organisational experts and controllers derives directly from their
organisational mandate to manipulate – bestow/withdraw – desired
resources. One must not be so fascinated by the 'under-life' of
organisations – the informal groupings and cultures – as to forget
the massive power and resources of the officially powerful.

Nevertheless, if we do find that officially subordinate and power-
less groups or levels within organisations manage to retain or
increase their intra-organisational muscle, we must ask where this
bargaining strength comes from. How is it that lower-level
organisational participants retain some organisational power? The
organisational hierarchy is a hierarchy of power: the higher the
position, the greater the power, so how is it that the lowest of all
retains some capacity to influence events and resist domination?

Clearly, part of the answer lies in the extra bargaining power
bestowed on organisational members by their membership of a
union. As Hyman has remarked:

*Individual employees, whatever their level of skill, responsibility or
expertise, are highly vulnerable when confronted with the concentrated economic power of capital (buttressed by extensive legal
sanctions) of which the employer is the embodiment. It would be
wrong to regard the individual as wholly impotent; but in general,
significant resistance to employer objectives – let alone the ability
to impose altogether different priorities – is on the agenda only
when strategies of a collective character are adopted. . . . Trade
unionism is the most obvious manifestation of such collective
action: for a trade union is a stable, formalised, hence highly
socially visible means of worker combination (Hyman, 1976,
pp.87–8).*

The threat of collective withdrawal of labour, or of a work to
rule, or other forms of industrial action will count heavily with

management, since management *depends* upon the availability of reasonably willing labour to achieve its purposes, just as the organisational employees depend upon management for various resources. (See the discussion earlier concerning varieties of organisational reward.) Furthermore, even less organised, more individual or spontaneous reactions and opposition probably carries some weight with senior members. Organisational executives are usually worried about absenteeism, turnover, sabotage, pilfering, and other signs of the withdrawal of commitment.

But lower-level members of organiations may manage to achieve some control without recourse to such actions or threats, by gaining for themselves some work autonomy. We have seen that employees frequently struggle to achieve and retain some self-control at work often through union activity. If they achieve it, such control is itself a source of power – which is exactly why senior organisational members strive to reduce members' autonomy. For autonomy can, in 'irresponsible' hands, lead to unpredictability.

The most famous example of this process is contained in Crozier's *The Bureaucratic Phenomenon*. He reports how groups within the organisation fight for work autonomy (see p.144 above). Such autonomy, once gained, gives *control over* uncertainty:

the power of A over B depends on A's ability to predict B's behaviour and on the uncertainty of B about A's behaviour. As long as the requirements of action create situations of uncertainty, the individuals who have to face them have power over those who are affected by the results of their choice (Crozier, 1964, p.160).

Crozier argues that the power of maintenance men in the organisation he studied followed from their power to handle the major sources of organisational uncertainty – technical break-downs. The engineer, writes Crozier, has 'control over the last source of uncertainty remaining in a completely routinised organisational system' (Crozier, 1964. p.109). This view of the basis of organisational power has been developed by Hickson *et al.* (1973). These authors argue that the more a sub-unit within an organisation copes with uncertainty, the greater its power within the organisation; but they add that such power will increase if the sub-units are not easily substitutable, and if the activity is particularly central to the overall activity of the organisation. The importance of this model of organisational power is not only that it reveals why senior organisational members go to such lengths to reduce the autonomy of low-level organisational members (see Section II) so as to reduce the power of such members, but it also points to the relationship between the installation of procedures which are designed to achieve routinisation (by reducing reliance on judgement and discretion) and the elimination of lower-level members' power. To routinise by laying down procedures or by incorporating these procedures in machinery or the work design, increases enormously the substitutability of personnel, for the decision-making has been removed from the employee and invested in procedures, regulations, machinery. The new less skilled job will require less training and expertise. This way of reducing the power of sub-units involves legislating – through various systems – for ways of reacting to and coping with the uncertainty; another method involves reducing the uncertainty itself. This might mean, in the case reported by Crozier, installing a system of planned maintenance. It might mean reducing the variability of the organisation's raw material through pre-selection or other controls. The result of both procedures is the same – the reduction of the sub-unit's intra-organisational power by reducing its control over uncertainty. It is precisely because of this consequence of processes of automation, 'rationalisation', work study, mechanisation and routinisation that such processes are resisted by the employees concerned. And it is because of the power implications of the discretionary element of organisational work that senior executives tend to impose prescription and standardisation. But they won't succeed, because, as Crozier reminds us, it is not possible entirely to eliminate discretion. Despite centralisation, automation and formalisation, some areas of potential autonomy, or uncertainty, remain. And it is on these that members base their efforts to regain sufficient unpredictability to increase their organisational power. The organisation of work and the organisation of control are two sides of the same basic process of organisational domination.

Roles

It is quite common for writers to conceptualise processes of power and control in organisations in terms of organisational roles. This concept refers to the fact that

human beings, as a result of occupying . . . statuses, play such roles as father, mother, factory worker, manager, friend and soldier. All these are separate and well defined roles . . . what makes the role of such importance is the fact that it largely determines how human beings will act in certain areas . . . the role of factory worker implies certain duties and certain rewards, certain relationships to management and its representatives, and other relationships to fellow workers (Schneider, 1969, p.14).

Others have seen organisational roles in very similar terms. Katz and Kahn suggest that role refers to recurring actions of an individual which are interrelated with the repetitive activities of others so as to produce a predictable outcome.

The concept role is usually proclaimed as the mediator between the individual and the organisation, which achieves and explains the

individual's production of office-related activities which are
external to the individual in the sense that he is merely 'filling' a
role, and could be replaced, but which he soon comes to regard as
proper and normal. Much role behaviour is probably not regarded
as such by the members who produce it.

Why do organisational actors perform activities and duties
associated with their organisational role? An organisational role,
according to this approach, exposes an incumbent to a series of
expectations which are held by certain significant and influential
colleagues. The role set – the persons most immediately affected by
the incumbent's role performance – depend upon the role
incumbent for their own role performance; they have a stake in it.
Because of this they mobilise rewards, encouragement, assistance,
instructions, and penalties to direct and elicit his role performance.
The role incumbent is surrounded by expectations governing
organisational behaviour, and unwillingness to disappoint the role
set, and a desire for the rewards and approval associated with
competent role performance, encourage his or her compliance. The
concept role refers, basically, to these patterned and regular
expectations, and the behaviours associated with them.

This concept has been extremely influential in organisational
analyses. So much so that it is common for people to refer to an
organisational title or position – foreman, manager, scientist – as
the foreman's role, the manager's role etc., as though it were
merely an established way of referring to these positions, and
without realising that the use of this concept carries certain
assumptions and problems.

It is true, as we have noted earlier, that organisations are, in
part, co-operative phenomena, characterised by subtle and implicit
processes of give-and-take and mutual adjustment and negotiation.
It is true that organisational life is not characterised by constant
reference to rewards and discipline, that members do get on with
their work without constant supervision and direction. Indeed one
of the most striking features of any organisation on first entering it,
is the *absence* of instruction and direction. And the concept role is
useful for highlighting this aspect of organisational life: the way in
which, and the extent to which, members monitor and direct their
own work behaviour in the light of what they know to be expected
of them. But this is only part of the story: and the other part is less
easily fitted into the role approach.

If organisational regularity is the result of members conforming
to the expectations of their role set, certain problems and questions
immediately come to mind. Firstly it is highly likely that members
may be exposed to more than one body of expectations. We have
seen that organisational members may be members of informal
work groups, unions, professional bodies, as well as incumbents of
organisational offices. Each and all of these memberships will carry

bodies of expectations. Even more crucially, we have seen that the relative weight of relevant expectations can vary enormously. Dahrendorf has remarked that at least three sorts of role expectation can be distinguished – 'must', 'shall' and 'can' expectations. These differ in the 'degree to which their associated expectations are compulsory' (Dahrendorf, 1968, pp.41–2).

Many writers have pointed to the weakness of the role approach. It has been noted that it is important to distinguish between role and position, in order to avoid circularity (Bradbury *et al.*, 1972, p.42); that we must be clear about to whom we are attributing the relevant expectations. There is a danger that society is reified in these analyses (Dahrendorf, 1968, p.44). We must separate the researcher's interpretive framework and the actor's interpretative procedures (Cicourel, 1970, pp.4–6). We must not assume that role expectations are consensual, or that the role incumbent is clear about the nature of these expectations, and their relative priority (Gross *et al.*, 1958; Kahn *et al.*, 1964). It is likely that the role incumbent will find it hard to know which conflicting set of expectations he should *activate* at any time (Pugh, 1973). Finally we have been warned to adopt a *creative* conception of roles, seeing role incumbents not as passively conforming with expectations, but as actively adjusting their behaviour in the light of their interpretations and experiences (Urry, 1970, p.360).

But the main problem with the concept, and approaches to control in organisations which employ it, is quite simple: many, possibly the majority, of organisational employees are not controlled in ways which can be subsumed under this concept. To talk of organisational roles places the emphasis on control through members' conformity with expectations, commitments and obligations. The role incumbent is seen as *morally* obliged to conform, and this obligation is backed up by his involvement in sets of organisational relationships which carry and transmit the expectations on which the incumbent depends for status, approval and esteem.

But it has already been stressed that many organisational members fill jobs where discretion is purposely eliminated or reduced, and where control through expectation would be inappropriate since it is built into the work itself, or carried by detailed rules and procedures. Low level organisational employees are not controlled through their moral commitment to the role expectations of their role set (except in the case of informal work groups). On the contrary they are frequently alienated from such expectations and the values and interests that lie behind them. Such members are controlled in more direct ways, by explicit, written rules and instructions, or through the design and mechanisation of work, not through moral compliance with *expectations*.

To use the concept role to understand processes of organisational control is to assume answers to the very question under consideration – how far is organisational control regarded as legitimate. The concept role sees all power as authority. But as we have stressed, this is empirically fallacious. Just because organisations do not demonstrate continual struggle, resistance and overt control, the fact should not be masked that lying just behind this apparent harmony is the reality of coercion. As Silverman put it, he who has the greatest power has the greatest ability to impose his definition and view of the situation. A preoccupation with organisational roles might be useful for investigating members' definitions of their own and other jobs, but it won't help uncover the part played by sheer power in the extraction of members' obedience.

Organisations and knowledge

Chapter 12

Organisational structure and ideology

Many organisations *make* knowledge, or information. All organisations *use* knowledge in their daily activities. And all organisations attempt to develop and disseminate definitions and moralities which describe and legitimate their structure and activities. No understanding of organisations – and especially processes of control within organisations – is possible without some consideration of the ways in which organisations construct and use knowledge. This section will attempt the outlines of such a consideration.

We are by now used to the suggestion that organisations *construct* knowledge; that the representations of reality presented by mass media organisations, universities, schools, religious institutions, publishers, information agencies and other bodies, are significantly structured and coloured by the nature, goals and orientations of the organisation concerned. Only those in senior positions within these organisations maintain the objectivity and truth of their products, for obvious reasons.

To a considerable extent what we 'know' about the world, ourselves, each other, the society we live in, and the organisations which employ us, is derived from organisations. Take the news for example. What passes for the news about current affairs, world events, political conflicts, etc., is what is disseminated by newspapers, news agencies, television and radio organisations. Can anyone seriously conceive of news as 'an objective body of events which occur and which the journalist pursues, captures in his notebook or newsreel and takes back triumphantly to his editor'? (Cohen and Young, 1973, p.15). Most people would now accept the more relevant and accurate picture of news – and other mass media products – as the result of an active selection process whereby the newsman, or other media employee, selects 'angles' and edits his material in the light of *bureaucratic* exigencies, constraints and knowledge (of what is marketable, acceptable, newsworthy, safe, interesting), and *ideological* priorities and definitions, which encourage the selection of some items, the rejection of others, the value of some treatments, the irresponsibility of others (Cohen and Young, 1973). Furthermore, as Stuart Hood has usefully remarked in his analyses of the BBC, the values and assumptions which lie behind, and are reflected in, the claimed impartiality of this organisation (i.e. the assumption of middle-class consensus politics) are not necessarily overt and imposed. The new recruit to the BBC – or other media organisations – soon learns what is permitted and what is not from 'the conversation, comments, anecdotes and reactions of his fellow workers' (Hood, 1968). He will learn, if he is to be successful, that the good BBC man anticipates the unstated rules and requirements, and he will master the art of knowing what he 'can get away with' and what he must refer to his seniors. In these ways processes of ideological control become transmuted into personal sensitivity, discretion and, finally, personal success or failure.

We should be equally sceptical of other authoritative organisational information, produced by those bodies which Kitsuse and Cicourel call 'rate producing agencies', that is organisations that create and disseminate statistical rates, or other information, such as government agencies or information departments (Kitsuse and Cicourel, 1963). And Douglas has sounded the same warning with respect to official statistics, when he writes of the enormous powers of control that follow from the capacity to create authoritative knowledge about the world. Such remarks, of the essentially ideological and social status of organisationally produced knowledge, are of course even more applicable to the most important of all such social processes – education.

As well as making knowledge, organisations use knowledge. This aspect of organisational functioning constitutes the prime concern of the decision-making approach. Within organisations there is a constant and continuing process of data creation, storage, application and communication. Information of levels of performance is collected in all organisations – the number of cars made per month; of patients treated; of students examined, passed or failed; of newspapers printed, distributed, sold; of applications processed; houses built. Information on levels of success and failure – on waste rates, empty beds, unused capacity, labour turnover, absenteeism – and on organisation's costs – per item, per man-hour, per product, on quantities of energy, resources, materials, commodities used – are typically collected. Records are kept of levels and costs of performance – for personnel and machines, for it is a basic tenet of organisational thinking that control is only possible in the light of information. The data gathered are utilised in decisions (or non-decisions) about alterations to process, personnel, organisation, material, market or clients.

It is a defining feature of modern bureaucracy, Weber writes, that 'Administrative acts, decisions and rules are formulated and recorded in writing, even in cases where oral discussion is the rule or is mandatory. . . . The combination of written documents and a continuous organisation of official functions constitutes the 'office'

which is the central focus of all types of modern corporate action'
(Weber, 1964, p.332). There are few organisations where
considerable effort is not committed to formulating, discovering,
and recording information on all aspects of organisational structure,
process and achievement.

Just as the capacity and possibility of official decision-making is
not spread evenly throughout the organisation, but is concentrated
in senior positions within the structure, so the flow and distribution
of information is hierarchically determined. Senior members of
organisations strive to maximise the information from subordinate
levels and groups: to discover how production, or teaching, or
reporting, or diagnosis, is going: to isolate levels of personal
commitment, performance, co-operation; to assess the nature and
variability of raw materials, customers, patients, clients; to discover
the state of 'morale', and employees' attitudes, etc.

Wilensky has suggested that the sort of information of most
concern to an organisation depends on the major problems it faces
– the more important the environment, the greater the effort that
will be committed to 'intelligence'; when the commitment and
support of organisational personnel is seen to be crucial, internal
communications will be emphasised; and when the efficiency and
productivity of the organisation is crucial, 'facts and figures' men
will dominate. In other words organisations emphasise different
types of organisational knowledge, depending on senior members'
assessment of major areas of organisational salience or vulnerability.

Wilensky also points to the *political* nature of this form of
organisational knowledge: that it is used to impose, or avoid,
control (1967). We are familiar with the fact that subordinates and
organisations tend to 'cover up' their departmental, or personal,
failures or misdemeanours, to 'rig' the figures to present a more
rosy picture than might otherwise appear. On the other hand
seniors can be deliberately flooded with information, when
subordinates withdraw their 'gatekeeping' function. (See Scheff,
1970, and Chapter 11.) Or subordinates may modify their work
behaviours so as to emphasise recorded activities at the expense of
more elusive but more primary goals. Wilensky remarks that the
inaccuracy of senior members' information, or the development of
obstacles to the flow of organisational information follow from
three basic organisational features – hierarchy, specialisation and
centralisation (Wilensky, 1967). Blau's study of performance
statistics (Blau, 1963) illustrates the political origins and
consequences of such information.

Culture

So far we have concentrated on formal knowledge which is used
and produced by organisations. Such knowledge constitutes only a

fraction of the ideational and moral world of organisations. Distinctive cultures – both organisational and specialist – occur in all organisations, and play an important part in the distinctive and discrete character of different types of organisations. The difference between a military regiment and an electronics factory, or a university department and an insurance company, is not composed only of differences in structure, activity, technology and control mechanisms. It includes different ways of thinking and evaluating, different moralities and cultures. It is this difference we are referring to when we talk of the 'feel' of an organisation, or the 'atmosphere', or 'climate'; the distinctive and habitual ways in which members of the organisation (or departments, or sections, or specialities) relate to each other, think, evaluate, know and conceptualise themselves, each other, their work, organisation and their objectives.

Such organisational cultures are least obvious to current members of the organisation, who take their confident mastery of, and competence at, the culture of their employing organisation entirely for granted. So much so that it is confused with normality – with the way things are, and must be. But their inconspicuousness does not extend to outsiders, or to their members. As we shall see, members of the organisation go to considerable lengths to recruit new members with some apparent predisposition towards the receiving culture; and once within the organisation the recruit is exposed to considerable formal and informal training and socialisation. Membership of, and commitment to, the organisational culture or sub-culture is no optional extra. It is critical for the recruit's ability to operate 'efficiently' and reliably within his employing organisation. It is, indeed, an essential component of the structure of organisational control of middle level and expert members.

Ideology and rationality

Another highly significant, and related, element of the moral and ideational world of organisations is the body of ideas which is used to validate and legitimate the hierarchy, structure of control, distribution of rewards and privileges within the organisation. As Mills expresses it, 'The demand of the bureaucracies has been not only for intellectual personnel to run the new technical, editorial and communication machinery, but for the creation and diffusion of new symbolic fortifications for the new and largely private power these bureaucracies represent' (Mills, 1956, p.153).

Elsewhere Mills argues that modern organisations attempt to increase their control over their members at the same time as they disguise this control in forms which senior organisational members of their personnel and work experts hope will achieve greater control through neutral, insidious and inconspicuous ways. Some of these methods were considered in the previous chapter. The ideological aspect of this effort will be discussed later in this section. Both within organisations and without, ideas and attitudes exist and are energetically propounded by organisational executives and their spokesmen and apologists, that justify the form of organisation, the locations of people in their various positions with their associated rewards and deprivations, and that claim the inevitability and neutrality of the organisation and the design of work, and proclaim the functional necessity of this form of organisation and the value of the organisation's goals. A variety of ideas and moralities are pressed into the service of these functions, as we shall see.

The development of such ideologies is in itself a considerable organisational achievement, and one that requires the active assistance of special experts and advisers. Mills is just one of a number of writers who have noted that the size, number and importance of modern organisations has produced a demand for new justifications and ideologies. He writes: 'Many an intellectual earns a good income because of that fact. The whole growth of ideological work is based on the need for the vested interests lodged in the new power centres to be softened, whitened, blurred, misinterpreted to those who serve the interests of the bureaucracies inside, and to those in its sphere outside' (Mills, 1956, p.154).

Much of this growth of ideological work has relied upon social science knowledge, or assistance, either directly through consultancy work, personnel activities and communication experts, or indirectly through the generally supportive nature of most social science research in the field of organisations and work (see Baritz, 1975). Such ideological assistance is presented as 'objective' by those concerned. Mills suggests, somewhat charitably, that such postures of objectivity and integrity might be the result of intellectuals' difficulty in locating their masters in the impersonal machineries of authority in which they work. Somehow we have to explain how it is that the most striking inequalities and injustices of organisational activity and structure have for so long been presented and accepted as inevitable, neutral, even just. 'When irresponsible decisions prevail and values are not proportionately distributed, universal deception', writes Mills 'must be practised by and for those who make the decisions and who have the most of what values there are to have' (Mills, 1956, p.155).

Organisational structures, decisions, technologies, procedures, and systems are frequently defined – by senior members and others – as rational, or the result of 'rationalisation'. By this they imply that the decision or event or technology is: (*a*) related to, or deriving from, scientific, modern, efficient principles and criteria; (*b*) an inevitable and unavoidable aspect of modern life, of progress; (c) beyond choice or politics. The only choice is to ignore such pressures towards rationalisation, and run the risk of inefficiency, competitive defeat, or commercial vulnerability. Since the interests of all organisational members are defined as coincident, such problems would adversely affect all members of the organisation. Therefore, to resist the technological or organisational implications of rationalisation is to oppose progress and to damage your own interests (i.e. the organisation's). To the extent that the results of rationalisation, or decisions regarded as essentially rational in terms of their technical, scientific logic, are agreed to be 'unfortunate' (redundancies, deskilling, loss of control etc.), such 'costs' are regarded as more than outweighed by the advantages in output, costs, and the improved performance of the organisation.

Many recent writers have pointed to the ideological aspects of this sort of 'rationality'. Weber's distinction between two types of rationality is important. We must overcome our conviction that something rational is reasonable. Rationality, Weber remarks, may be either 'formal' or 'substantive'. Formal rationality involves certain processes or operations which are seen as rational. When these processes or operations are employed, it can, in this highly limited sense, be said to be rational. These processes are, essentially, the conversion of situations, problems and decisions into numerical, calculative terms, or the application of technical rules. For example, when talking about the 'formal rationality of economic action' Weber remarks that this expression 'will be used to designate the extent of quantitative calculation or accounting which is technically possible and which is actually applied' (Weber, 1964, pp.184–5). It is in this sense that the application of, say, Scientific Management principles, or work study systems, or numerical appraisal schemes, can be regarded as rational. They are not necessarily rational in the 'real' sense (i.e. efficient in achieving goals, or reasonable in terms of the various parties' needs and expectations). Weber notes that formal rationality can be at odds with 'real' rationality (Albrow, 1970, p.64). 'Substantive' rationality involves a relation to the ends that are sought –

a relation to the absolute values or to the content of the particular given ends to which it is orientated. In principle there is an indefinite number of possible standards of value which are 'rational' in this sense. Socialistic and communistic standards which, though by no means unambiguous in themselves, always involve elements of social justice and equality, form only one group among the indefinite plurality of possible points of view. Others are action in the interests of a hierarchy of class distinctions or in furtherance of the power of a political unit (Weber, 1964, pp.185–6).

This is a crucial distinction which, exactly because of its importance, is not made by those who choose organisational goals, strategies, techniques and structures. If all debate can be restricted to questions of 'formal' rationality, while insisting that these are rational in the second sense, organisational decisions can be imbued with inevitability and inexorability. However, if goals and objectives of the organisation can be defined as rational, debate about alternative activities, or alternative forms of society in which such goals would be unnecessary, would be possible.

Weber's distinction warns us to distrust the rationality (i.e. reasonableness) of modern organisations' goals or strategies. Both are chosen, both are avoidable, both are political. Indeed the rationality of organisations, their goals and their structure, must, we have argued, be seen as a result and reflection of class society and class interests. The 'formal' rationality of organisations must be seen, argues Marcuse, as part of efforts to mobilise, organise and exploit technical, scientific and mechanical principles and advances in order to maintain and secure the supremacy of the senior executives. Furthermore, not only must we question the reasonableness of organisational structured goals, but even the scientific (neutral?) knowledge which underlies much organisational-technological development must be suspect:

Scientfic management and scientific division of labour vastly increased the productivity of the economic, political and cultural enterprise. Result: the higher standard of living. At the same time and on the same ground, this rational enterprise produced a pattern of mind and behaviour which justified and absolved even the most destructive and oppressive features of the enterprise.

Scientific-technical rationality and manipulation are welded together into new forms of social control. Can we rest content with the assumption that this unscientific outcome is the result of a specific societal application of science? I think that the general direction in which it came to be applied was inherent in pure science even where no practical purposes were intended (Marcuse, 1972, pp.120–21).

The importance of this suggestion cannot be exaggerated. By doubting the 'neutrality' of the science that is so often applied to organisational technique and structure Marcuse is adding yet more weight to the critique of the reasonableness of organisational rationality. (See also Habermas, 1976, pp.330–47.)

Two final points must be made. We have considered the rationality of organisational means (technology, work design, structure), but what of organisational *ends*? How rational are they? Weber's remarks on 'substantive' rationality should warn us that no one goal is any more intrinsically rational than any other. Goals are derived from ethics and morality, not reason. In these terms we

may doubt the rationality of many organisations' goals.
Consumerism, materialism, alienation, the trivialisation of issues
and culture through the mass media, the destruction of the environment, the unbelievable stockpiling of grotesquely destructive
armaments, the establishment of increasingly elaborate health
systems and hospitals in conjunction with deteriorating standards of
health care, the use of education as preparation for work roles etc.,
where is the rationality of such organisational achievements? These
are rational goals only in forms of society with definite conceptions
of value.

A final feature of the rationality of modern work organisations is
the extent to which the ideological nature of organisational
decisions and events, or structures and processes, is mystified, disguised and denied by the very structures which advance and
perpetuate the oppression of organisational members. For it is often
argued that members of organisations are constrained and frustrated not by human agency, or sectional interests, but by neutral
technology, inevitable market pressures, unavoidable scientific-
technical advances, the need to 'rationalise'. In this way individuals
are made incapable of 'seeing "behind the machinery those who use
it, those who profited from it, and those who paid for it"'
(Marcuse, 1972, p.153). Beynon's *Working for Ford*, and Nichols
and Armstrong's *Workers Divided*, are two important recent
empirical accounts of this process of mystification and its impact,
and of the efforts of the organisational members concerned to
understand and oppose the interests and structures that oppress
them.

Such mystification extends even to the structure of the
organisation itself. Despite assurances that organisational structure
is an inevitable consequence of the technologies employed, or the
size of the organisation, ideologies and values play a significant role
in the design of organisations. Class-based values and assumptions,
notions of the nature of types of personnel, varieties of
management principles, or organisational imperatives influence
organisational structure at both conscious and subconscious levels.

Burrage has described the moral and ideological bases of
organisational structure with respect to British public corporations –
the BBC, British Airways, Central Electricity Generating Board, the
nationalised industries, etc. He remarks that these are some of the
largest organisations in the world, and that they were established in
an 'intuitive' manner, based upon a professional model or ideal.
This model contained certain valued elements – a relatively fixed
sphere of operations, a 'moral unity' and identity, and a
considerable degree of autonomy (Burrage, 1973, p.259). The really
significant point about the choice of structure of these enterprises is
that the choice of the professional ideal as a model for
organisational design reveals the considerable impact of cultural

ideological factors. The form of the public corporation, Burrage argues, 'expresses, in part at least, a cultural preference, especially as, by contrast with the French, Italians, Swedes and others, they seem to have been very consistent in this respect' (Burrage, 1973, p.253).

The importance of cultural factors in determining organisational structure has also been shown by Hinings and Foster in their investigation of the structure of Church organisations. They remark that their model of the determinants of church ' "structure" . . . is essentially a goal model giving causal priority to the purposes, *belief systems* and aims of the organisation' (Hinings and Foster, 1973, p.102, our emphasis). The point is also made by Thompson (1973).

If organisational structure is based upon cultural and ideological assumptions and preferences it also communicates these to organisational employees. Of course this communication is mediated by the way in which work and control are designed and organised, and by the orientation and definitions of members. But we must remember that members' organisational experiences – their rewards, delights, achievements, deprivations and frustrations – carry meanings for members. The experience of work and control are especially important socialising influences. It is from their treatment within organisations that members gain an understanding of the value placed on them by senior management (see Fox, 1974, and Nichols and Armstrong, 1976).

Chapter 13

Organisational cultures

Culture, write Eldridge and Crombie,

is a characteristic of all organisations, through which at the same time, their individuality and uniqueness is expressed. The culture of an organisation refers to the unique configuration of norms, values, beliefs, ways of behaving and so on that characterise the manner in which groups and individuals combine to get things done. The distinctiveness of a particular organisation is . . . manifested in the folkways, mores, and in the ideology to which members defer, as well as in the strategic choices made by the organisation as a whole (Eldridge and Crombie, 1974, p.89).

From the point of view of senior organisational members it is important that new organisational members become committed to the formal supportive organisational culture, and therefore amenable to organisational control, oriented towards organisational rewards, involved in organisational identities and groups. This commitment can be achieved by two interlocked processes: selection and socialisaton. Organisational selection can be seen, to a great extent, as a search for candidates who display some degree of anticipatory socialisation. As Merton notes: 'For the individual who adopts the values of a group to which he aspires but does not belong, the orientation may serve the twin functions of aiding his rise into that group and of easing his adjustment after he has become part of it' (Merton, 1957, p.265). Furthermore there is a relationship between successful organisational socialisation once a recruit joins the organisation and the prior selection of candidates who show preparedness to accept the values of the organisation, or some previous anticipatory socialisation into them.

A major goal of the organisation's socialisation efforts is to gain the newcomer's acceptance of the organisation's ideology, which once accepted, 'creates a sort of psychological barrier prohibiting the individual's desertion of the organisation' (Van Maanen, 1976, p.88).

A similar point has been made by Sofer in his analysis of mid-career managers (1970). He notes that organisations are people-processing institutions which he defines as institutions which attempt to change the person, to encourage him to define and develop himself in ways that are congruent with organisational interests, and to get him to identify with the values and interests of the senior members of the organisation. (See also Sofer. pp.229–30.)

Organisations contain a variety of cultures, organised around a number of axes. For example, Turner (1971) has described the nature of what he calls 'the industrial subculture', which he defines as the 'distinctive set of meanings shared by a group of people whose forms of behaviour differ to some extent from those of the wider society' (Turner, 1971, p.1). He argues that despite differences between industrial organisations, it is possible to observe certain broad similarities of a sub-cultural sort, which set off the industrial sub-culture from the culture of the larger society. This sub-culture contains both unofficial and official elements: it is the customary and traditional way of thinking and doing things which is, more or less, accepted by all members of the industrial organisation. As Turner notes, it is transmitted by the exposure of new recruits to patterns of evaluation, ways of thinking, forms of language, myths, which they must learn if they are to become competent and confident members of the organisation.

Turner is concerned with a sub-culture which can be observed within industrial organisations. Other writers have remarked on the more specific and discrete culture of professional organisations, particular types of organisation (for example military organisations) or of groups within organisations. It is possible that these various types of organisational culture: of types of organisation, or specific organisations, reflecting their particular history and circumstances, of definite groups within organisations and so on, vary in their dynamics, and in their attitude towards the structure and functioning of the organisation. Some are, presumably, more legitimating than others, though it would probably be a mistake to regard even the most apparently critical organisational sub-cultures as being entirely opposed to the existing structure and activity of the organisation. Nevertheless, a distinction must be drawn between organisational sub-cultures of groups and departments within the organisation – which may, to varying degrees, be antithetical to the activities and priorities of the organisation's elite, or to the hierarchical structure of the organisation – and what may be called the organisational culture, of the sort described by Eldridge and Crombie above, which if it doesn't characterise the organisation as a whole, nevertheless is distinctive of the organisation as a whole, is concerned with the organisation as a whole, and is largely supportive of the organisation and its structure and activity.

Such organisational cultures contain a number of elements. Members of the same organisation, despite their many differences, share a language, ways of thinking and communicating, notions of their organisation, and its relationship with others, values, knowledge and history. It is important to separate, at least conceptually, technical and ideological elements in these cultures, or what passes for relatively neutral knowledge, from sheer evaluation. Speaking of the industrial sub-culture Turner remarks: 'The knowledge held by members of the industrial sub-culture about their work is not disinterested knowledge. It is permeated by value elements. . . . Also the systems . . . contain elements of "ought": at many points they prescribe desirable behaviour, or they offer critera by which it can be judged whether behaviour is desirable or not' (Turner, 1971, p.92). The same mixture of knowledge and evaluation – both of which are ultimately evaluative – characterises organisational cultures.

Socialisation

Newcomers learn mastery of their organisation culture – they 'learn the ropes' – through a process of socialisation. This process exists, Geer *et al.* suggest, in at least four forms. Trainees learn from formal instructors, from peers, from clients or subordinates and from several different groups (Geer *et al.,* 1968). Furthermore, this process can be formal or informal. In some organisations considerable explicit attention is given to induction sessions for new recruits. Even here, however, further (possibly more important) learning will occur outside the formal training. Van Maanen has pointed to the variety of formal organisational processes whereby newcomers learn the ropes – apprenticeship, formal training, induction, probationary periods etc. But most important of all, in understanding how recruits learn the 'ropes' about 'persons, places and things which the trainee thinks relevant to mastering his situation' (Geer *et al.,* 1968, p.230), is the simple fact of the recruits' exposure to the ongoing cultural life of the organisation.

Failure to master it not only makes the recruit look ridiculous (and many organisations have well-established practical jokes which test newcomers' grasp of organisational lore and language), it can cause total personal failure. The recruit is exposed as the 'wrong sort of person', as unable to fit in. Such failure will be attributed to the personal incompetence and intransigence of the recruit.

Van Maanan notes the link between acceptance of organisational culture and involvement in social networks within the organisation. He remarks how the new recruit initially survives the culture shock caused by exposure to organisational culture because of his commit-ment to become a member of the organisation and to establish a career and receive formal organisational rewards. Gradually he begins to establish social relationships with his colleagues, and to value and enjoy these. These relationships not only depend upon his 'normal' grasp and acceptance of the language and culture of the organisation, they also buttress and transmit them. As Presthus has remarked, within organisations

the individual's learned deference towards authority is evoked and interpersonal relations are ordered in ways that honour organisational claims for loyalty, consistence, and dispatch. Organisations are composed of congeries of small groups that have a similar influence on behaviour. They inculcate majority values in their members; they reward compliance and punish those who resist their demands. In many cases, group values contribute to the organisation's manifest goals. In others, they conflict with them' (Presthus, 1978, p.113).

Undoubtedly, acceptance of the organisational culture is not the result simply of exposure. Recruits are encouraged, pressured, rewarded to make them regard the culture and all its elements as normal and sensible. And they are rewarded, formally and informally, for such a commitment. Becker has noted the ways in which commitment to organisational values and identities is influenced by the individual's contributions of time, money, ego, pride etc. These 'side bets' become contingent upon the individual's success (Becker, 1968). The individual's conception of himself can become dependent on his successful mastery of the organisational culture, his competence as an 'old hand', and his establishment of an organisational career. Such commitment is encouraged by the organisation and its structure:

certain organisational conditions ensure the individual's dependency. Hierarchical control of status rewards and resulting status anxiety encourage the cheerful acceptance of existing patterns of distribution. The use of the co-optation principle in appointing successors and the fact that long tenure in a single organisation is now the modal career pattern enhance dependency. Individuals become extremely sensitive to the opinions of their immediate superiors, who control their career chances (Presthus, 1978, p.125).

Of particular importance in achieving mastery of organisational cultures is the individual's aspiration to establish an organisational career. Recruits know that how they are evaluated during their early, training period may have long-lasting effects on their career within the organisation. They soon learn that their preparedness to 'learn the ropes' will have significant career implications. To be labelled as unco-operative or resistant, or as having inflexible, antagonistic attitudes, can be very serious indeed.

As noted by Etzioni and others, organisations vary in their efforts to socialise their recruits into new cultures, and the cultures themselves vary in their concern with extra-organisational activities and interests. While some organisational cultures are entirely parochial, others are concerned with society-wide issues. Furthermore, as Goffman has noted, organisations vary in the extent to which they encompass many or few aspects of members' lives. And this factor too is related to the nature and pervasiveness of the organisation's culture (Salaman, 1974).

Organisational members are ambivalent about their organisational cultures. Sometimes, defensively, they will insist that organisational methods, structure, activities and decisions are not culturally based, but *rational,* deriving from neutral, non-evaluative principles of efficiency (see above). At other times the organisation's way of doing things – the distinctive and discrete culture, is complacently paraded as a source of pride and delight available only to those fortunate and clever enough to have gained entry to the occupation.

This ambivalence is particularly evident during processes of organisational selection. At this time, the selectors are searching for candidates with a predisposition towards, or some anticipatory socialisation into, the organisational culture. This 'match' has important practical consequences. At the same time selection is, increasingly, subject to the 'universalistic' rhetoric of personnel experts, who insist on translating organisational roles into the ostensibly value-free language of work-study and personnel. Such language with its vocabulary of 'skills', personal qualities, 'attainments', educational achievements etc., might seem to be at odds with the process of cultural, or ideological, choice. But the problem is resolved by the translation of cultural items into personal or social qualities. So, despite the apparently rigorous and systematic nature of organisational selection procedures, the really salient qualities derive not from some neutral process of job study, but from a desire to pick recruits with the 'proper', responsible attitudes and appropriate values. Nichols gives an example of the translation of cultural items into personal qualities in his research into managerial ideologies. He asked his respondents what made a good manager: 'the answers given did make one thing quite clear, that "character", "personality" and social skills and personal characteristics in general, were considered to be more important than technical skills. By far the largest category of responses contained references to "leadership" or some supposed aspect of this, like "being firm but fair" or "commanding respect"' (Nichols, 1969, p.127).

Very little data exists on the nature and function of organisational cultures, or their role in processes of organisational selection. However, some illustrations of the translation of cultural items into personal qualities under the legitimating rubric of 'scientific' selection can be drawn from some Open University course materials on selection processes in the British army and Ford. These are elusive processes: implicit and subtle. They are, however, displayed in these materials. We shall consider them in some detail.

The selection of British army officer candidates is remarkably thorough. Selection takes place over three-and-a-half days, and the candidates are put through a number of different sorts of exercise, interview, group discussion and tests. The selecting officers, who work full time on selection, assess the candidates on three major dimensions: training potential, applied ability, and character. Each of these is broken down into constituent elements. Character is composed of eleven elements, including 'coolness', 'sense of urgency', 'military compatibility', 'sense of responsibility', 'liveliness', 'dominance', and others.

These qualities are themselves culturally based and determined. And their interpretative use by the selecting officers shows how they can be employed to isolate and reward cultural qualities.

The qualities are cultural in the sense that the value the officers place on these qualities derives from their conception of the work of army officers, and their responsibilities, authority, tasks, exigencies, etc. As with any job, such values are derived from the culture of the incumbents. Even when, as in this case, the qualities and dimensions are worked on by outside 'experts', they cannot diverge too far from the conceptions and values of current incumbents. For these are the future colleagues of the successful candidates. And too great a divergence would result in candidates being selected for an army that was different from our own.

The qualities are cultural in that the behaviours, responses, reactions, attitudes and performances which the selectors take to be examples of these qualities, are much more likely to be demonstrated by boys from particular class-cultural backgrounds. The expression 'dominance' doesn't make much sense until one has some idea of the sorts of behaviours and attitudes which the selectors consider operationalise this concept. Such a process of interpretation demonstrates marked cultural preferences, in this organisation and others.[1]

The officers' interpretation of these essentially cultural concepts was, in itself, directly related to their shared culture. Take 'dominance' and 'coolness', for example. The transcripts suggest that the officers felt both these qualities were aspects of a central value in their culture: natural leadership. It seems that officers must be *natural* leaders. Only then can they be sure of the respect and obedience of soldiers. Such a belief has obvious ideological

---

1. We shall draw on recordings of selection interviews, assessment procedures, discussions with the participants. The material was gathered as part of Open University course DT352, *People and Organisations*. The nature and status of the material is discussed in two media booklets contained in the course. Quotations are from the transcripts edited by Mary-Anne Speakman. These materials prove nothing: they are for illustration only. However, I am convinced of the typicality of the processes depicted.

implications: which group is most likely to have this capacity? Furthermore, it is interesting to see the sorts of attitudes and behaviours which the officers felt were evidence of this quality. Consider the following two passages in which the officers consider a successful and an unsuccessful candidate, both of whom had done badly in their 'command tasks' – when the candidate under inspection takes command of the group and attempts to solve a practical problem:

F   I thought this boy yesterday, during his command task when things went wrong and they kept dropping things into the water, remained remarkably cool and he persevered although he couldn't see how to do it – and this we've taken into account already – um, I thought he was remarkably cool and I'd like to go for a good rating.

T   Well I thought he was remarkably cool as well.

F   After all, he's only seventeen – he's what –

T   Seventeen one.

F   – seventeen one, isn't he? That's all.

T   I thought he was remarkably cool . . . (Television Programme 6 or transcript.)

On the other hand, the behaviour of the other candidate (who appeared less congenial to the officers in terms of their culture) was defined very differently. *The manner in which he failed* worried the officers:

L   . . . I feel this is because of a later box (reservation) basically but he couldn't really see his way through that task and he required help from the group and if you recall during the briefing it developed into an open discussion. Er, he hadn't planned his way through that task, he wasn't able to tell the group what he wanted. Er, and I'm afraid it was, er, a rather disastrous affair subsequently.

F   Yes, that was disappointing and I believe probably, um, a lack of coolness –

L   I think this was –

F   – would account for it.

L   It stems basically from that but the evidence that I could produce, had he produced a sensible, practical plan for that task and the answer to me there I'm afraid was No.

F   Obviously when he has time and can think, he can put it down on paper.

T   Oh I – I mean with that brain box, I think he's a planner on paper.

F   But when he has to think under pressure, as he did outside, then there are shortcomings. (Television Programme 7 or transcript.)

The concern for 'coolness' and 'dominance' suggests an emphasis on the candidate's manner of self-presentation, in particular his confidence in his 'natural' superiority regardless of how well deserved it is in terms of knowledge, skill or competence. The important thing is to maintain composure and the impression of confidence – the assumption of a right to lead, regardless of efficiency. Such attitudes are indicative of a certain class-cultural socialisation, one that is closely related to the military culture.

The selection scheme focuses the officers' enthusiasm for a particular sort of social and cultural background which, for them, supplies evidence (or at least increases the likelihood) that the candidate will be compatible with military life, discipline, culture, institutions and traditions. For example:

F   He may have a slight problem later on –
T   – maybe later on, yes, I agree –
F   – passing promotion standards and, er, getting into the Staff College –
T   I feel that –
F   Certainly at lower level –
T   But he's got potential –
F   – he's got plenty of personality and character.
L   I have no doubts in him as a young officer . . .
F   . . . Would you be happy to have him in your corps, Henry?
L   Glad to, sir. (Television Programme 6 or transcript)

and:

T   And he'd certainly fit in.
F   I can see him fitting very happily.
T   And here he fitted in well with the group.
F   Mm.
T   There were no problems there.
F   No, well, I'm happy with an 'Adequate'. I don't think really we ought to go higher than that.
T   **OK.**
F   I don't know, perhaps we could; um, he was a senior chap in the – in the –
T   Well, he is, he's a cadet . . . isn't he, in the corps, I mean he is the senior cadet, he runs the organisation under the orders of the – of the staff.
F   On the other hand, there is no real military background in his family.
T   No military background.
F   Er, his father was a wartime 8th Hussar. He's got a serving uncle in REME. Um –
T   Well, let's go through – 'the high rating should be reserved for those candidates who have – a sound background of military family and/or experience of military life, have a genuine interest and therefore good knowledge of what the military life entails. Give good reasons for and show enthusiasm for wanting a military career, provide positive evidence that they are likely to settle down to a military life.' This is what we're grading for 'Good'. And 'Adequate' is: 'give sound

reasons for wanting a military career; provide positive evidence; likely to settle down'.

F It's – it's jolly nearly good, isn't it? Very nearly good. I think probably not quite enough to qualify.

T Not quite. . .

F . . . He mixed well with the other chaps in the group, didn't he.

T I think he'd go up and down actually.

F But I can see him conducting conversations with –

T Oh yes.

F – people senior to himself and people outside the services as well – can't you?

L I think he – he accepts that degree of thickness because, um, he showed himself to be quite flexible actually and he was never dogmatic.

F Can you, can you see him earning the respect of soldiers?

L Oh, very much so.

T Oh, yes.

F There's no doubt –

C Oh, yes –

F So can I . . . (Television Programme 6 or transcript.)

The selectors *use* the selection scheme to achieve the result they favoured in terms of their shared officers' culture. Very similar behaviours produced by desirable (i.e. compatible) and undesirable (incompatible) candidates were treated very differently. The inevitable ambiguity of the selection concepts was used to restrict, or magnify, the implications of failure or weakness, to achieve the desired outcome. An uncongenial background which gave rise to (and in this particular case was related to) behaviours and attitudes which could be regarded as incompatible with the officers' emphasis on a sense of natural superiority, unfaltering confidence and assured social manner, was defined as follows:

C . . . Travel to and from school prevents him taking part in many extramural activities there and he has not had the opportunity to visit foreign countries. He is not gregarious by nature, events in the world seldom interest him and he is limited for awareness.

T I agree, I must say, I found him very narrow actually.

F Did you take into account a certain amount of voluntary service he did?

T Yes.

F Particularly as it was organised by the school.

T Mm, and the environment and so on and so forth but still with – I thought with the current affairs score as well. (Television Programme 7 or transcript.)

F Right, liveliness. You're both 'Limit' there. Er –

T I – I –

F   – and I agree with you too.

T   Yes, I thought he was a bit dull, I must say.

L   He wasn't lively in the group situation, he couldn't overcome his – his – his, um, inherent shyness and – and lack of cool.

T   And it came out both in face to face – certainly in my interview – and in the group situation more like John's.

C   Mm. As far as the interview was concerned, he would speak to him but he didn't really contribute anything very lively at all –

F   There was no sparkle.

C   No, no sparkle I'm afraid.

L   He – he's had a very narrow life I'm afraid. (Televison Programme 7 or transcript.)

These passages can be seen to illustrate the subtle and elusive manner in which the design, interpretation, utilisation and application of selection systems, and their outcomes, relate to and derive from the shared culture of the selectors. We have looked in some detail at these processes among British army officers for they are only evident in the details of discussion, but we must remember that they are common to all organisations. The officers show a cultural preference for certain qualties and social backgrounds which to them suggest a compatibility with military institutions, values and traditions. And they demonstrate a predilection for candidates who display the behaviours and attitudes which they regard as evidence of natural leadership, untroubled superiority and a sympathy for a highly stratified organisational life. The officers' use of the selection scheme is informed by their common 'knowledge' of the necessary qualities of an army officer and their common culture.

The significance of organisational, cultural values in selection processes is also most evident in recordings of selection interviews and assessments in Ford.[2] The Ford selectors are concerned with the following qualities: 'communication, social skills, and in that I mean the ability to adapt behaviour to industrial circumstances and flexibility, motivation, attitude towards industry, realism of career aspirations, general level of intelligence' (Transcripts, 3, p.14).

The Ford selectors' description of the qualities of the successful candidate reflect their conception of their employing organisation, and themselves. These are cultural statements since such conceptions derive from the shared beliefs and knowledge of committed members of the company:

Well I personally am looking for, first of all, the ability to get things done, but quickly, and obviously this requires a level of

---

[2] These quotations are taken from transcripts of recorded interviews between discussions with Ford Managers and graduate recruits. They were gathered as part of *People and Organisations*.

general intelligence which is not necessarily, doesn't necessarily have
to be a very high IQ rating but has to be a level of general
intelligence which is consistent with the sort of job situation a
graduate is going to experience. The individual has to be ambitious,
he has to have drive, he has to be able to get on with people and
that tends to be the sort of phrase which is used over-frequently by
lots of people, not only in industry but elsewhere. He has to be able
to get on with people in the sense that he has to be able to persuade
them to do things which they may not want to do. He has to be
able to adapt his behaviour, in other words he has to be flexible but
has to have perseverance . . . In terms of personality an
individual . . . has to have the capacity for hard work, to attack the
grimble as well as the exciting work, he has to be able to use his
initiative, he has to be what I like to call a self-starter. . . . The guy
obviously has to be motivated towards industry (Transcript 2,
p.18).

These analyses reflect the culture and self-conceptions of
members of the organisation. It is only necessary to compare these
attributes with those of the successful army officer, to realise that
the considerable difference reflects more than differences of
structure and activity between the two organisations.

The Ford selectors were themselves quite aware of the importance
of a predisposition towards, or a commitment to, the values and
priorities of their organisation:

. . . what's important for us when we're interviewng candidates is
to look for people who are, have their minds made up and have
genuine reasons for wanting to work in the sort of company that
we are. And the sort of activity they say they want to work in, or
what goes with working in this sort of business environment; and
what we found in the past is that people who aren't generally
motivated to work in the sort of, in industry, but who eventually
join us through one reason or another, are less successful than
people who are, who are genuinely motivated. So it's very
important to start looking at the roots of the motivation and the
shape the motivation takes (Transcript 2, p.15).

Elsewhere the selectors emphasise the importance of 'motivation
towards a working sort of environment, he's got to gain satisfaction
from the sort of business environment that we offer' (Transcript 2,
p.17).

When they talk of motivation, the Ford managers are stressing
the importance of the candidate's knowledge of, and sympathy
with, the values and beliefs current within the organisation, and
which lie behind organisational events and decisions. Their scrutiny
of candidates is largely a search for appropriate attitudes and self-
conceptions. These purposes underlay the selectors' questions, and

their reactions to candidates' answers. Consider these questions: 'Do you think your experience both academic and extra-curricular at university, um, is going to help you to become a successful manager in. . .?' 'If Ford were to take you onto a graduate training scheme, um, what sort of ambitions do you have within the company; where do you see yourself, say, in ten years' time?' 'Why did you apply to Ford?' 'Can I go back to your original decision to apply to industry in the first place. Obviously you could have an alternative; you could go to, to other studies, you could go into teaching or whatever. Now, what's the attraction of industry?' 'You said you're interested in finance, and obviously your experience as treasurer would help. What do you think makes a good finance manager? What's his role in the company?' And so on. These questions are attempts to gain information about the candidate's attitudinal and cultural predilections. Is he going to be compliant to organisational reward systems? Will he fit into the cultural system of the organisation? Will he find the organisation's values congenial? Will the current managers find his attitudes and priorities appropriate?

The selectors are looking for candidates who show an ability to internalise and respect the reactions of others – who show a quality of *self*-control within the constraints of organisational policy and culture. Such candidates will *anticipate* the demands made of others and censor and regulate themselves:

self analysis is probably the most important, um, because we ask, ask a lot of questions about why do you think you, you'll be suitable for the particular activity you said you'd be most interested in, um, what changes would you make to your life to date, um, why do you think you're good at various things, why have you participated in the social activities (Transcript 2, p.14).

The managers emphasised that this capacity to accept and internalise the moral principles of the organisation was critical in later success:

We found, in looking at the people who leave us, graduates who leave us, that a number of people leave us because they're disillusioned with industry and the sorts of things it means. And they have done it because basically we've been bad at selecting them, perhaps because they're people who really weren't the sort of people who could survive in an industrial environment. They weren't really keen on industry but perhaps the monetary rewards, for example, were important to them and they have just not been able to adapt, and it has been a traumatic experience for both them and us when they've left (Transcripts 2, p.20).

Later, the same manager adds: 'There's no point in someone joining a firm and not being prepared to work with the things that make that firm successful' (Transcripts 2, p.21).

The candidates were well aware of the importance of demonstrating their sympathy with the organisation's culture. To a considerable extent they defined their biographies and preferences in terms of what they felt to be the company's major moral preferences. Such processes are very common. One interviewee remarked: 'You try and come across as yourself but whilst submitting that you're trying to sell yourself to that individual company. Different companies have different approaches; you try to sell yourself to that' (Transcript 2, p.23). Later, the same candidate remarks: 'I'm talking to people here who are representatives of the system and therefore I ought to bias my argument along those (conservative) lines. And I think I was guilty of doing that actually' (Transcript 2, p.24).

These quotations illustrate, with reference to a very different organisation, the same processes that are evident in the army material: organisational selection processes and decisions reflect the culture of the selecting organisation. This is not an accidental or peripheral feature of selection: it is basic to it. Despite the use of apparently neutral, scientific concepts and procedures; when responsible organisational personnel are entrusted with the critically important job of recruiting new members to the organisation they attempt to ensure that the people they select will, as a result of their sympathy with, knowledge of, and some degree of commitment to, the organisation's culture, be congenial colleagues, and reliable employees.

We can see, as Sofer remarks, that processes of mutual selection and rejection take place between organisational representatives and applicants (or recruits) for middle level organisational positions. These processes, which we have illustrated with materials from two organisations, constitute efforts to reduce discrepancies between organisational members and organisational cultures. Senior management, Sofer maintains, have a notion of what constitutes a 'right' or 'good' sort of person, or orientation. Once within the organisation, new members find they are exposed to systematic efforts to mould and structure their attitudes, values and identities. Such efforts continue throughout members' organisational careers. These processes frequently reinforce earlier experience. And the values and attitudes in question follow the individual's existing predispositions. Exact content – language and myths – might be specific to the organisation. But the basic values of organisations, argues Presthus, follow directly extra-organisational values:

'Socially validated beliefs and behaviour are instilled in the young through the anxiety-conformity-approval syndrome. In this way "culturally defined and interpersonally imposed patterns of behaviour come to motivate human beings as imperiously as biologically determined requirements" (Miller and Shanson, 1958,

*p.55). This process, moreover, persists throughout life as the
socialization role of the family is reinforced by the small group, the
school, and the church. Success now requires extended university
training, and such training is the prerogative of middle-class
families who employ child-rearing practices that give their children
the inside track by emphasizing striving, punctuality, and the
suppression of unprofitable emotions. These attributes prove
functional in big organisations, now among the main sources of
mobility status and prestige. As a result, those who possess these
attributes assume power and tend to replace themselves with men
who reflect their own image. In such ways the socialization process
is tuned to the demands of modern society and its organisations for
consistency, conformity, and the muting of conflict (Presthus, 1978,
p.112).*

It would be misleading to imply that organisations consist of one
major cultural system which is shared by all members. The
quotations from Strauss *et al.* earlier demonstrated an important
feature of organisations: the *variety* of competing cultures which
co-exist within any organisation. Elger has noted the significance of
competing conceptions and utilisations of the organisational goals –
which operate, as was noted earlier, as an overall legitmating
symbol. Understanding organisational members' attempts to protect
and advance their interests within the organisation, Elger notes,
'requires consideration of . . . those overt strategies, involving
explicit reference to some version of the organisational goal, by
which members may defend or advance their interests in organisational bargaining' (Elger, 1975, p.101).

Versions of the organisational goals may differ very considerably,
with each competing group insisting on its prerogative to define and
achieve the essential organisational objective. And organisational
cultures may reflect the different, and often conflicting, conceptions
and moralities of organisational specialities (research, sales,
engineering), disciplines, regiments, wards, departments, and so on.

Organisational cultures contain more than mere morality and
conceptions of persons and purpose. They contain knowledge.
Various accounts of inter-organisational cultures have emphasised
their close relationship with members' knowledge of the nature of
the organisation, its personnel, objectives, clients and processes.

For example, Sudnow, in his account of the organisational
knowledge and culture of Public Defenders in the USA, notes how
they use and apply the penal code in the light of their 'knowledge'
of the nature of typical crimes and typical criminals. Sudnow calls
normal crimes

*those occurrences whose typical features, e.g. the ways they usually
occur and the characteristics of persons who commit them (as well
as the typical victims and typical scenes), are known and attended*

to by the PD. For any of a series of offence types the PD can provide some form of proverbial characterisation. For example, burglary is seen as involving regular violators, no weapons, low-priced items, little property damage, lower class establishments, largely negro defendants. . . . A major task in socialising the new PD deputy attorney consists in teaching him to recognise these (normal, familiar and typical) attributes and to come to do so naturally. The achievement of competence as a PD is signalled by the gradual acquisition of professional command not simply of local penal code peculiarities and courtroom folklore, but, as importantly, of relevant features of the social structure and criminological wisdom (Sudnow, 1973, pp.351–3).

Bittner's study 'The police on skid row' (1973) supplies further examples of the ways in which organisational cultures contain knowledge as well as morality: knowledge of what members are *really* meant to be doing, of the nature of their colleagues and their clients. Like army officers and Ford managers and members of other organisations, such shared organisational knowledge constitutes a significant bond between organisational members, as well as reflecting, in non-evaluative form, the preferences and philosophies of members. This is also true of organisational sub-cultures. When 'informal' work groups, such as those studied by Roy (1973) and Roethlisberger and Dickson (1964), reward and value some behaviours, and disapprove of others, or when they 'bend' the rules, 'fix' the rate, ignore clearly stated rules, avoid regulations or procedures, they do so in the light of their knowledge of the organisation, its purposes and nature. While management may proclaim that the organisation is a unitary, unified enterprise committed to the achievement of all members' needs, lower level members' knowledge of the place and events in it confirms their 'sub-cultural' moralities.

Chapter 14

Organisational ideologies

Selznick has noted that

Among the many and pressing responsibilities of leadership, there arises the need to develop a Weltanschauung, *a general view of the organisation's position and role among its contemporaries. For organisations . . . the search for stability and meaning, for security, is unremitting. It is a search which seems to find a natural conclusion in the achievement of a set of morally sustaining ideas, ideas which lend support to decisions which must rest on compromise and restraint (Selznick, 1966, p.47).*

This chapter will consider these 'morally sustaining ideas', and will attempt to isolate some recurring and pervasive constituents. Organisations persist, Katz and Kahn argue, because people are induced to become members, and because, as members, they accept their expected activities and duties. How is such acceptance achieved? Why is it that members of organisations accept the inevitability or morality of their location within hierarchic and inegalitarian structures?

Recognition of the ways in which higher authorities develop mechanisms intended to sustain organisational activities which match their priorities must . . . be coupled with an assessment of the knowledge and resources deployed in such strategies, appreciation of the strategies employed by lower participants in response to such managerial initiatives, and the practical limits to recalcitrance which the elite will tolerate before disbanding the organisation (Elger, 1975, p.99).

Many of these issues have been discussed earlier. It is important to stress, with Elger, the real power and sanctions which lie behind organisational ideologies. It is also necessary to consider the ideas and themes which characterise these processes of ideological control – never losing sight of the fact that ideological domination is extremely important but is not in itself responsible for obedience within organisations. The power of those who own and control organisations (which is confirmed and buttressed outside the organisation) is also crucial. (See Rose, 1975, pp.243–50.)

Clearly, any consideration of the 'knowledge' values and ideas which make up the justifying ideologies in all sorts of employing organisations will have to occur at a general level. The precise ideas which are employed to justify the nature and operation of hospitals, armies, civil service departments, universities, banks, factories, etc. will vary, depending on the culture of the organisation concerned. Nevertheless, there are some very definite ideas which, if not common to all organisations, recur with marked frequency, in various guises. And it is these common elements of organisational ideologies which we will now consider.

1. Structuralism

The basic feature of the structuralist theme is a simple one: the way in which organisations are structured is beyond choice. Structure is simply the consequence of the necessary application of modern, scientific, rational principles, and of outside forces which are beyond anyone's control. Organisational positions and jobs are similarly the result of neutral principles of management. The function of management itself is defined as an expert function, with managers operating as referees of a variety of competing demands and pressures. Management, administration, hierarchy, are simply technical activities, politically neutral.

Far from being a source of inequality, organisational structuring is presented as the elimination of personal capriciousness, bias and arbitrariness. The systematic, scientifically based establishment of organisational structures and procedures removes the irrationality of personal responses and prejudices, in just the same way as the application of sacred canons of administrative and organisational theory eliminates the traditionalism and despotic, particularistic, idiosyncratic quality of pre-scientific organisations.

Within organisations, the argument runs, people are allocated positions on the basis of their expertise, achievements or knowledge. Since all middle and senior jobs are now defined as expert (including management itself), incumbents of these jobs are defined as having expert knowledge. This is the justification for personal location within organisations: expertise. Such knowledge of course must be *achieved* by the incumbent. The knowledge itself is complex and mysterious, frequently involving the mastery of a new language. Gaining the knowledge is a tough, competitive and demanding process, requiring more than average amounts of intelligence. Once it has been gained, therefore, it is, in itself, a sign of the moral worth of those who hold it. Organisational compensations must be distributed in accordance with personal achievement. This is the ideology of achievement, which, as Habermas remarks, now legitimates professional or organisational success in terms very similar to those used to justify market success in previous eras (Habermas, 1976, pp.381–2)

Offe has recently exposed the ideology of achievement to rigorous critique. In contemporary capitalist society, the system of 'offical self-imagery and self-explanation is dominated by the concept of the achieving society' (Offe, 1976, p.11). Offe bases his critique on three arguments: first, that the actual distribution of life chances is at variance with occupational work, since classes, economic power, racial and sexual factors and the economic system play a hugely significant role in 'affecting and regulating the constitution, let alone the exercise, of individual abilities' (Offe, 1976, p.134). Secondly, Offe points to the way in which the fetish norm of productivity (which is related to the emphasis on achievement as a basis for social and moral worth) overwhelms alternative bases and objectives of production. Thirdly, Offe argues that development of bureaucratic structures and procedures, and technologically-based and dominated work, reduces the validity of the norm of achievement, since these, and other developments (of the sort described earlier as designed to reduce *discretion*) also serve to reduce the need for, and reliance on, the achievement principle.

Despite these alterations in the objective bases of the achievement principle, Offe argues that the idea of societal or organisational position and rewards being based on achievement, retains its salience. This is an ideological significance: 'it is turning into a disciplinary technique which rewards loyalty to the dominant interests and forms of life. It perpetuates cultural divisions and creates and stabilises the appearance of an "objective" or "technical" legitimacy of organisational hierarchies' (Offe, 1976, p.138).

The location of individuals within organisational hierarchies is presented as a consequence of their achievements in gaining complex and relevant expertise and knowledge, knowledge which is required for the difficult, technical job of management and administration: i.e. the technical aspects of the work, plus the surveillance, directing and controlling of subordinates.

Another important element of organisational ideologies stresses the neutrality and inevitability of the organisation's environment, and the inevitability of hierarchic organisations. Hierarchy is presented as necessary for efficiency; to reduce hierarchy would be to risk 'anarchy' and chaos. No doubt many – possibly most – organisational employees accept this argument to some extent.

The pressures to accept the inevitability of hierarchical, inegalitarian organisational structures are very considerable. As Fox has remarked, if subordinate members of organisations accept – to some extent – the principles on which the work organisation is constructed and the conventions by which management operates it, this must be seen in the light of the fact that

the values of wealth, position, and status shape much of the content of public communication in newspapers, magazines, radio,

*television, advertising, public relations, education and training, all
of which manifest either explicitly or implicitly these dominant
ideas and assumptions (about the design of work, the structure of
organisations, and the distribution of organisational rewards) (Fox,
1974, p.17).*

Nichols and Armstrong (1976) describe, in empirical terms, the
point made by Fox: that while many members may not grant
complete legitimacy to hierarchical, inegalitarian organisational
structures, they regard it as something which just *is*, as they put it.
Something which is an inevitable – and unpleasant – fact of life.
This reflects fatalism as much as legitimacy. Fox stresses that when
employees accept their organisational structure (and their position
within it) they do so not as a result of free choice, but because they
are aware of the power of their employers and because 'their social
environment induces them . . . to see it as "natural", "realistic",
and "only to be expected"' (Fox, 1974, p.18). Nichols and
Armstrong illustrate these tendencies in their study. They remark:

*These workers can see imperfections, illogicalites, differences in
living standards, can even think sometimes of better societies. What
they lack is the faith and certainty that these better societies are
possible: that the differences in living standards could ever be overcome; that the illogicalities are illogical, that the imperfections are
imperfect. They lack knowledge (Nichols and Armstrong, 1976,
p.58).*

In short, what I have called *structuralism* is a body of
interrelated ideas – some of which have been discussed earlier in the
book – which assert that: (*a*) The structure of organisations
(especially the basic features of differentiation, hierarchy and control) is neutral, beyond choice, and inevitable. To break the
management and administrative laws that assert the necessity for
hierarchical organisations would be to plunge the organisation into
inefficiency. (*b*) Many aspects of organisational life are the result of
the organisation's environment – especially the market. This is seen
as a natural force over which the organisation has no say. It is just
there. If market events mean a reduction in demand for a product,
and therefore redundancies, or the need to install new technologies
or whatever, these events are beyond control. (*c*) The position of
people within the organisation is based on their achieving mastery
of organisationally relevant and valuable knowledge and expertise.
The implication of this for subordinates is clear: their lowly status
is their responsibility, their own failure. Finally, (*d*) organisational
structure, and positions within it, are beyond politics in that they
involve on the one hand the elimination of personal, arbitrary
'irrational' decisions and preferences, and impose the equitable
principles of universalism, science and calculation, and on the other
hand, consist of the expert and rational application of technical

rules to complicated matters of organisational process, or structure. Both the structure of the organisation, and the nature of senior positions within it, are seen as direct features of social progress. The fact that employees have little if any control over their work, their product, their activities and objectives is presented as the embodiment of reason, but a reason which means submission to the facts of life (Marcuse, 1972, p.23). 'The efficiency of the system', writes Marcuse, 'blunts the individual's recognition that it contains no facts which do not communicate the repressive power of the whole' (p.23). And he adds that this suggestion is the result not of the laws of physics (or engineering, or management) but of society.

2. Psychologism

When the structure of organisation is regarded as the result of neutral principles and pressures (not ideologies and interests), events within the organisation, and individuals' positions and experiences, must be seen as the result of members' attitudes, abilities and competence. The structure of the organisation is given; therefore what must be changed, if change is desired or necessary, is members' behaviours. This excessive emphasis on the individual as responsible for organisational performance, I call *psychologism*.

It is not hard to see the ideological advantages that follow organisational efforts to define the nature of the organisation, and levels of performance, as a result of individuals' qualities, strengths, abilities and training, at the expense of a consideraton of the basic structural features of the organisation. As Argyris notes, it is highly convenient, when things go wrong, for management to think that 'the fault lies in the employees (not in the company, management's leadership, management controls, and human relations programs). It is the *employee* who must be changed' (Argyris, 1957, p.143). This sort of psychologism involves a consideration and treatment of organisational personnel as though they were *objects*, or *resources*, entirely amenable to the same sort of 'rational' measurement and utilisation as is applied to work processes, techniques and materials.

Psychologism is ideological not only in that it encourages the translation of structural features and problems into personal qualities of commitment, motivation, ability etc. (and therefore avoids any questioning of the nature, efficiency and justice of the organisation's structure), but also in that it exposes the individual to pressures to change himself in line with organisational realities. So that the individual is encouraged to regard himself as an organisational resource, and one which must be 'polished', adjusted and trained to fit his position. As Sofer remarks, within organisations there are efforts to

alter the person, to encourage him to define and develop himself in a particular way in line with what are considered to be the interests of the employing organisation, to get him to adopt the values and purposes of the organisation (senior management) as his own, to give these priority over certain other life interests (Sofer, 1970, p.37).

Sofer's book is a useful account of these processes: recruitment, selection, induction, appraisal counselling, training etc.

Organisational members are encouraged to see themselves as organisational resources which require constant scrutiny and adjustment. As a manager remarked of his attitude towards a lengthy management training course: 'I, I, treated it as, are we going to finishing school to get polish because I've been in the commercial environment say for two years and I thought I knew a lot about it, so I thought, well, I'm going there, they're going to polish me up, finish me off, ah, mm, I've learnt something.'[1]

The importance of such courses for influencing members' attitudes and motivation must be stressed. Training occupies an increasing number of expert organisational personnel, and most members will be sent on courses of some sort at some stage of their organisational careers. The function of these courses is to adjust organisational members to organisational demands and realities; to encourage members to gain 'insight' into themselves, their colleagues and the organisation ('insight' of a rather limited sort, usually); to inform members about the organisation, and to develop new skills. They achieve insidious control. One manager remarked of a training course he had experienced: 'I think you become more a part of the company after a course like this, you realise the company's future and aims and everything else and you feel more involved and go . . . a different way to try and help the company to achieve its aims, now that you've found out what the aims of the company are.' The following exchange shows managers' awareness of the 'correct' reaction to the course. The consultant/instructor asks whether private sessions with one course member had been helpful. He replied:

Manager: 'In the same way that we've been, we've just been saying, I think it's all part and parcel of this relaxing and 'nothing minuted' makes for the much freer exchange of ideas and thoughts and . . .
Instructor: But did you find that you got rid of a lot of perhaps irrelevant ideas, misconceptions and so on?
Manager: Oh, yes, indeed. It took the chips off our shoulders.
Instructor: Which probably might have been piling up over several months because you are somewhat isolated from head office?

---

1. These quotations are taken from transcribed recordings of a management training office and interviews with the participants. These materials were gathered as part of an Open University course: *People and Work* DE 351.

One increasingly common organisational activity which reflects in explicit form this theme of psychologism is management development or appraisal. These schemes are, according to their traditional apologists and advocates, designed to achieve two interrelated objectives: to increase employees' *satisfaction* and their *satisfactoriness,* through the systematic collection of information on members' levels of performance, attitudes, cooperation, integrity, work knowledge etc., and the communication of this information to the manager concerned. It is assumed that members will gratefully accept clear and impartial accounts of their strengths and weaknesses, in their eagerness to learn from this 'feedback' and adjust their behaviour. It is also assumed that the responsibility for levels of performance rests with the individuals concerned – their skills, sensitivity, ability, knowledge, and that since organisations are consensual goal-directed phenomena, it is only necessary to redirect individual members' activities and targets to achieve increased organisational efficiency.

Drucker has stated a pervasive conception of the relation between individual and organisation which is basic to those schemes.

Any business enterprise must build a true team and weld individual efforts into a common effort. Each member of the enterprise contributes something different, but they must all contribute towards the common goal. Their efforts must all pull in the same direction, without friction, without unnecessary duplication of effort (Drucker, 1968, p.150).

Management development, appraisal and target setting schemes are intended to achieve these objectives. Objectives are important because, as a manager remarked,

the alternative is disaster without a doubt; if we don't know where we're going, we're in trouble. It's vital to have objectives as a base. Because we know the direction in which we go. It's vital to have objectives because if management has objectives it enforces a very careful appraisal of the suitability of its resources to reach that objective.

Such remarks reflect a main element of *psychologism:* that individual goals and targets can and must be coincident with the organisation's objectives. The achievement of this coincidence of organisational and individual needs and direction is gained through a variety of techniques, including appraisal schemes, training, and job design. It is ideological in that it ignores the complexity, ambiguity and variability of organisational goals, and assumes a highly consensual view of organisations, and places the responsibility for organisational performance on the individual members, thus ignoring the structural aspects of organisations. As Sofer remarks,

*Effective performance is affected not only by one's personal
attributes, but also by the attributes of one's colleagues and the
precise character of one's relations with them. Most organisational
outcomes are a function of group processes and some of one's
attributes manifest themselves in one set of relations but not
another (Sofer, 1970, p.26).*

The main elements of *psychologism* can be briefly stated: The
responsibility for organisational performance is placed on
individual members. Members are moulded and adjusted to fit in
with organisational priorities and goals. Individual qualities and
abilities are emphasised instead of structural arrangements, and the
procedures and language of organisational rationality – calculation,
measurement, specification, feedback, etc., are applied to the
'human resources' of the organisation, which is regarded in such a
way as to eliminate the possibility of structural conflicts of interest
or objective. Such an emphasis on the psychological qualities of
organisational members are allied to a concern for selecting,
measuring, developing and training the 'right' qualities,
commitments, attitudes, values, and personalities, and so achieving
a 'fit' between organisational structures and hierarchies and
individuals.

Psychologism is closely related to another element of organisational ideologies: consensualism, to which we shall now direct our
attention.

3. Consensualism

This is a very common idea: that organisations are consensual
entities, where conflict, when it occurs, is the result of the
pathological psychologies of members – their incompetence or
recalcitrance – or of communications problems. Despite the
differentiation and specialisation that characterises organisations
they are presented to their members as unified and unitary
phenomena – the interests of the organisations are the interests of
all – where harmony must prevail, unless disrupted by fools or
knaves. As Fox remarks,

*To the extent that they convince their employees their job is made
easier; to the extent that they convince the public they gain
sympathy whenever their policies are challenged by their workers.
Finally, the propagation of the idea that the interests of the rulers
and the ruled are identical helps to confer legitimacy on the regime
(Fox, 1971, p.126).*

These remarks need not be restricted to industrial organisations:
they have a more general application.

The propagation of consensualism usually centres around some
statement of the overall organisational goal and its general utility

and neutrality. The attainment of this goal is presented as benefiting all organisational members, and conflicts between members as resulting not from any structural or endemic conflict of interests or ideology (for how can anyone fail to understand that organisational structure and hierarchy is inevitable and necessary for efficiency?), but from problems of communication, or of attitude.

The idea of consensualism has particular appeal because it has *some* basis in reality. There *are* occasions when the activities of an organisation can be seen to benefit all members. And even in industrial organisations there is a sense in which the survival of the enterprise is significant for all the members. What is less obvious however is that this survival, or the achievement of genuinely shared objectives, is dependent on the existing structure of the organisation, and the current distribution of rewards, the organisation of control, work, etc. However, the claim of consensualism is used to justify these aspects of organisations.

When conflict and dissension occur, senior members find it hard to understand how subordinate members can persist in their erroneous conception of the organisation. It must be the result of poor communications, or stubborn bloody-mindedness. Hence the emphasis on communications programmes. These are probably more successful with those whose commitment is more assured. The following remarks of a manager on his new orientation after undergoing a management course illustrate the expected response:

we have got a lot broader concept on what we are trying to achieve. Um, we have seen what head office is trying to achieve and they have brought us into their circle say for us to help them achieve it. Before we were just engineers doing a particular piece in a particular field. Um, outside the circle of head office. . .

Another manager felt that his conversion to a more responsible perspective could justify the admission of some previous doubts:

I've found that a lot of things that have been brought up I've had put to me before. And when it was originally put to me some years ago, I was, had a tremendous resistance to change. I fought it. I was down at the bottom and management were pushing me and the accountants wanted these figures and someone else wanted this done and I had to learn everything you've been teaching us.

His colleague added: 'this awareness of what's going on, ahmm, does help you feel involved, you know what the company's doing, you've got more involvement in the company. It's not brain washing, it's, ahmm, it's an interest, you know'.

Members who see their interests as being in conflict with the organisation's are less likely to find such instructional sessions motivating and reassuring. On the contrary, Argyris has suggested that they may feed the very resistance they are designed to reduce: 'if the employees feel a basic conflict of interest between management and themselves, if they feel, for any reason, that they cannot trust management, then it is possible that the communications programmes used by management may serve to increase these feelings rather than decrease them' (Argyris, 1957, pp.143–4). For an example of this process, see Beynon, 1973, pp.277–9.)

Finally, it is important to note that this rather bland view of organisational life; astructural and ahistorical (and unempirical in its dismissal of the easily apparent fact of organisational conflict) is not restricted to senior members of organisations. It is also evident in writings of some organisation theorists. Hyman and Fryer have pointed out that many writers on organisations appear to have identified with management's interest in achieving the smooth, continuous and efficient co-operation of all employees in the achievement of the official organisational goals, ensuring obedience and maximising performance (Hyman and Fryer, 1975, p.157).

4. Welfareism

I use this expression to refer to the various practices whereby senior members of organisations attempt to engage subordinates' commitment through the apparent delegation of authority and decision-making, the enlargement or enrichment of jobs, or other deliberate deviations from conventional organisational principles of work design or control. Child has noted, in his useful review of British Management Thought (1969) that 'in much human relations writing a form of neo-paternalism stood together with slogans of "participation", and even of democracy', and goes on to argue that the pervasiveness of this sort of human relations thinking was simply because it ' . . . appeared to afford the best method of maintaining, and even extending, control, managerial control in the new (full employment) situation' (Child, 1969, pp.125–6). The same point has been made by many writers and Trade Unionists: much if not all moves to participation, job-enrichment, etc. represent managerial solutions to problems of employee motivation, and hence control, rather than anything else. (See Nichols, 1976; and Nichols and Beynon, 1977.)

Welfareism of various sorts is applied to organisational members of all levels. Middle-level organisational careers can be seen as involving high levels of welfareism as successful careerists receive (and expect) even greater amounts of organisational attention and privilege. Furthermore organisations typically seek to persuade their career members that their interests and futures will be well and fairly protected and advanced by their all-seeing, ever benevolent, employer.

Once again the transcripts quoted earlier supply some nice

illustrations of typical management attitudes towards current personnel ideas such as democratic management, participation etc. First a delightful statement, from a manager on the course, on the advantages (in control terms) of the 'personal touch':

if the managing director lets it be known that he can be spoken to then the guy can say I've got a problem I'd like to see you, and he can say right I'll make an appointment for you. People need that sort of contact with management. If they don't get it, if they feel isolated, a 'them and us' situation, they can't get through to see 'them' at all, then you develop tremendous problems.

We may doubt how far this sort of communications exercise might prevent a 'them and us' situation developing (see Fox, 1974, pp.56–62).

The main question for senior members of organisations is described, by a senior manager on the course, as follows: 'how can a manager . . . get optimum performance from staff working for him?' His answer is to consider various 'styles' of management which he distinguishes: *autocratic, laissez faire,* and *democratic.* The interesting thing about his analyses of these styles is that it is clear they are being evaluated in terms of their efficiency at maximising subordinates' performance. They are explicitly considered for their productivity, nothing else. Furthermore, the expressions don't mean quite what they may seem to mean – control is never to be really delegated. The following quotation nicely catches the ideological implications of discussions of participation:

The democratic style of management is where the manager does not completely let the situation go, but where he controls it in a much more participative way. He involves his staff in any areas of decisions that concern them, that would change their working patterns, he will involve them and get their views on the materials to be used, the methods to be used. He would discuss the objectives which he thinks they have as a group in order to achieve whatever the particular task is that they have in hand. He will not allow them to run away on their own, he will carefully bring them back if he feels. . .

Furthermore, not only does democratic management not mean quite what it implies, but managers are advised to employ different styles of management under different situations, in order to maximise efficiency. Once again a quotation from the management course illustrates the calculating way in which various strategies are considered, selected and used: managers are advised to use the various management styles so as to maximise their efficiency and the commitment of their subordinates. Democracy is advocated only so far as it is useful. The senior manager remarks:

*In the system that I am calling democratic management, you use
many different approaches to situations, you don't have a
absolutely stereotype approach to every situation. There are
disciplinary situations where the only answer is to bawl somebody
out. Don't let's believe that you have a soft approach to every
situation. Because that is the demands of that particular situation at
that point in time.*

The main inspiration behind recent interest in 'democratic'
management, or other aspects of current management thinking –
'participation', job enrichment and so on – is, not surprisingly,
quite clear: that within organisations, as we have noted earlier,
principles of organisational structure are increasingly alienating employees. This results in the much-heralded 'problem of motivation'.
The solution to this problem is seen as involving some or all of the
various ingredients of *welfareism*: an emphasis on personal relations
at work, on less onerous and oppressive forms of control, on more
relaxed supervisory methods, on some changes even in the organisation of work – or rather in the combination of work tasks (see
Nichols and Armstrong, 1976; Nichols and Beynon, 1977; Nichols,
1976). The prime objective of these techniques was nicely stated by
an instructor on the management course: it is to get 'inside' the employee, and reactivate a relationship of 'high trust'. The instructor
remarks:

*motivation is not something that's imposed on you, it's not a carrot
that's dangled in front of you and somebody runs around.
Motivation comes from inside you. And it's very important you
understand this. I cannot motivate somebody else, I can only
produce a situation where they become self-motivated.*

The impact of these efforts to re-establish high-trust relations is
probably less than management desires. Their failure only serves to
re-confirm senior members' jaundiced view of the stubborness and
'bloody-mindedness' of subordinate members. But, as Goodrich
notes, 'Control implies initiative; . . . forms of control entirely
initiated from above must be ruled out unless or until they are
shown to involve workers' *activity* as well as *acquiescence*. . . . Real
control of industry cannot be presented like a Christmas-box'
(Goodrich, 1975, pp.254–5).

Nevertheless welfareism constitutes an important element of
organisational ideologies since it seems to show the neutrality of
organisational structures, and the eagerness of senior members to
sacrifice a total concern for organisational efficiency for some increase in the well-being and happiness of subordinate members. In
this way the beneficence of senior members is displayed, and the
inherent unitariness of the organisation demonstrated.

5. Legalism

This idea, which has been mentioned earlier in the book, is the last element of organisational ideologies. Simply, it asserts that members of organisations have legally contracted to sell their skills, labour and commitment to the organisation, and that this contract was fair and equal, and therefore binding. While both parties should be allowed some (similar and equal) freedom to renegotiate or terminate the contract, the existence of the contract puts both parties under definite and fair obligations – the employer to reward the member for his services (the value of which will be calculated by systematic and rational calculations), and the employee willingly and co-operatively to make available his labour, skill and knowledge.

Often legalism is allied with the idea that ownership of the organisation confers 'rights' on the owners – or their agents, managers (see Fox, 1971, p.40). Management's 'right' to manage is founded upon their function as representatives of the ownership, when the organisation has an owner; on their necessary and important function, as expert managers, administrators and experts; and on their personal achievement (see above) in gaining these important organisational roles (upon which the livelihood of all members depends). Employees' obligation to comply with their seniors' requests is based not only on their 'right' to manage or lead, but on subordinates' 'agreement' (which is seen as inherent in the employment contract) to obey instructions. Fox quotes Ross to the effect that

in entering into a contract of employment, the employee legitimises the employer in directing and controlling his activities 'especially in relation to time, place, content and method of work' (Ross, 1969, p.13) and legitimises, too, the employer's use of sanctions if necessary to maintain this obedience (Fox, 1969, p.40).

This is the language of ideology; to describe the employment contract as an arrangement whereby parties with equal resources freely, clearly and self-consciously come to a balanced arrangement whereby one sells to the other control and direction over his labour in exchange for a wage, is misleading in that it ignores the essential imbalance in the arrangement: an imbalance that stems from the unequal power of those who hire labour, and those who sell it. A formalistic conception of the employment contract, which considers only management's right to manage and direct the labour they have 'freely' bought, is in danger of ignoring the numerous ways in which organisational employees seek, by official and unofficial, collective and group, action, to achieve some control over their own work conditions, design, rewards etc., and thus constantly challenge management's rights. The obvious advantages of this formalistic, legalistic view, however, is that it effectively attaches the burden of blame for any deviation or attempted alteration in working conditions or whatever, on the employees, who are defined as having broken a contract they had themselves agreed to (see Hyman, 1972, pp.36–42, 45).

While any change management might wish to achieve – technological change, de-skilling, new work processes, more onerous supervision, redundancies, closure, dismissal or whatever – can be seen either as an aspect of their 'right' to insist on certain standards of performance or behaviour, or of their quite proper search for greater efficiency (or of their need to react to market or political pressures), the employees find that any effort they might make to resist change, or to improve their working conditions, is likely to be seen as a breach of contract, a breach of trust, or a betrayal. Obviously this makes opposition all the more difficult. A good example of this sort of thinking is contained in a letter from R.J. Ramsey, Director of Labour Relations, Ford Motor Co., to striking Ford workers, quoted in Huw Beynon's, *Working for Ford:*

As you know the 1967 wage agreement signed by all trade unions expires next July. Nevertheless the company agreed last October to begin discussion on a new wage agreement. These discussions resulted in a pay package proposal that offered an increase of $7\frac{1}{2}$ per cent to 10 per cent as well as security against lay-off, extra holiday pay and so on. A lot of discussion has surrounded the 'penalty' clause, but there was no 'penalty' in this clause. It was in fact a bonus clause because all it did was offer additional benefits to everybody who kept their word. Most of our employees live by this code. It is only the exception who doesn't and he would not get the benefits (Ramsey, quoted in Beynon, 1973, pp.277–9).

Later in the same letter there are some good examples of some of the other ideological themes we have considered: *structuralism, psychologism, consensualism,* and so on. Indeed it is rare to find a public statement by senior organisational members about the nature of the organisation and its personnel which doesn't employ one or more of these themes. Ramsey remarks at one stage: 'The major concern in our relationship is to provide something that is good for everybody in Ford. . . .'

I have tried to isolate some of the main elements of organisational ideology, and to illustrate these when possible, with remarks from members of organisations. Obviously these quotations are for illustration only. But they serve to give some feel of the ways in which senior organisational members articulate, to each other, the nature of their organisation, their understanding of the nature of the organisation and its personnel. The ideological elements described above probably do not exhaust all possible ideas and values that can be pressed into the service of organisational legitimation, especially since this is now a well-rewarded expert activity. But they cover most of the common themes. The basic notion, and one which is quite remarkably pervasive and well entrenched, is the coincidence of hierarchy and centralisation, and efficiency. This notion is not restricted to industrial organisations, nor is it limited only to overtly capitalist apologists. But the strength and pervasiveness of this idea should not blind us to certain other possibilities:

1. If, as we have suggested, the hierarchic structure of organisations is, to some extent, the result of class-based values, the need for control of an alienated workforce, is based upon class assumptions about the nature of organisational personnel, and their characteristics, then it is surely possible that the general acceptance and 'obviousness' of the link between centralisation and efficiency could also be the product of certain unquestioned assumptions, rather than of any necessary relationship.
2. We must consider just what we mean by efficiency in this context. Efficient for whom, or for what? What values and interests are served by these notions of efficiency? Whose needs are met?
3. Is the link a real one? What is the evidence that centralisation is necessary in large modern organisations? If it seems that work processes and technologies limit the design of organisations then we must consider the interests that lie behind the choice, design and installation of work principles and technologies.
4. If we can find some degree of variation in the degree of centralisation and differentiation, and if this variation does not seem to be related to differences in efficiency (however defined) then we must direct our attention to discerning the nature and determinants of these differences, rather than dismissing them as evidence of some hopelessly impractical traditionalism.

Conclusion

This book has ranged over a wide variety of issues and topics, but it is to be hoped that the diversity of detail has not obscured the major theme of the book – i.e. the political nature of organisational structure and functioning. Essentially, the purpose of this book has been to argue for the inherently conflictful, sectional, and political nature of organisational structure and process, and to attempt to relate these events and processes to certain aspects of the surrounding society – its class nature. This purpose has required constant reference to research and theory from industrial sociology, and, occasionally, elsewhere. And it has required that interest be restricted to employing, or work, organisations. The traditional focus of interest on the fact of organisation itself, regardless of type, which is closely related to the attempt to develop a discreet speciality, with its attendant 'theory', solely concerned with forms or organisation, has been, it is argued, an obstacle to the development of a genuinely sociological approach to work organisations. The history of organisation theory is a striking example of the perils and pathologies of academic specialisation.

The book began by noting that despite much public interest in organisations, and mass media and governmental discussion and theorising about the nature and implications of particular work forms, bureaucratic red-tape, etc., a sociological interest in, and account of, work organisations could not rely simply on the obvious problematics of these phenomena. Certain key issues of considerable interest to sociological theory about organisations were noted: the determinants of organisational structure and process, and the relationship between these and the society within which they occurred. The writings of Marx and Weber were considered for their relevance to a current understanding of work organisations. Despite the important differences between these writers certain common areas of interest were isolated. Both saw organisations as structures of control. Both regarded the organisation of work as inherently concerned with control. Both saw organisational structures as reflecting interests and priorities of powerful groups outside the organisation. Both attempted to delineate the major principle underlying organisational structure.

Most of these notions have been forgotten by more recent

organisation theory, but within the last few years there have been signs of a welcome re-emergence of a genuinely sociological interest in organisations. The main contributors to this development were discussed in Chapter 3.

It is to be hoped that this book will constitute a further contribution to, and support of, this new approach to organisations. By considering the meaning of organisational membership, and the forces, internal and external, that structure that experience (an enterprise which requires reference to the everyday impact of class-based conflicts and interest), this book attempts to de-mystify organisational structure and experience, to assert the simple point that organisations are man-made, and, in their nature and operation, reflect definite interests and values.

Section II of the book was concerned with establishing the main elements – or principles – of organisational structure, and their determinants. A number of classifications of types of organisations were considered, and the heuristic role of such notions as effectiveness, efficiency, and performance was noted. At the risk of overlooking many useful studies which describe significant inter- and intra-organisational structure it was suggested that in order to be able to establish the major elements of organisational structure, and the factors which these revealed, it was useful to regard organisational structure as consisting of three elements: the design of work and of control, and the body of knowledge and ideas which exist within organisations – the organisation culture(s). It was further argued that organisational structure revealed one major feature – the divison between design and execution. A great deal of organisational structure and process could be seen to be closely related to the distinction between those who designed work and control systems, and those to whom these systems were applied, or whose work consisted of executing decisions made elsewhere. Using Fox's distinction between high- and low-discretion work, this aspect of organisational structure was explored. Clearly it relates closely to what other sociologists in other specialist traditions would describe as class distinctions.

Chapter 7 considered possible determinants of this distinction. The explanation in terms of organisation goals was discussed, for example, and some serious deficiencies described. Of particular importance is the argument in terms of organisational technology. It was pointed out that the determinant role of such technologies have been overstated, and that technologies themselves are chosen, designed, rejected, in terms of the interests and assumptions of dominant groups. Choice of technology reflects other priorities and values, often of a class sort. 'Efficiency' and control are tightly linked. To a considerable degree technologies – and organisational structures – are chosen for what are regarded as their control functions and benefits, and for their role in advancing class interests and conflicts.

The following section of the book considered processes of control within organisations. Such control can be exercised in a variety of ways: mechanisms of control, and forms of control, vary considerably, in line with the distinction between high- and low-discretion work. Again the class implications of differences in types of control, and rewards and deprivations associated with types of control (which themselves often constitute rewards or deprivations) was discussed.

It is usual to distinguish certain distinct and opposed forms of control: through formalisation of rules and procedures, or through centralisation of decision-taking, and through delegation to reliable professionals and experts, or through bureaucratic forms. Chapter 10 considered these distinctions, and while again remarking the class implications of the distinctions, went on to argue that while *forms* of control may vary in ways which are highly significant to those involved, this should not be taken to mean that any organisational groups were in any sense free of organisational control of some sort. The apparent autonomy of organisationally-employed experts and professionals was questioned. Even the most privileged members of organisations must (because of their very importance) be reliable. Their 'autonomy' must not carry any risks of serious mis-calculation or misdemeanour.

In this book, organisations are regarded as arenas of conflict and dissension. In view of what has been said about the 'political' nature of organisational structure, and processes of control, it will be clear that such features of organisation will not only reflect conflict (actual or potential), they will constitute objects of conflict and struggle. Such developments are normal within hierarchic, inegalitarian organisations. Nevertheless various mechanisms within organisations serve to disrupt, obstruct and muddle such conflicts, and some of these mechanisms were considered.

Of particular importance in determining the nature, indeed the occurrence, of such conflicts, are the ideas and values which occur within organisations. Organisations are, among other things, structures of knowledge and beliefs, and Section IV looked at some of these ideas, with particular attention to the legitimating or mystifying function of such ideas – or their role in assisting processes of organisational control. The very 'rationality' of organisations is itself highly vulnerable to charges of masking, and advancing, sectional interests in the name of neutrality, science and technology. Also important are organisationally specific cultures which tend to establish 'ways of thinking' which structure and influence individuals' decision-taking, and ensure the reliability of well socialised members of the organisation. Materials from Open

University films on organisational selection were used to illustrate the cultural nature of organisational recruitment, and the implications for processes of 'insidious control'.

The last chapter attempted a brief delineation of some of the main ideas used to buttress organisational structures and inequalities. Again drawing on Open University film transcripts, it was argued that certain well-developed themes occurred with some frequency: structuralism, psychologism, legalism etc.

The book started with a rediscovery of the political, sectional nature of modern work organisations. It argues for a return to the preoccupations of Marx and Weber, and for a re-integration of theory and research from organisation theory and from industrial sociology and the sociology of work. Above all it tries to re-establish the political nature of organisational structure and organisational process. What occurs within organisations, the ways in which work is designed, control applied, rewards and deprivations distributed, decisions made, must be seen in terms of a constant conflict of interests, now apparent, now disguised, now overt, often implicit, which lies behind, and informs, the nature of work organisations within capitalist societies. The book is an attempt to argue against the inevitability of the 'iron cage' of bureaucracy and organisation, to assert that the world of work, and all the deprivations which, for many, are associated with it, is man-made, and reflects definite and sectional interests and values. If we are to make any progress towards alleviating the miseries, deprivations and injustices of work, we must first understand how these are systematic products of larger social conflicts and distinctions.

References

Aiken, Michael and **Hage, Jerald** (1970) 'Organisational Alienation: a comparative analysis', in Grusky, Oscar, and Miller, George A. (eds), *op cit.*, pp. 517–26.

Albrow, Martin (1968) 'The study of organisations – objectivity or bias?', in Gould, Julius (ed.), *Penguin Social Sciences Survey 1968*, Penguin Books, Harmondsworth.

Albrow, Martin (1970) *Bureaucracy,* Macmillan, London.

Allen, V.L. (1975) *Social Analysis: a marxist critique and alternative,* Longman, London.

Argyris, Chris (1957) *Personality and Organisation,* Harper, New York.

Argyris, Chris (1968) 'The organisation: what makes it healthy?', *Harvard Business Review,* **36**, pp. 107–16.

Argyris, Chris (1973) 'Peter Blau', in Salaman, Graeme, and Thompson, Kenneth (eds) (1973), *op. cit.*, pp. 76–90.

Baldamus, W. (1961) *Efficiency and Effort,* Tavistock, London.

Baran, Paul A. and **Sweezey Paul, M.** (1972), *Monopoly Capital,* Penguin Books, Harmondsworth.

Baritz, L. (1975) 'The servants of power', in Esland, Geoff, *et al.*, (eds), *op cit.*, pp. 325–37.

Barnard, Chester I. (1968) *The Functions of the Executive,* Harvard University Press, Cambridge, Mass.

Becker, Howard S. (1968) 'The Self and Adult Socialisation' in Norbeck, Edward, Price-Williams, Douglas, and McCord, William, M. (eds), *The Study of Personality,* New York, Holt, Rinehart and Winston.

Bell, Daniel (1974) *The Coming of Post-Industrial Society: A Venture in Social Forecasting,* Heinemann, London.

Bendix, Reinhard (1963) *Work and Authority in Industry,* Harper and Row, New York.

Benson, Kenneth J. (1977a) 'Innovation and crisis in organisational analysis', *The Sociological Quarterly,* **18**, No. 1, pp. 3–16.

Benson, Kenneth J. (1977b) 'Organisations: a dialectical view', *Administrative Science Quarterly,* **22**, pp. 1–18.

Berle, A.A. and **Means, G.C.** (1932) *The Modern Corporation and Private Property,* Macmillan, New York.

Beynon, Huw (1973) *Working for Ford,* Allen Lane, Penguin Books, Harmondsworth.

Bittner, Egon (1973) 'The police on skid row: a study of peace-keeping', in Salaman, Graeme, and Thompson, Kenneth (eds) (1973), *op. cit.*, pp. 331–45.

Blackburn, Robin (1972) 'A brief guide to bourgeois ideology', in Edwards, Richard C. *et al.* (eds) (1972) *op. cit.*, pp. 36–46.

Blau, Peter (1963) *The Dynamics of Bureaucracy,* University of Chicago Press, Chicago.

Blau, Peter M. (1970) 'Decentralisation in bureaucracies', in Zald, Mayer N. (ed.), *Power in Organisations,* Vanderbilt University Press, Nashville, Tenn, pp. 150–74.

Blau, Peter M. and **Schoenherr, Richard A.** (1971) *The Structure of Organisations,* Basic Books, New York.

Blau, Peter M. and **Scott, Richard W.** (1963) *Formal Organisations: A Comparative Approach,* Routledge and Kegan Paul, London.

Blauner, R. (1964) *Alienation and Freedom,* Chicago University Press, Chicago.

Bosquet, Michel (1977) 'Prison factory', in Bosquet, Michel (ed.), *Capitalism in Crisis and Everyday Life,* The Harvester Press, Hassocks, Sussex, pp. 91–101.

Bowles, S. and **Gintis, H.** (1976) *Schooling in Capitalist America,* Routledge and Kegan Paul, London.

Bradbury, M., Heading, B. and **Hollis, M.** (1972) 'The Man and the Mask: a Discussion of Role Theory,' in Jackson, J.A. (ed.) *Role,* Cambridge University Press, pp 41–64.

Braverman, H. (1974) *Labour and Monopoly Capital,* Monthly Review Press, New York.

Brown, R.K. (1967) 'Research and consultancy in industrial enterprises', *Sociology,* **1,** No. 1, pp. 33–60.

Brown, Richard (1977) 'The growth of industrial bureaucracy – chance, choice or necessity?', in *Human Figurations: Essays for Norbert Elias,* Amsterdam's Sociologisch Tijdschrift, pp. 119–120.

Burns, T. (1967) 'The comparative study of organisations' in Vroom, V. (ed.), *Methods of Organisational Research,* University of Pittsburg Press, Pittsburg, pp. 113–70.

Burns, Tom and **Stalker, G.M.** (1961) *The Management of Innovation,* Tavistock, London.

Burrage, M. (1973) *'Nationalisation and the professional ideal',* Sociology, **7,** No. 2, pp. 253–72.

Child, J. (1969) *British Management Thought,* Allen and Unwin, London.

Child, John (1973a) 'Organisational structure, environment and performance: the role of strategic choice', in Salaman, Graeme, and Thompson, Kenneth (eds) (1973), *op. cit.,* pp. 91–107.

Child, John (1973b) 'Strategies of control and organisational behaviour', *Administrative Science Quarterly,* **18,** No. 1 pp. 1–17.

Chinoy, E. (1955) *Automobile Workers and the American Dream,* Doubleday, New York.

Cicourel, A. (1958) 'The Front and Back of Organisational Leadership' in *Pacific Sociological Review,* Vol. 1 pp. 54–8.

Cicourel, A.V. (1970) 'Basic and normative rules in the negotiation of status and role', in Dreitzel, H.P. (ed.), *Recent Sociology,* No. 2, Macmillan, New York, pp. 4–48.

Clegg, Stewart and **Dunkerley, David** (1977) *Critical Issues in Organisations,* Routledge and Kegan Paul, London.

Cohen, Stanley and **Young, Jock** (1973) 'Introduction', in Cohen, Stanley, and Young, Jock (eds), *The Manufacture of New Social Problems, Deviance and the Mass Media,* Constable, London, pp. 9–11.

Collins, Randall (1975) *Conflict Sociology: Toward an Explanatory Science,* Academic Press, New York.

Crouch, Colin (1977) *Class Conflict and the Industrial Relations Crisis,* Heinemann Educational, London.

Crozier, Michel (1964) *The Bureaucratic Phenomenon,* Tavistock, London.

Dahrendorf, R. (1968) *Essays in the Theory of Society,* Routledge and Kegan Paul, London.

Daniel, W.W. (1969) 'Industrial Behaviour and the Orientation to Work,' *Journal of Management Studies,* 6.

Dalton, Melville (1959) *Men Who Manage,* Wiley, New York.

Davis, Louis E. (1972) 'The design of jobs', in Davis, Louis E., and Taylor, James C. (eds), *op. cit.,* pp. 299–327.

Davis, Louis E., Canter, Ralph R. and **Hoffman, John** (1972) 'Current job design criteria' in Davis, Louis E., and Taylor, James C. (eds), *op. cit.,* pp. 65–82.

Davis, Louis E. and **Taylor, James C.** (eds) (1972), *Design of Jobs,* Penguin Books, Harmondsworth.

Davis, Louis E. and **Taylor, James C.** (1976) 'Technology, organisation and job structure' in Dubin, Robert (ed.), *Handbook of Work, Organisation and Society,* Rand McNally, Chicago, pp. 379–419.

Deutsch, Isaac (1969) 'Roots of bureaucracy', in Milliband, Ralph, and Saville, John (eds), *The Socialist Register,* The Merlin Press, London, pp. 9–28.

Dickson, David (1974) *Alternative Technology,* Fontana/Collins, London.

Douglas, Jack D. (1970) 'Freedom and tyranny in a technological society', in Douglas, Jack D. (ed.), *Freedom and Tyranny: Social Problems in a Technological Society,* Alfred A. Knopf, New York, pp. 3–30.

Dreyfuss, Carl (1952) 'Prestige grading: a mechanism of control', in Merton, Robert K., Gray, Ailsa P., Hockey, Barbara, and Selvin, Hanan C. (eds), *Reader in Bureaucracy,* Free Press, New York, pp. 258–64.

Drucker, Peter F. (1968) *The Practice of Management,* Pan Books, London.

Edwards, Richard C., Reich, Michael and **Weisskopf, Thomas E.** (eds.) (1972) *The Capitalist System,* Prentice-Hall, New Jersey.

Edwards, Richard C. (1972) 'Bureaucratic organisation in the capitalist firm', in Edwards, *et al.* (eds), *op. cit.,* pp. 115–19.

Eldridge, J.E.T. and **Crombie, A.D.** (1974) *A Sociology of Organisations,* Allen and Unwin, London.

X **Elger, Anthony J.** (1975) 'Industrial organisations: a processual perspective', in McKinlay, John B. (ed.), *op. cit.,* pp. 91–149.

Elliott, Philip (1972) *The Sociology of the Professions,* Macmillan, London.

Elliott, Philip (1975) 'Professional ideology and social situation', in Esland, Geoff, *et al.* (eds), *op. cit.,* pp. 275–86.

Esland Geoff, Salaman, Graeme and **Speakman, Mary-Anne** (eds) (1975) *People and Work,* Holmes McDougall, Edinburgh.

Etzioni, Amitai (1961) *A Comparative Analysis of Complex Organisations: On Power, Involvement, and their Correlates,* Free Press, New York.

Fox, Alan (1971) *A Sociology of Work in Industry,* Collier-Macmillan, London.

Fox, Alan (1974) *Beyond Contract: Work, Power and Trust Relations,* Faber and Faber, London.

Fox, Alan (1976) 'The meaning of work', in *People and Work,* an Open University course, Open University Press, Milton Keynes.

Freidson, Eliot (1970) *Professional Dominance: The Social Structure of Medical Care,* Atherton, New York.

Geer, B., Vivona, C., Haas, J., Woods, C., Miller, S. and **Becker, H.** (1968) 'Learning the ropes', in Deutscher, I. and Thompson, E.M. (eds), *Among The People,* Basic Books, New York, pp. 209–33.

Giddens, Anthony (1973) *The Class Structure of the Advanced Societies,* Hutchinson, London.

Goldthorpe, J.H, Lockwood, D., Bechhofer, F. and **Platt, J.** (1968) *The Affluent Worker: Industrial Attitudes and Behaviour,* Cambridge University Press, Cambridge.

Goodrich, Carter I. (1975) *The Frontier of Control: A Study of British Workshop Politics* (with a new foreword and notes by Hyman, Richard), Pluto Press, London.

Gorz, Andre (1972) 'Technical intelligence and the capitalist division of labour', *Telos,* No. 12, pp. 27–41.

Gouldner, A.W. (1954) *Patterns of Industrial Bureaucracy,* Free Press, New York.

Gouldner, A.W. (1955) 'Metaphysical pathos and the theory of bureaucracy', *American Political Science Review,* 49, pp. 496–507.

Gouldner, A.W. (1971) *The Coming Crisis of Western Sociology,* Heinemann Educational, London.

Gross, N., Mason, W.S. and **McEachern, A.W.** (1958) *Explorations in Role Analysis,* Wiley, New York.

Grusky, Oscar and **Miller George A.** (eds) (1970) *The Sociology of Organisations: Basic Studies,* Free Press, New York.

Habermas, Jurgen (1975) 'Technology and Science as 'Ideology'', in Esland, Geoff, *et al.*(eds) *op. cit.* pp. 33–48.

Habermas, Jurgen (1976) 'Theory and practice in a scientific civilisation', in Connerton, Paul (ed.), *Critical Sociology: Selected Readings,* Penguin Books, Harmondsworth, pp. 330–47.

Haddon, Roy (1973) 'Foreword' in Kerr, Clark, Dunlop, John T., Harbison, Frederick, and Myers, C.A., *Industrialism and Industrial Man,* Penguin Books, Harmondsworth, pp. 1–27.

Hage, Jerald and **Aiken, Michael** (1967) 'Relationship of centralisation to other structural properties', *Administrative Science Quarterly,* **12**, No. 1, pp. 72–92.

Hage, Jerald and **Aiken, Michael** (1972) 'Routine technology, social structure, and organisation goals' in Hall, Richard (ed.), *The Formal Organisation,* Basic Books, New York, pp. 55–72.

Hall, Richard H. (1963) 'The concept of bureaucracy: an empirical assessment', *American Journal of Sociology,* **69**, No. 1, pp. 32–40.

Hall, Richard H. (1972a) *Organisations: Structure and Process,* Prentice-Hall, Englewood Cliffs, New Jersey.

Hall, Richard H. (1972b) 'Introduction' in Hall, Richard (ed.), *The Formal Organisation,* Basic Books, New York, pp. 3–11.

Hall, Richard H. (1973) 'Professionalisation and Bureaucratisation' in Salaman, Graeme, and Thompson, Keneth (eds), *op. cit.,* pp. 120–33.

Heydebrand, Wolf (1977) 'Organisational contradictions in public bureaucracies: toward a marxian theory of organisations', *The Sociological Quarterly,* **18**, No. 1, pp. 83–107.

Hickson, D.J. (1973) 'A convergence in organisation theory' in Salaman, Graeme, and Thompson, Kenneth (eds), *People and Organisations,* Longman, London, pp. 108–19.

Hickson, D.J., **Pugh, D.S.** and **Pheysey, Diana C.** (1972) 'Operations technology and organisation structure: an empirical reappraisal', in Azumi, Koya, and Hage, Jerald (eds), *Organisational Systems: A Text-Reader in the Sociology of Organisations,* Heath, Lexington Mass. pp. 137–50.

Hickson, D.J., **Hinings, C.R.**, **Lee, C.A.**, **Schneck, R.E.** and **Pennings, J.M.** (1973) 'A strategic contingencies' theory of intraorganisational power', in Salaman, Graeme, and Thompson, Kenneth (eds), *op. cit.,* pp. 174–89.

Hinings, C.R. and **Foster, B.D.** (1973) 'Organisational Structure of Churches: A Primary Model', *Sociology,* **7**, No. 1, pp. 93–106.

Hood, Stuart (1968) 'The BBC: not so much a corporation, more an attitude of mind', *The (London) Sunday Times Colour Magazine,* July 1968.

Hyman, Richard (1972) *Strikes,* Fontana Collins, London.

Hyman, Richard (1975) *Industrial Relations: A Marxist Introduction,* Macmillan, London.

Hyman, Richard (1976) 'Trade unions, control and resistance', in *People and Work,* an Open University Course, Open University Press, Milton Keynes.

Hyman, Richard and **Fryer, Bob** (1975) 'Trade unions: sociology and political economy', in McKinlay, John B. (ed.), *op. cit.*

Ingham, G.K. (1970) *Size of Industrial Organisation and Worker Behaviour,* Cambridge University Press, Cambridge.

Jaques, Elliott (1972) *Measurement of Responsibility: A Study of Work, Payment, and Individual Capacity,* Heinemann, London.

Kahn, R.L., **Wolf, D.M.**, **Quinn, R.P.**, **Shoek, J.D.**, and **Rodenthal, R.A.** (1964) *Organisational Stress,* Wiley.

Katz, Daniel and **Kahn, Robert L.** (1966) *The Social Psychology of Organisations,* Wiley, New York.

Katz, Fred E. (1973) 'Integrative and adaptive uses of autonomy: worker autonomy in factories', in Salaman, Graeme, and Thompson, Kenneth (eds), *op. cit.,* pp. 190–204.

Kerr, Clark, Dunlop, John, T., Harbison, Frederick, H. and **Myers, Charles, A.** (1973) *Industrialism and Industrial Man,* Penguin Books: Harmondsworth.

Kitsuse, J.I. and **Cicourel, A.** (1963) 'A note on the use of official statistics', *Social Problems,* **11**, pp. 131–9.

Langer, E. (1970) 'Inside the New York Telephone Company and the women of the Telephone Company', in *New York Review of Books,* March 12, pp. 16–24, and March 26.

Lenin, V.I. (1965a) *The State and Revolution,* Foreign Languages Press, Peking.

Lenin, V.I. (1965b) 'The Immediate Tasks of the Soviet Government', in *Collected Works,* **27**, Progress Publishers, Moscow.

Levison, Andrew (1974) *The Working Class Majority,* Coward, McCann and Geoghegan, New York.

Lockwood, David (1958) *The Blackcoated Worker,* Allen and Unwin, London.

Luxembourg, Rosa (1972) 'The role of the organisation in revolutionary activity' in Looker, R. (ed.), *Rosa Luxembourg: Selected Political Writings,* Jonathan Cape, London.

Mackenzie, Gavin (1975) 'Work images and the world of work', in Esland, Geoff, Salaman, Graeme, and Speakman, Mary-Anne (eds), *op.cit.,* pp. 170–85.

McKinlay, John B. (ed.), (1975) *Processing People: Cases in Organisational Behaviour,* Holt, Rinehart and Winston, London.

Mann, Michael (1973) *Consciousness and Action Among the Western Working Class,* Macmillan, London.

Mannheim, Karl (1936) *Ideology and Utopia,* Harcourt Brace, New York.

Mansfield, Roger (1973) 'Bureaucracy and centralisation: an examination of organisational structure', *Administrative Science Quarterly,* **18**, pp. 477–88.

Marcuse, Herbert (1972) *One Dimensional Man,* Abacus/Sphere Books, London.

Marglin, S.A. (1976) 'What do bosses do?', in Gorz, Andre (ed.), *The Division of Labour,* Harvester Press, Hassocks, Sussex, pp. 13–54.

Martin, Roderick and **Fryer, R.H.** (1973) *Redundancy and Paternalist Capitalism,* Allen and Unwin, London.

Marx, Karl (1954) *Capital: A Critical Analysis of Capitalist Production,* **1,** Progress Publishers, Moscow.

Merton, R.K. (1957) *Social Theory and Social Structure,* Free Press, Glencoe, Ill.

Meyer, Marshall W. (1972) *Bureaucratic Structure and Authority,* Harper and Row, New York.

Michels, Robert (1970) 'Oligarchy', in Grusky, Oscar, and Miller, George A. (eds), *op. cit.,* pp. 25–43.

Miller, George, A. (1970) 'Professionals in bureaucracy: alienation among industrial scientists and engineers', in Grusky, Oscar, and Miller, George A. (eds), *op. cit.,* pp. 503–16.

Mills, C. Wright (1940) 'Situated actions and vocabularies of motive', *American Sociological Review,* **5**, pp. 904–13.

Mills, C. Wright (1956) *White Collar: The American Middle Classes,* Galaxy Books, Oxford University Press, New York.

Mouzelis, Nicos P. (1967) *Organisation and Bureaucracy: An Analysis of Modern Theories,* Routledge and Kegan Paul, London.

Nichols, T. and **Beynon, H.** (1977) *Living with Capitalism,* Routledge and Kegan Paul, London.

Nichols, Theo (1969) *Ownership, Control and Ideology,* Allen and Unwin, London.

Nichols, Theo (1975) 'The sociology of accidents and the social production of industrial injury', in Esland, Geoff, *et al.* (eds), *op. cit.,* pp. 217–29.

Nichols, Theo (1976) 'Management, ideology and practice', in *People and Work,* an Open University course, Open University Press, Milton Keynes.

Nichols, Theo and **Armstrong, Peter** (1976) *Workers Divided: A Study in Shopfloor Politics,* Fontana/Collins, London.

Offe, Claus (1976) *Industry and Inequality,* Edward Arnold, London.

Parker, S.R., Brown, R.K., Child, J. and **Smith, M.A.** (1977) *The Sociology of Industry,* Allen and Unwin, London.

Parsons, Talcott (1970) 'Social systems', in Grusky, Oscar, and Miller, George A. (eds), *op. cit.,* pp. 75–82.

Perrow, C. (1961) 'The Analysis of Goals in Complex Organisations' in *American Sociological Review* Vol. **26,** pp. 854–66.

Perrow, Charles (1970) *Organisational Analysis: A sociological View,* Tavistock, London.

Perrow, Charles, (1972a) 'A Framework for the Comparative Analysis of Organisations' in Brinkerhoff, Merlin, B., and Kunz, Phillip, R., (eds), *Complex Organisations and their Environments.* Wm. C. Brown, Dubuque, Iowa, pp. 48–67.

Perrow, Charles (1972b) *Complex Organisations: A Critical Essay,* Scott, Foresman, Glenview, Illinois.

Pettigrew, Andrew M. (1975) 'Occupational specialisation as an emergent process', in Esland, Geoff, *et al.* (eds), *op. cit.,* pp. 258–74.

Presthus, Robert (1978) *The Organisation Society,* St. Martins Press, New York.

Pugh, D.S. (1973) 'Role activation conflict: a study of industrial inspection', in Salaman, Graeme, and Thompson, Kenneth (eds), *op. cit.,* pp. 238–49.

Pugh, D.S. and **Hickson, D.J.** (1973) 'The comparative study of organisations', in Salaman, Graeme, and Thompson, Kenneth (eds) *op. cit.,* pp. 50–66.

Roethlisberger, F.J. and **Dickson, William** (1964) *Management and the Worker,* Wiley, New York.

Rose, Michael (1975) *Industrial Behaviour: Theoretical Developments Since Taylor,* Allen Lane, London.

Ross, N.S. (1969) *Constructive Conflict,* Oliver and Boyd, Edinburgh.

Roy, D. (1954) 'Efficiency and 'the Fix': the Informal Intergroup Relations in a Piecework Machine Shop,' in Lipset, S.M. and Smelser N.J. (eds) *Sociology: The Progress of a Decade,* Prentice-Hall, New Jersey.

Roy, D. (1973) 'Banana time: Job satisfaction and informal interaction', in Salaman, Graeme, and Thompson, Kenneth (eds), *op cit.,* pp. 205–22.

Salaman, Graeme (1974) *Community and Occupation: An Exploration of Work/Leisure Relationships,* Cambridge University Press, Cambridge.

Salaman, Graeme (1977) 'An historical discontinuity: from charisma to routinisation', *Human Relations,* **30,** No. 4, pp. 373–88.

Salaman, Graeme and **Thompson, Kenneth** (eds) (1973) *People and Organisations,* Longman, London.

Salaman, Graeme and **Thompson, Kenneth** (1974) *Media Booklet* 1 and 2, *People and Organisations,* DT 352, Open University Press, Milton Keynes.

Salaman, Graeme and **Thompson, Kenneth** (1978) 'Class culture and the persistence of an elite', *Sociological Review,* **26,** No. 2, pp. 283–304.

Scheff. Thomas J. (1970) 'Control over policy by attendants in a mental hospital', in Grusky, Oscar, and Miller, George A. (eds), *op. cit.,* pp. 329–40.

Schneider, Eugene V. (1969) *Industrial Sociology: the Social Relations of Industry and the Community,* McGraw-Hill, New York.

Selznick, Philip (1952) 'A Theory of Organisational Commitments' in Merton, Robert, K.; Gray, Ailsa, P., Hockey, Barbara; and Selvin, Hanan, C., (eds) *Reader in Bureaucracy,* Free Press, New York, pp 194–201.

Selznick, Philip (1966) *TVA and the Grass Roots: A Study in the Sociology of Formal Organisation,* Harper and Row, New York.

Shroyer, Trent (1970), 'Towards a Critical Theory for Advanced Industrial Society,' in Dreitzel, Hans, Peter (ed.), *Recent Sociology, No. 2,* Macmillan, New York pp 209–234.

Sills, David L. (1970) 'Preserving Organisational Goals', in Grusky, Oscar, and Miller, George A. (eds), *The Sociology of Organisations: Basic Studies,* Free Press, New York, pp. 227–36.

Silverman, David (1970) *The Theory of Organisations,* Heinemann, London.

Sofer, Cyril (1970) *Men in Mid-Career: A Study of British Managers and Technical Specialists,* Cambridge University Press, Cambridge.

Stinchcombe, Arthur L. (1970) 'Bureaucratic and craft administration of production', in Grusky, Oscar, and Miller, George A. (eds), *op. cit.,* pp. 261–72.

Strauss, Anselm, Scatzman, I., Ehrlich, D., Bucher, R. and **Sabshin, M.** (1973) 'The hospital and its negotiated order', in Salaman, Graeme, and Thompson, Kenneth (eds), *op.cit.,* pp. 303–20.

Sudnow, David (1973) 'Normal crime: sociological features of the penal code in a public defender office', in Salaman, Graeme, and Thompson, Kenneth (eds), *op. cit.,* pp. 346–57.

Szymanski, Al (n.d.) 'Braverman as a Neo-Luddite?: A Critique of the uses of *Labour and Monopoly Capital.*

Taylor, Frederick W. (1972) 'The principles of scientific management', in Davis, Louis E., and Taylor, James C. (eds), *op. cit.,* pp. 27–31.

Thompson, E.P. (1968) *The Making of the English Working Class,* Penguin Books, Harmondsworth.

Thompson, James D. and **McEwen, William J.** (1973) 'Organisational goals and environment: goal-setting as an interaction process', in Salaman, Graeme, and Thompson, Kenneth (eds), *op. cit.,* pp. 155–67.

Thompson, Kenneth (1973) 'Religious Organisations: The Cultural Perspective', in Salaman, Graeme, and Thompson, Kenneth (eds), *op. cit.,* pp. 293–302.

Touraine, Alain (1972) 'An historical theory in the evolution of industrial skills', in Davis, Louis E. and Taylor, James C. (eds), *Design of Jobs: Selected Readings,* Penguin Books, Harmondsworth, pp. 52–61.

Turner, Barry (1971) *Exploring the Industrial Subculture,* Macmillan, London.

Udy, Stanley H. (1959), ' "Bureaucracy" and "Rationality" in Weber's organisation theory', *American Sociological Review,* **24**, No. 6, pp. 791–5.

Ure, A. (1835) *The Philosophy of Manufacturers,* Charles Knight, London.

Urry, J. (1970) 'Role analysis and the sociological enterprise', *Sociological Review,* **18**, No. 13, pp. 351–63.

Van Maanen, John (1976) 'Breaking in: socialisation to work', in Dubin, Robert (ed.), *Handbook of Work, Organisation and Society,* Rand McNally, Chicago, pp. 67–130.

Walker, C.R. and **Guest, R.H.** (1952) *Man on the Assembly Line,* Harvard University Press, Cambridge, Mass.

Wamsley, Gary L. (1970) 'Power and the crisis of the universities', in Zald, Mayer N. (ed.), *Power in Organisations,* Vanderbilt University Press, Nashville, Tenn.

Weber, Max (1964) *The Theory of Social and Economic Organisation,* edited with an introduction by Talcott, Parsons, Free Press, New York.

Wedderburn, Dorothy and **Craig, Christine** (1975) 'Relative deprivation in work', in Esland, Geoff, *et al.* (eds), *op. cit.,* pp. 59–69.

Wilensky, H.L. (1967) *Organisational Intelligence,* Basic Books, London.

Wilensky, H.L. (1968) 'Careers, life-styles and social integration', in Glaser, Barney (ed.), *Organisational Careers: A Sourcebook for Theory,* Aldine, Chicago, pp. 50–53.

Woodward, Joan (1969) 'Management and technology', in Burns, Tom (ed.), *Industrial Man: Selected Readings,* Penguin Books, Harmondsworth, pp. 196–231.

Yeo-chi King, Ambrose (1977) 'A voluntarist model of organisation: the maoist version and critique', *British Journal of Sociology,* **XXVII**, No. 3, pp. 363–74.

Zald, Mayer N. (ed.) (1970) *Power in Organisations,* Vanderbilt University Press, Nashville, Tenn.

Zimmerman, Don (1973) 'The practicalities of rule use', in Salaman, Graeme, and Thompson, Kenneth (eds), *op. cit.,* pp. 250–63.

Index